John Lennon

Printed in the United Kingdom by MPG Books Ltd, Bodmin

Published by Sanctuary Publishing Limited, Sanctuary House, 45-53 Sinclair Road,
London W14 0NS, United Kingdom

www.sanctuarypublishing.com

Distributed in the US by Publishers Group West

ISBN: 1-86074-487-7

John Lennon

Alan Clayson

Sanctuary

About The Author

Born in Dover, England, in 1951, Alan Clayson lives near Henley-on-Thames with his wife, Inese, and sons, Jack and Harry. His portrayal in the *Western Morning News* as "the AJP Taylor of the pop world" is supported by *Q*'s "his knowledge of the period is unparalleled and he's always unerringly accurate". He has written many books on music, including best-sellers *Backbeat* (subject of a major film) and *The Yardbirds*, as well as for journals as diverse as *The Guardian, Record Collector, Mojo, The Times, Mediaeval World, Eastern Eye, Folk Roots, Guitar, Hello!, The Independent, Ugly Things, The Times* and, as a teenager, the notorious *Schoolkids' Oz*. He has also performed and lectured on both sides of the Atlantic, as well as broadcast on national TV and radio .

From 1975 to 1985, he led the legendary group Clayson And The Argonauts and was thrust to "a premier position on rock's Lunatic Fringe" (*Melody Maker*). As shown by the formation of a US fan club – dating from a 1992 *soirée* in Chicago – Alan Clayson's following has continued to grow, as has demand for his talents as a record producer and the number of cover versions of his compositions by such diverse acts as Dave Berry – in whose Cruisers he played keyboards in the mid-1980s – and new-age outfit Stairway. He has also worked with The Portsmouth Sinfonia, Wreckless Eric, Twinkle, The Yardbirds, The Pretty Things and the late Screaming Lord Sutch, among others. While his stage act defies succinct description, he is spearheading an English form of *chanson*. Moreover, his latest album, *Soirée*, may stand as his artistic apotheosis, were it not for the promise of surprises yet to come.

Further information is obtainable from www.alanclayson.com.

Contents

"He's dead but he won't lie down"
– Old music-hall song

Prologue

"I Only Learnt To Play To Back Myself"

Just what the world needs, eh? Another book about John Lennon.

You probably know at least the bare bones of the story backwards, but for that aged Tibetan monk who still hasn't heard of him, Lennon is recognised generally as the leader of a 1960s pop group called The Beatles, who sold – and still sell – millions of gramophone records. If Lennon – arguably, the group's chief creative pivot – had shed most of his artistic load by 1968, he'd left such an ineradicable impression on the complacency of post-war pop that certain of his more jaw-dropping public activities were dismissed initially as the prerogative of celebrity.

Although the world become wiser to his failings – mainly via a decidedly erratic post-Beatles career – his omnipotence is such that veneration has yet to fade for countless fans in a languid daze from the fixity of gazing – figuratively, anyway – at the Dakota Building, the luxury apartment block in New York that was his family home for the final years of a life that was as triumphant as it was tragic. As a 1960s myth, rather than the mere man who was shot dead by a nobody called Mark David Chapman on 8 December 1980, John Lennon was built to last.

As early as 1963, a certain Billy Shepherd was preparing his *The True Story Of The Beatles*, the first of more biographies of The Beatles – together and apart – than anyone could have imagined then. Described by BBC radio presenter John Peel as "the engine room of The Beatles",[1] Lennon has been particularly well served. Indeed, the principal events of almost every day of his life since 1962 have been accounted for in some publication or other, and even as sources of "new and rediscovered facts" continue to dry up, there are presently nearly 70 books concerning him alone still in print. How many have you read already?

Even before his hasty cremation, publishers were liaising with authors about posthumous explorations of every nook and cranny of John's four decades on this planet. Raw information has been chronicled over and over again, whether cornucopias of listings – say, the 700 pages of Keith Badman's day-by-day diary, *The Beatles After The Break-Up* – or Bill Harry's vast, meticulous and culminant *John Lennon Encyclopedia*, which deals with people, places and things concerning the subject as accurately and as adequately as anyone might reasonably expect.

While these books cater for the devotee who derives deep and lasting pleasure from studying basic data, more opinionated tomes have ranged from near-hagiographies – such as *Lennon* by Carole Lynn Corbin – aimed at those for whom the former art student sits at the right hand of God to the likes of *Every Sound There Is: The Beatles' Revolver And The Transformation Of Rock And Roll*, a collection of essays pitched at the consumer who attends a concert in order to chat about how "interesting" it was in licensed premises afterwards. In the privacy of his own home, he reads a lot, thinks a lot, but does nothing. Perhaps the word I'm looking for is *intellectual*. Dripping from the pens of college academics from across the globe, titles like "A Flood Of Flat-Sevenths", "Premature Turns: Thematic Disruption In The American Version" and "Rearranging Base And Superstructure In The Rock Ballad" telegraph that you might need to have a dictionary of musicological terms – or at least a plain dictionary – close to hand.

At another point on the spectrum is *The Lives Of John Lennon* by the late Albert Goldman, a best-seller that depicted Lennon as barking mad after a lifetime of incredible human frailty. Forgive my xenophobic paranoia, but I've read few books concerning British pop written by North Americans that have come anywhere near capturing the peculiarities of being British. I'm not even sure whether a non-Liverpudlian like myself is qualified to write about a Beatle, but I don't waste sentences explaining what I mean by "winkle-pickers" and "not half". I do not revolt readers by juxtaposing imagined British colloquialisms like "all of a blessed sudden" with hip Americanisms such as referring to a sex orgy as a "fuckfest". I don't think Ascot is a suburb of London. Crucially, anyone who refers to John Lennon's "cockney chirpiness" – as a *Rolling Stone* journalist did in a biography of Paul McCartney – is a bit suspect.

In Canadian Geoffrey Giuliano's *Dark Horse*, a "secret life of George Harrison", Pete Best's dismissal in 1962 is over in half a sentence, and not long afterwards The Beatles are winding up a world tour in San Francisco four years later. Furthermore, did John really shout, "Sieg heil, you mothers!" at the Kaiserkeller audience? And what's all this about "after leaving Quarry Bank High School For Boys in 1953, George was enrolled at the Liverpool Institute"? Maybe Giuliano thinks "high school" means "primary school" over here. In any case, it was Lennon, not Harrison, who went to Quarry Bank. That was among Giuliano's more glaring gaffs, but with self-interested vigilance I stumbled on a few other testaments to Rudyard Kipling's "what should they know of England who only England know?" but, overall, *Dark Horse* was an untaxing read with little that was particularly new or significant revealed.

Yet, when I was approached to write this present account, I wondered how difficult it would be for me too to say anything fresh or valuable about John Lennon without taking liberties with the old backstage plot, treating his most flippant remarks as gospel or squeezing paragraphs from, say, drummer Jim McCarty's observations when his Yardbirds secured a support spot with The Beatles' during their 1964 season at Hammersmith Odeon. During an intermission, he saw Lennon standing at the top of a fire-escape at the back of the building in the teddy-bear costume he wore for one of the comedy sketches, which then filled part of the show. John was considering the purchase of one of a fleet of limousines from a London showroom. As it was inconvenient for the pop star to visit the garage during opening hours, its bowing, scraping proprietor had arranged for the vehicles to nose past the twilit foot of the metal stairway.

Another problem I had is this: I don't know about you, but Lennon's more orthodox music – both solo and with The Beatles – has become so embedded by 40 years of availability and airplay that I hear most of it nowadays no more than a sailor hears the sea. To ask my opinion about 'She Loves You', 'Strawberry Fields Forever' or 'Imagine' is like asking me about railway lines or donkeys' false teeth because I can't say anything objective about them any more. They're just there.

For reasons connected vaguely with this, and for psychological stimulation, I Blu-Tacked a picture of John Lennon on the wall. It hung there until I got sick of the wretched fellow gazing reproachfully at an untidy room that my piano and writing desk dominate like twin castle sinisters while, like a medieval scribe at his parchment, I deciphered exercise books full of scribble and transcribed interview tapes. While I was still establishing an order peculiar to myself, Lennon witnessed too the occasional wild-haired search for some mislaid jotting or other that had me ready to kill someone.

Bear in mind also that, as a soldier going over the top in the Great War, I have to screw myself up before talking to various members of the *dramatis personnae* about events that took place up to half a century ago – although over the years, I've become more desensitised about asking incisive questions that stop just short of open impertinence. If some of my interviewees here were politely evasive on occasions, that very silence often illuminated the back stairs of John Lennon's life as surely as if they'd actually named names and told tales.

You see, I'm determined that this will be the last word on Lennon – or at least the last word on those aspects of Lennon and his associates that intrigue me. However, in a dark and lonely corner of my mind, a still, small voice tells me that it won't be, because all publications to do with The Beatles and John Lennon remain such sound marketing exercises that I wonder if there's ever going to be a cutting-off point. Apparently, someone's at work on a biography of Mal Evans, one of the group's road managers. Will there also be a book each from every act on the same label? Everyone who ever covered or revived a Lennon–McCartney song? The foresters who felled the trees to make the paper on which they were written?

I'll stop being facetious for long enough to state that interest in John Lennon – for what he was and for what consumers think he has become – will endure because his influence as a vocalist and composer is and has been acknowledged by every pop artist that has mattered, and his lyrics are still quoted like proverbs.

During the four-year sabbatical before the brief re-emergence that climaxed in his sudden death, Lennon had become as unreachable an object of myth as Elvis Presley. There wasn't a newspaper editor in the world who wouldn't promise a fortune for a Lennon exclusive or an up-to-the-minute photo. Rock stars passing through the Big Apple made at least token efforts to gain an audience with the Grand Old Man, despite his many dubious antics in the past and the hearsay circulating about peculiar goings-on in the Dakota.

Having gouged so deep a wound in pop culture, it might not have mattered if, in the years left to him since the sundering of The Beatles in 1970, Lennon had not continued even a sporadic recording career, let alone one containing odd sparks of the old fire that used to power him when The Beatles were stuck on the Liverpool–Hamburg treadmill. At that time there had been so many ideas – and not only musical ones – chasing through his mind that it was all he could do to note them down. Flames of inspiration would kindle during a 20-minute dawdle to Hamburg's main railway station to buy yesterday's *Daily Express*. Others jerked him from a velvet-blue oblivion back into the dungeons where The Beatles slept during their maiden visit in 1960.

Even after the group made it, tomorrow would seem a year away as with McCartney, more often than not, John would figure out a chord sequence to fragments of melody or rhymes to form a couplet. From a mere title, the ghost of maybe a sketchy chorus would smoulder into form and a red-eyed objectivity and private quality control might engross him and Paul until evening became morning with the two surrounded by cigarette butts, smeared coffee cups and pages full of scribbled verse and notation peculiar to themselves.

As he'd never learned to sight-read or write musical script, John was untroubled by the formal dos and don'ts that traditionally affect creative flow. There were only the stylistic clichés and habits ingrained since his teenage self had positioned as-yet-uncalloused fingertips on the taut strings of his first guitar. "I only learnt to play to back myself,"[2] he'd admit later.

On 9 December 1980, a BBC television reporter asked George Martin, The Beatles' producer, if he thought that the deceased was a great musician.

"He was a great man," replied the diplomatic Martin.[3]

John Lennon wasn't a virtuoso, far from it, but he functioned fully (most of the time) according to his capacity within the context of The Beatles and was able to cross the demarcation line of John (rhythm guitar), Paul (bass guitar), George (lead guitar) and Ringo (drums) when it was necessary to cut corners. He played lead, for instance, on both 'The Ballad Of John And Yoko' – on which neither Harrison nor Starr were present – and 'Get Back'. He was no slouch on keyboards, either, having been hunched over a Vox Continental organ when necessary – admittedly, unheard above the screams – during The Beatles' final tour.

Yet John Lennon hadn't had all that much going for him when he trod the boards as an amateur with the skiffle outfit The Quarry Men in 1957. While he could just about find his way around his instrument then, he aroused little fervour for either his singing or his first attempts at composition. On the surface, he wasn't that brilliant at anything then. And yet...

Alan Clayson
December 2002

1 *"Who Am I To Regard As Mother?"*

At 6:30pm on Wednesday 9 October 1940, John Winston Lennon was prised into the world at Liverpool's Oxford Street Maternity Hospital. The BBC Home Service weatherman had forecast that the night and the next day would be dull but mild, which they were. Dull but mild it remained for more or less the next fortnight. But one evening before the baby was brought home, wailing sirens and flares illuminated the sky as the Luftwaffe dropped ton upon booming ton of death and destruction in and around the slip-slapping wharfs of the docklands where the Mersey sweeps into the Irish Sea.

The following morning, brick dust crunched beneath the hooves of dray horses dragging coal through mean streets to rusty ships, but Julia Lennon's firstborn was destined for a comfortable middle-class home – with a fitted dining-room carpet, not lino – in Menlove Avenue, one of the main thoroughfares of Woolton, a village-like suburb that aligned itself more with rural Lancashire than Merseyside, embracing mock-Tudor colonies, golf clubs and boating lakes.

After his father, Freddie, a seaman of Irish extraction, vanished to all intents and purposes when John was five, so soon did the concept that there is no God but Mummy, and Daddy is the prophet of Mummy. With Freddie represented – perhaps unfairly – as the villain of the piece, the subsequent complications of his wayward mother's love-life and domestic arrangements made it more convenient for the child to grow up in Mendips, the semi-detached villa of Julia's childless sister, Mary Smith (whom John would always call by his cradle articulation "Mimi") and her ex-serviceman husband, George, once an infinitesimal cog in the global hostilities but now running his late father's dairy business. George was to die suddenly when his nephew by marriage was 14.

As John was to discover, Julia lived nearby with her second family, and bound by the invisible chains that shackle child to parent he used her council house as a bolthole whenever strait-laced Mimi's rearing methods became oppressive. The innate confusion of "Who am I to regard as mother?" affected John's ability to trust adult authority figures, whom he mocked and abused as a defence against being rejected by them – particularly after Julia was killed in July 1958 by a car with a policeman, late for his shift, at the wheel.

Moreover, despite the extenuating circumstances, he felt that he'd been cast out by his mother as well as by Freddie, having had enough experience of her to know what he was missing, hence the bitterness inherent in outbursts against teachers, friends and his devoted aunt. She usually blamed doubtful company for John's mischief when, short-trousered and gaberdine-raincoated, he began his formal education on 12 November 1945 in the kindergarten at Moss Pits Lane Infant School, a few streets' dawdle from Mendips.

The following April, John was expelled for disruptive behaviour and, chastened by this disgrace, commenced a less wild career at Dovedale Road Primary School. For a while, he modelled himself on "William Brown", Richmal Crompton's outrageous 12-year-old from a well-to-do rural family, whose first exploit, *Just William*, was published in 1917.[4] Lennon, however, was to go beyond the rough-and-tumble of acceptable boyhood larks on passing his 11 Plus and gaining a place at Quarry Bank, a grammar school nicknamed "the Police State" by the Liverpool Institute, Prescot Grammar, the newer Liverpool Collegiate and other more liberal seats of learning for its pretentious affectations and Draconian rigmarole. An Eton-like house system was in full force there and so was corporal punishment, administered as often as not with the swish of a bamboo cane on buttocks or outstretched palm.

John might have fared better at a secondary modern, where 11 Plus "failures" went, or better still a comprehensive, had one been established on Merseyside by the early 1950s with the schools' more pronounced "education for all" concept theoretically enabling children to follow what best suited their abilities and inclinations as they developed. As it was, it didn't take long for John to transform from a capable if uninvolved pupil to a C-stream hard case, hanging onto his place at Quarry Bank by the skin of his teeth. By the end of his second year there, he had become a sharer of smutty stories and magazines of female lingerie and a mainstay of the smoking club behind the bicycle sheds. Indeed, the adult Lennon would be tearing the cellophane off up to three 20 packs a day.

As well as overt offences, John was a more insidiously bad influence on others via his insulting "politeness" to teachers, his red-herring time-wasting tactics in class, his copied homework and his dumb insolence when directed to spit a sweet into the litter bin during lessons.

Similarly leading by example outside school, Lennon had some kind of vice-like grip on his allies in delinquency, some of whom weren't so much friends as disciples whom he could usually persuade to do almost anything. Among them was the type of specimen that might be lured into some shaming *faux pas*, sent on a fool's errand, driven to near-suicide with mind games and slapped hard on the back or around the face under the flag of aggressive friendliness so that he'd have to grin at John with tears in his eyes. He'd want to join the gang, but he'd be a figure of fun at best, at worst the arbitrary object of aggression, and in between an outsider denied the social intercourse that king-bee Lennon and his alpha-boys took for granted. Outwardly unbothered and faithful, he struggled not to put his foot in it when John threw down a few words like small change to a beggar, before that butterfly concentration alighted elsewhere.

Some of Lennon's "victims", however, either weaned themselves off him or started to snap back. A few went so far as to put up their fists and look fierce, noting how swiftly their antagonist would back down. "I used to beat them up if they were small enough," John was to admit, not especially ruefully, "but I'd use long words and confuse them if they were bigger. What mattered was that I stayed in charge."[5]

Not standing when he could lean, hands rammed in pockets and chewing gum in a half sneer, the attitude of that Lennon boy – lazy, destructive, narcissistic and, as far as he dared, a bully – was also reflected in further extra-curricular activities that had little bearing on what he was supposed to be learning at school. Absorbing a hidden curriculum, he'd developed a messy aptitude as an illustrator and writer of comic verse and stories since Dovedale Primary. On a par with this at Quarry Bank, however, was his interest in the guitar, the instrument that Elvis Presley hung around his neck. Lennon didn't only like Presley; he worshipped him – no other word would do. John Lennon worshipped Elvis Presley – the Hillbilly Cat, the Memphis Flash, the King Of Western Bop – from the moment he heard 'Heartbreak Hotel', the Tennesseean's debut entry in the newly established *New Musical Express* record charts, and saw the first photograph of him published in Britain[6] as a hybrid of nancy boy and amusement-arcade hoodlum. As far as John was concerned, Elvis was to die metaphorically when manager Colonel Tom Parker's smoothing of his rough diamond began in 1958, with the stressing of an uncomplaining diligence while the young star was on National Service in the US Army.

Other of the Quarry Bank schoolboy's rock 'n' roll heroes went down, too. Little Richard, a chart fixture with such set-works as 'Rip It Up,' 'Long Tall Sally' and 1958's 'Good Golly Miss Molly' – all dominated by his vamping piano and declamatory vocals – eschewed pop for the Church. Whilst at theological college and a subsequent ministry, he was to issue little but religious material for several years.

Jerry Lee Lewis, meanwhile, was also prone to vigorous bouts of evangelism, but he continued to play the devil's music after 1957's 'Whole Lotta Shakin' Goin' On', and attendant electrifying appearances on US television catapulted him to international attention. The momentum was sustained with such as 'Great Balls Of Fire' and 'High School Confidential' before a tour of Britain brought to light his bigamous third espousal to an under-aged cousin.

Chuck Berry would be off the air, too, after 'Roll Over Beethoven', 'Sweet Little Sixteen', 'Johnny B Goode' and other self-penned items, which celebrated in song the pleasures that were available to American teenage consumers. In 1959, Berry was to serve the first of two jail terms, which put temporary halts to his career. Nevertheless, this incarceration served to boost his cult celebrity status in Britain where he'd been seen "duckwalking" derisively with a crotch-level guitar only in *Jazz on A Summer's Day*, a film documentary about the Newport Jazz Festival.

Buddy Holly And The Crickets also wrote their own songs and this ability, plus the compact sound of two guitars, bass and drums on the group's only UK tour, was one of the major elements that coalesced to produce the British beat boom. This 1958 visit was in the wake of a string of international smashes, which began with the previous year's 'That'll Be The Day'. However, in the aftershock of his fatal aeroplane crash in 1959, US obituarists tended to write off Holly as a has-been in professional as well as absolute terms.

It was no coincidence that, after Buddy's British trek and subsequent death, sales of guitars boomed at Frank Hessy's music shop in central Liverpool. John Lennon, however, had acquired one as a result of an earlier craze traceable to "king of skiffle" Lonnie Donegan being permitted to sing one or two blues-tinged North American folk tunes to the accompaniment of washboard, double bass and his own guitar strumming while a member of Chris Barber's Jazz Band. "Really, it was me doing impressions of Big Bill Broonzy, Leadbelly, Josh White and Lonnie Johnson," confessed Lonnie when I interviewed him two years before his death in November 2002, "as well as Woody Guthrie, Hank Snow, Hank Williams...but they came out as Lonnie Donegan."

From a 1954 Barber album on Pye Records, there were sufficient BBC Light Programme airings of Lonnie's 'Rock Island Line' to warrant its issue as a grudging spin-off single in autumn 1955. Its alarming climb into the sleepy Top 20s of both Britain and the United States made it expedient for the 24-year-old to go solo. "I didn't see success in the USA as long term," estimated Donegan. "I had every intention of coming back and rejoining Chris Barber, but the agent booked me for all sorts of rock 'n' roll shows all over America. The first one was with Chuck Berry in Cleveland. I was doing very well, but then I received a telegram from Pye saying, 'Come Home. "Lost John" at Number Two.' I was shocked at all the skiffle clubs that had opened everywhere and the thousands of guys trying to imitate Lonnie Donegan. It was uncanny how much John Lennon sounded like me on that Quarry Men tape that turned up a few years ago."

When 'Rock Island Line' boomed from the loudspeakers just before the main feature in a Grantham cinema, Roy Taylor, a member of The Harmonica Vagabonds with fellow members of the YMCA, claimed, "I couldn't believe my ears! Next morning, I bought the record. Then I bought a guitar and started a skiffle group called just The Vagabonds. For our repertoire, Lonnie couldn't turn out records fast enough."

Future Trogg Chris Britton in The Hiccups in Andover, Van Morrison with Belfast's Sputniks, Peter Smith (later Crispian St Peters) of Swanley's Hard Travellers and other hitmakers-in-waiting listened hard to Donegan, who bossed the ensuing craze throughout its 1957 prime and beyond. Backed by his own Skiffle Group, Donegan's driving whine and vibrant personality lacquered further adaptations of similar North American material, which, if failing to further his cause in the land from whence it came, kept him in domestic smashes, even after he offended purists by tilting for wider acceptance with chestnuts from the golden days of Empire, such as chart-topping 'Putting On The Style' and 'My Old Man's A Dustman', an adaptation of the Merseyside folk ditty 'My Old Man's A Fireman On The Elder–Dempster Line'.

"The platform for working at that time was the variety theatres to a very general public," explained Lonnie. "You could work half the year, and spend the rest doing nothing. I was headlining over dancing girls, comedians, jugglers, whatever, and couldn't just stand there like one of Lowry's Matchstick Men, because I had to learn to back-project, announce and get laughs. You had to perform, not just play. Otherwise, you died and got no more work."

No skiffle purist, John Lennon didn't mind Lonnie thus broadening his appeal. After a fashion, he too was extending himself beyond US folk songs. At first, he hadn't played his new guitar much, although Julia – who plinked a banjo – had taught him a few less-than-full chords before she died. Rather than progress beyond these, he'd focused more on cultivating a lustrous, brilliantined pompadour tapering to sideburns like scimitars, even going through a phase of flicking back his quiff just like Elvis, pretending that it wouldn't stop falling over his eyes.

Sometimes, in a time-honoured ritual of thwarted eroticism, he'd place a Presley single on the record player in his bedroom and arrange himself in front of the wardrobe mirror, standing there with his guitar. From the opening bars to the coda, he'd curl his lip and pretend to slash chords and pick solos with negligent ease. He'd mouth the lyrics, *yeah*-ing and *uh-huh*-ing to thousands of ecstatic females that only he could see.

Once, an only-too-real female burst in. Gaping at the arched eyebrow and crooked smile in the doorway, John felt no end of a fool. Then Aunt Mimi gazed into the middle distance and spoke in generalities. The gist was that it's heartbreaking to see people struggling desperately to be something they can never hope to be. Their vain attempts to scale the heights of their dreams give glimpses of high comedy to someone watching but bring themselves nothing but misery. Tragi-comedy is only truly funny to the truly heartless – but there's no tragedy in being untalented if you've no knowledge of it. It's a bearable state, even a happy one, until someone opens your eyes to it. Ignorance – or arrogance – can be a very protective shell.

This embarrassing episode may have goaded John to make a more cursory go at learning his instrument properly, bringing him to realise that certain basic chord cycles recurred over and over again in skiffle and classic rock. Yet the fascination of holding down an E major chord didn't interfere with his work on the visuals, getting all the Elvis Presley moves off too, even though there wasn't room in the bedroom for feigning a collapse and crawling to the edge of a imaginary stage. The chief motivation for his efforts, of course, was connected with the fleeting flashes of knicker as girls jived in gingham whenever he went to a dance.

A hard-won mastery of basic musical and choreographic techniques, combined with the rising sap of puberty, therefore found him at the central microphone – indeed, the only microphone – with The Quarry Men, as a perk of being in a pop group was, so he understood, readier licence to talk to girls, at least, than most of the other chaps who'd paid to shuffle about in the gloom beyond the stage with a built-in sense of defeat.

Almost as a matter of course, John had a walkover in whatever power struggle there was in The Quarry Men. As well as an ingrained bossiness, he could claim real and imagined genealogical links with showbusiness. There was, apparently, a Liverpool-Irish grandfather, Jack Lennon, who'd emigrated to North America and been in a touring revue called Andrew Robertson's Kentucky Minstrels prior to returning to Merseyside as a pub entertainer. However, John kept quieter about The Lennon Sisters –

Dianne, Peggy, Kathy and Janet – who came to national attention in the USA as featured vocal group on light orchestral supremo Lawrence Welk's weekly television show, all scripted grinning and harmless fun. And when they were signed to Coral – Buddy Holly's label – in 1955, they became known as singers of catchy tunes with jaunty rhythms, as demonstrated in their US novelty hit a year later with 'Tonight You Belong To Me'.

This Lennon sisters had no place in John's index of possibilities as a Quarry Man. In the burning glare of the footlights – if there were any – at what posters then billed as "swing sessions" in this village institute or that social club, he sometimes incurred the dislike of the expected cluster of teddy boys and other male riff-raff on one side of the hall, keeping up a baleful barrage of catcalls and barracking, whilst the girls danced round each other's handbags opposite. Narrow-eyed with frustration and alcohol, if they could get it, their objective for being there might metamorphose into more brutal sensual pleasure than the pursuit of sex.

Such attention was partly self-inflicted because of John's visible and omnipotent hold over the other Quarry Men, just like Lonnie Donegan had held sway over his Skiffle Group. If Lonnie looked like a used-car salesman offstage, the King of Skiffle could be mesmeric in concert, creating true hand-biting excitement as he piled into numbers that the Group didn't know, taking on and resolving risky extemporisations and generating a sweaty, exhilarating intensity never before experienced in British pop. In retrospect, it's not silly to put Lonnie Donegan on a par with Jimi Hendrix.

More typical of the genre than either hitmaking Donegan or raw amateurs like The Quarry Men was Ricky Richards' Skiffle Group, resident in the Skiffle Cellar, a stone's throw from the 2 I's, central London's more renowned shrine of British pop. After nearly half a century, their entire recorded output – 12 hitherto-unissued tracks, taped mostly in the double-bass player's Wembley home – was made available for public consumption on a small record label in 2002.

In all conscience, I cannot resort to cheap laughs at Ricky and his ensemble's expense because, as well as being a slice of cultural history, the CD entitled *Shake It Daddy* is also entertaining, but not because it's so bad it's good; as well as making a fair lo-fi fist of numbers that were common property of other outfits all over the country, the lads turn in two Richards originals – including the title song – which stand as tall as their workman-like versions of 'John Henry', 'Wreck Of The Old '97', 'Putting On The Style' *et al*.

Give him credit, too. Ricky's fretboard picking was held in high regard by the discerning Tony Sheridan, then emerging – albeit briefly – as one of Britain's most sensational rock 'n' roll guitarists. Both were destined for walk-on parts in Lennon's life after he left Quarry Bank in July 1957.

When the predictably poor results of John's GCE O-levels fluttered onto the doormat a few weeks later – he'd failed all of them, albeit by only one grade – Aunt Mimi made an appointment to discuss her charge's future with the headmaster, Mr William Pobjoy, who informed her that John's most legitimate contribution to school affairs had been when The Quarry Men performed during the interval at the sixth form's end-of-term party.

Mimi hadn't realised until recently, she said, that John's wretched skiffle group even had a name, let alone gone beyond just messing about with guitars. His fooling around on the Spanish model she'd been badgered into buying him was all right as a hobby, she'd told him, but she'd thought she'd die of shame if he ever appeared onstage with a pop group. He'd answered back that a boy he knew called George Harrison only had to ask for one of these electric guitars and it was his. Well, that's as may be, but showbusiness isn't a reliable living, is it? You couldn't see it as a career unless you'd been born into it.

Even then, Mr Pobjoy chipped in, if you were a vocalist in the popular style, you had to "mature" with an output that veered between sentimental ballads and singalong ditties. Look at Lonnie Donegan and, before him, indigenous entertainers like Max Bygraves, Ronnie Hilton, Donald Peers ("the Cavalier of Song") and the neo-operatic Lee Laurence.

Again, that's as may be, replied Mimi, but John's nonsense about wanting to make his way as a "pop star" was nearly as appalling as a girl announcing that she wanted to shake her backside in a burlesque troupe. In the perceived moral decline of the country since the war, such a viewpoint was to remain the norm in decent provincial households, where patterned wallpaper was the only hint of frivolity and where the 1950s wouldn't end until about 1966.

That was one reason why John was a nuisance at school. That he was one, Mimi had suspected from the beginning, if only because his behaviour there impacted at home in constant turmoil over his choice of friends, his insolence, his speech, his manners, his slouch, those crude drainpipe jeans and him sculpting his hair in that stupid quiff-and-ducktail style, with side-whiskers like one of these teddy boys: secondary modern ne'er-do-wells who, garbed in seedy flash finery, prowled the evening streets in packs, looking for things to destroy and people to beat up.

Lately, Mimi continued, she'd started to position herself at the front window whenever she'd deduced that John was about to leave the house. He didn't have to catch her eye; even sensing her glaring, quivering and tight-lipped disapproval was enough for him to return and change out of the more ridiculous clothes he'd got past her quality control.

When he next got a word in edgeways, Mr Pobjoy – who had given the boy a kinder written testimonial than either he or Mimi might have expected – suggested that the Youth Employment Centre might not find John beyond redemption and that an apprenticeship of some kind wasn't out of the question. Alternatively, he recommended that John could do worse than join the Regular Army.

However, as Aunt Mimi wouldn't hear of her fallen angel entering the world of work before she considered he'd completed his "education", the outcome of a rather fraught discussion was that John was to be enrolled at Liverpool's Regional College of Art that September. Entry standards for the establishment were particularly lax, to the point of being non-existent beyond evidence of a slight artistic turn.

The Quarry Men survived their leader's transfer to the higher-education establishment in the city centre, although by then he had come to seek the particular company of a lad named Paul McCartney, enlisted into The Quarry Men in July 1957. The fact that his elder son was joining a group fronted by that John Lennon was a severe test of paternal support, but McCartney's widowed father accepted Paul's case for the defence, that John had been a square peg in a round hole at Quarry Bank and that he was a fine fellow when you got to know him.

Moreover, for all his loutish affectations, Lennon knew how he was supposed to behave when introduced to other boys' parents. McCartney, forever rejoicing in his council-estate origins, "never realised John put on this 'working-class hero' stuff. Nobody had a set of Winston Churchill books. Nobody had an aunt, 'cause we called 'em 'aunties'. 'Aunt' was very posh. Nobody had relatives who were dentists or worked at the BBC, as two of John's Scottish relatives did. Nobody had relatives in Edinburgh, my dear! This was a middle-class structure in which John was very much part of. When symphonies came on the radio, my family just went, 'Oh bloody hell!' and switched the station."[7]

The Quarry Men's new pianist, John Duff Lowe, was in the same form as Paul at Liverpool Institute and met John in the McCartney living room in the city suburb of Allerton. "It wasn't a particularly momentous encounter," he recalled, "though when you're 16, anyone 18 months older is often a bit intimidating. John also used to dress in what you'd loosely describe as teddy-boy gear. Paul's father – like all parents – was paranoid that his children were going to turn into teddy boys, pushing bottles into people's faces and creating mayhem in the clubs. The uniform indicated someone who was looking for trouble. John gave the impression of being like that but was actually quite a nice guy.

"George Harrison came into the group a week or two after me. Prior to us, the band had Rod Davis on banjo, Pete Shotton on washboard, Eric Griffiths on guitar, Colin Hanton on drums, Len Garry on tea-chest bass, John Lennon and, right at the end of the skiffle era, Paul McCartney."

Without the others, Paul and John began to practise and even write songs together, sometimes truanting to do so. They even lugged their instruments with them when, on the spur of the moment, they went hitch-hiking in the south of England one Easter holiday. That was when they'd really become friends.

Although their style was based on blues, hillbilly and further subdivisions of North American folk music, the pre-McCartney Quarry Men also embraced rock 'n' roll, and it was this element that had impressed Paul when he'd attended a performance in 1957 at Woolton summer fête (which someone taped for then-unimagined posterity, as well as the ears of an elderly Lonnie Donegan). So began one of the most crucial liaisons in pop. Not long afterwards, George Harrison deputised for and then superseded original lead guitarist Eric Griffiths, who, like most of the other personnel, regarded skiffle as a vocational blind alley, a trivial pursuit to be thrust aside on departure to the world of work, marriage or National Service.

John Duff Lowe's growing disinclination to remain a Quarry Man, however, was mostly because of geography: "I lived in West Derby, on the opposite side of Liverpool to all the others. Whereas Paul could easily bike round to John's house, it was a journey on two buses for me. I didn't tend to get involved during the week. We'd rehearse on Sunday and perform the following Saturday if anyone would have us. Also, whenever we turned up anywhere, the quality of the hall pianos varied so much. They were often either out of tune or had notes missing. This especially annoyed John, as the guitars had to be retuned to the piano."

Hundreds more than could actually have been there were to reconjure a night within the Mersey hinterland at maybe a church youth club with a wholesome, self-improving reek about it. They'd handed over the sixpence (2 1/2 p) admission to a with-it vicar in a cardigan, who'd booked The Quarry Men to perform in a playing area with a solitary white bulb as the lightshow and a microphone and two of the three guitars plugged perilously into one amplifier via two shared jacks. The other was fed through something soldered together from a kit advertised ("with a ten-watt punch") in *Melody Maker*.

This latter arrangement was the work of George Harrison, a bus driver's son, happy just to be around the beery breathed John, three years his senior and a fully fledged rock 'n' roller who boasted about how he'd tilted successfully for the downfall of some girl's underwear. An educated guess, however, is that John Lennon at 17 was probably still a virgin, like the vast majority of his adolescent peers. In days before the birth-control pill and the Swinging '60s, pre-marital sex was a much bigger issue. To sceptical cronies, a changing-room lothario at Quarry Bank would boast of carnal capers that everyone guessed were tall tales. He might have got to "third base" after a lot of effort, but only a "cheap" girl didn't "save herself" for her future husband. Until recently, John had imagined that girls went all the way only if they really loved you, and even then a true daughter of the 1950s would have none of it while yet unwed. Nevertheless, through some undignified fumblings, Lennon discovered that even a youth club's most arch proto-feminist – the sort who looked as if she couldn't wait for a game of ping-pong, followed by a chat about life after death over an orange squash – her whole tweedy, earnest being was screaming for sex just as much as any bloke.

Although George Harrison was the most heterosexual of males too, his heart would feel like it had burst through its ribcage whenever the great Lennon lowered himself to actually speak to him, no matter how nastily. Once, George brought a friend to be introduced to Lennon, but without looking around the cocky so-and-so outstretched his fingers over his left shoulder for the newcomer to shake. Had John then offered anything other than slights, exploitations and jokes at his expense, George might have been worried about his position as the lowest of the low in The Quarry Men hierarchy. Unaware that Lennon was an inwardly fearful youth whose successful promotion of himself as a physical and verbal fighter had brittle substance, it gave young Harrison a feeling of belonging.

Yet while George was looked down upon by John, this was balanced by the former's freshly acquired skills as a trainee electrician, notably ensuring that overloaded amps with naked wires were rendered less lethal and less likely to cut out halfway through a number. George had also taught himself ripostes to counter John's sarcasm, his callous teasing and, more recently, the near-impossibility of having a sensible conversation with him.

Of all The Quarry Men, John Lennon was the loudest in praise of BBC radio's *The Goon Show*, a development of the offbeat humour and topical parodies of an earlier series, *Crazy People*, which starred Spike Milligan, Peter Sellers, Michael Bentine and Harry Secombe, veterans of entertainments organised by the armed forces from their own ranks. Incongruous parallels, casual cruelty and stream-of-consciousness connections not only made *The Goon Show* different from mainstream series like *Educating Archie* and *The Clitheroe Kid*, but also ushered in that stratum of fringe-derived comedy that culminated in the late 1960s with *Monty Python's Flying Circus*. Aspects of The Goons became apparent, too, in the stylistic determination of such as Scaffold, The Bonzo

Dog (Doo-Dah) Band and, less directly, The Beatles, particularly in their first two films. It was also evident in Lennon's associated slim volumes, *In His Own Write* and 1965's *A Spaniard In The Works*. Many of the assorted oddments that filled these books dated from the first broadcasts of *The Goon Show* and John's habit of scribbling nonsense verse and surreal stories supplemented by Milligan-esque cartoons and caricatures, a habit that intensified with exposure to the programme.

John was also among those irritating people who re-enacted *Goon Show* sketches the next day during the programme's high summer, which was reflected in spin-off double-A-side hit-parade entries in the UK in 1956 for 'I'm Walking Backwards For Christmas'/'Bluebottle Blues' and 'The Ying Tong Song'/'Bloodnok's Rock 'n' Roll'. While these singles were released on Decca, solo records by Milligan, Sellers and Bentine, as well as two album anthologies entitled *The Best Of The Goon Shows*, came to be issued by Parlophone, a subsidiary of EMI, another of Britain's four major record labels. The discs were produced by George Martin, elevated to headship of Parlophone in 1954 at the age of only 29.

To The Quarry Men, George Martin was an unknown figure in an unknown future in 1958, when the group was a vehicle for John Lennon's self-projection as an aspirant Donegan or Presley. Because John imagined himself a firm enforcer of his own discipline at rehearsals, there had been disenchantment amongst certain of the others, exemplified by premature departures motivated by his ruthlessness in sticking to the job in hand. Over-sensitive souls walked out, mortally offended, to dissect his character and musical ability with bitter intensity.

Yet middle-aged ex-Quarry Men from the Woolton Fête era would reunite and perform again for fun and profit. Moreover, hardly a day would go by without them remembering with doleful affection one who had been the Woolton Flash as surely as Elvis had been the local equivalent light years away in Memphis.

2 *"There Was Something Slightly Worrying About Him"*

"The Quarry Men wasn't that special a thing," reckoned John Duff Lowe, "and I was getting fed-up with the hour-long journey from West Derby to rehearsals, and my girlfriend used to moan. Also, A-levels came along, plus parental pressure."

Among the principal assets of a fragmenting Quarry Men was the vocal interplay between Lennon and McCartney. Yet, while composition was then an eccentric diversion, at most, to nearly all working British pop musicians, the power structure whereby George Harrison was to be subordinate to John and Paul for as long as they stayed together was founded on the handshake that had now formalised the Lennon–McCartney songwriting partnership – or so you'd read when the myth gripped harder.

Unlike such composer/lyricist teams of the Gilbert and Sullivan or Andrew Lloyd Webber and Tim Rice persuasion, the functions of McCartney and Lennon were never so cut and dried. Even non-fans would be able to differentiate eventually between the work of either, especially after a sea-change *circa* 1967, after which they tended to compose separately, or at least present each other with numbers in more advanced stages of completion than before.

Yet it was an apparent McCartney–Harrison opus, 'In Spite Of All The Danger', that was to grace one side of the first Beatles-associated record, an ego-massaging pressing taped and cut on while-you-wait shellac in a studio customised on the ground floor of a terraced house in Liverpool's Kensington district. A quarter of a century later, a cluster of new streets in the area would be named in three of the participants' honour – John Lennon Drive, Paul McCartney Way, George Harrison Close.

Such a venture by an amateur skiffle outfit wasn't uncommon, of course; following a qualified triumph in a national skiffle competition in 1957, an echo-drenched and plummily inhibited single by Roy Taylor's Vagabonds exhausted an unrepeated self-financed run of 50 copies. However, The Quarry Men – by this time John, Paul, George, John Duff Lowe and Colin Hanton – shelled out for only one copy of 'In Spite Of All The Danger', which was coupled with an unimaginative reworking of 'That'll Be The Day', with Lennon as Buddy Holly.

"We rehearsed quite a long time for the session," recalled Lowe, "'That'll Be The Day' was the A-side. It was John's idea, but we all chipped in to pay for it. The studio was just a back room with these huge machines on the table, no overdubs, one microphone in the middle of the room and a piano. The guy, Percy Phillips, cut the acetate out there and then and we walked out with one copy. It didn't even have a proper sleeve; it was put in a 78rpm Parlophone sleeve. Nobody used it for any other purpose than lending it round. I ended up with it. Even after The Beatles had become well known, none of them then bothered to try and get it back."

The disc's existence alone was a bartering tool for engagements that were few and far between, and often undertaken for as little as a round of fizzy drinks. Moreover, Lennon's preoccupation with The Quarry Men – soon to rename themselves Johnny And The Moondogs – took its toll on his art studies. What did stereoplastic colour, tactile values and Vorticism matter when the group was filling the intermission spot that evening at, say, Stanley Abattoir Social Club or the Morgue Skiffle Cellar in Oak Hill Park?

A new-found college friend of Lennon's by the name of Bill Harry "put forward the proposal that the Students' Union used its funds to buy PA equipment for John's band to use". This seemed a practical suggestion as Lennon, McCartney, Harrison and a turnover of other musicians were also being engaged as a recurring support act at college shindigs headlined by the likes of The Merseysippi Jazz Band, then Liverpool's pre-eminent combo, and fully mobilised a decade before traditional jazz permeated the Top Ten via the toot-tooting of Acker Bilk, Kenny Ball *et al*. "In 1958, it was all jazz bands," sighed John Duff Lowe, "and we played mostly intervals during their beer breaks. We were always warned not to play too loudly."

The Quarry Men's only concession to the impending trad-jazz craze was Louis Armstrong's 'When You're Smiling', albeit with John singing in Harry Secombe's "Neddy Seagoon" voice and inserting cheeky references to college staff into its lyrics. Otherwise, nearly every item in the metamorphosing Quarry Men's repertoire now was a *salaam* to Elvis Presley, Gene Vincent, Jerry Lee Lewis, Chuck Berry, Little Richard and further behemoths of classic rock. "John wanted to put even more rock 'n' roll into it," recalled John Duff Lowe, "which meant that Pete, Rod and Len had to go because you didn't have washboard, tea-chest bass and banjo in rock. When I first became a Quarry Man, John was already squeezing out the skiffle-type music."

As it had always been, Lennon tended to be singled out as "leader" by both the casual listener and those Quarry Men still in terrified admiration of one who, as Philip Hartas, in charge of foundation sculpture, soon realised was "like a fellow who'd been born without brakes. His objective seemed to be somewhere over there that nobody else could see, but he was going, and in that process a lot of people got run over. He never did it to me, but he had this very sarcastic way of talking to people."[7]

When Lennon, in his first term at art college, attempted to change from a lettering course to graphics like Bill Harry, the head of that department, George Jardine, a pruny looking gentleman in sports jacket and patterned tie, wouldn't have it. Like some other members of staff, Jardine regarded Lennon as a nightmare of a young man, although it was recognised that many fellow students vied for John's attention, just as they had at Quarry Bank. Partly, it was to do with his strong personality, but also because The Quarry Men, if not the wildest act going on Merseyside, were starting to be noticed outside the comparative security of Students' Union bookings, having become adept at bypassing potentially ugly moments, often via Lennon's instinctive if indelicate crowd control.

With the music itself, the bars that linked choruses and bridges were cluttered and arrangements often shot to pieces, despite bawled off-mic directives. Yet every now and then, the group would be home and dry long before they reached the final number, in which either Lennon or McCartney on lead vocals might pull out every ham trick in the book, guarding a *pro tempore* stardom with the passionate venom of a six-year-old with a new bike.

However, it was enough that The Quarry Men/Johnny And The Moondogs survived at all at a time when talent scouts from London – where the country's key record companies were clotted – rarely found the time to listen to what was going on in other regions. Although it's true that most British regions had spawned at least one hit-parade entrant apiece during the 1950s, so parochial was provincial pop that there seemed to be few realistic halfway points between obscurity and the Big Time. But if you weren't to be a big name in a wider world, you could limit yourself to being cherished as one locally.

A hick outfit's transition to going semi-professional was usually assisted by the growth of a substantial fan following via regular performances in youth clubs, coffee bars, pub functions rooms and so forth. From one of the toughest districts in Liverpool, Gerry Marsden's Skiffle Group had worked a similar circuit to The Quarry Men, although Gerry confessed, "I didn't see them until Paul joined. Their sound was rubbish, but he and John stood out as talented. Somehow whatever John did was just *different*. He seemed to have absorbed all the rock 'n' roll influences and then come out the other side with entirely his own variation on them."

At a higher position in the local pop hierarchy than Lennon, Marsden's outfit had slipped into a routine of maybe two or three bookings a week within easy reach and with the occasional side trip into the next county. Meanwhile, the outer reaches of Johnny And The Moondogs' stamping ground didn't extend beyond the environs of Liverpool, at least until autumn 1959, when the group – which had by now boiled down to just John, George and Paul – made it through to the final regional heat of Carroll Levis's *Search For Stars* – the spiritual forerunner of *Opportunity Knocks* – under the proscenium at the Hippodrome Theatre in Manchester, "Entertainment Capital of the North", some 50km (30 miles) to the east.

The ultimate prize was the spot on Levis's ITV series, just as The Vagabonds had gained one on BBC TV's *Come Dancing* after being merely runners-up in the World Skiffle Championship the previous year. However, an obligation to catch the last train back to Lime Street Station in Liverpool put the tin lid on Lennon, McCartney and Harrison's chances, as it left too early for the three to be judged (by volume of applause) at the show's finale. Yet, while he didn't harp on about it at Mendips – advisedly – this crestfallen headway mattered more to John than any progress he was making at college.

To Mimi's dismay, John's career there was seeming to trace much the same ignominious trajectory as it had at Quarry Bank. Failure seemed inevitable from the start. In preparation for The Entrance on the very first morning, John had risen early to spend an inordinate amount of time combing his hair into a precarious quiff, gleaming with Brylcreem. For quick adjustments, he stuck a comb in the top pocket of a concessionary sports jacket buttoned over a lilac shirt that Mimi detested. He walked to the bus stop in approved Cavalry twills, but when he alighted he had a slightly pigeon-toed gait, having changed somehow during the jolting journey into the contentious drainpipe jeans, so tight that it looked as if his legs had been dipped in ink. Thus attired, he stood at the college portals and narrowed short-sighted eyes. He was too vain to be seen wearing the spectacles he'd needed for chronic short-sightedness since Dovedale Primary.

The undergraduate's self-image was at odds with the only subject he kept quiet about: his privileged upbringing in Woolton. An inverted snob, he'd already embraced the *machismo* values of both teddy boys and proletarian Merseyside males and generally came on as the Poor Honest Wacker – a working-class hero, in fact, although the only paid work he ever did, apart from as a musician, was as a labourer at local waterworks Scaris & Brick for a month during a summer recess. Nevertheless, by the end of his first term at college, he had started speaking in florid Scouse, laced with incessant swearing.

He'd also latched onto the notion that northern women were mere adjuncts to their men. John's overwhelmed new girlfriend – and future wife – Cynthia Powell seemed to tolerate this role, as well as the jealous anxieties that made him turn pale, clench his fists and make exasperating scenes if she said as much as a civil hello to a male not on his mental list of those that he considered to have no romantic interest in Cynthia.

And yet, however much he showered her with kisses and sweet nothings in private, Cynthia, a lass from over the river in Cheshire, was otherwise just one of an entourage in danger of being lost in his shadow as he continued to establish himself as a lecture-disrupting clown, and lunaticked around the city centre with his Moondogs and college sidekicks. Often, she and John would emerge from lectures for an intended tryst in, say, Rod Murray's bedroom in Gambier Terrace, just around the corner from the college, but they wouldn't have walked far before, say, George greeted them with his trademark whistle. With him and others in tow, endeavouring to monopolise her boyfriend, Cynthia's heart would sink to her boots – but then, from time to time, she'd catch John eyeing her in an uncharacteristically lovelorn fashion, perhaps because he had finally noticed that she'd allowed her blonde perm to go to highlighted seed so that she now looked a bit like Brigitte Bardot, who had emerged as France's national *femme fatale* thanks to a combination of unruly sexuality and doe-eyed ingenuousness.

Cynthia observed too that, when John was in the public eye, he played the fool as if on cue. "He worked so hard at keeping people amused, he was exhausting," said Rod Murray, another student. "One day, I saw him running down the street, holding a steering wheel – no car, just the wheel. He said he was driving down to town."[7]

Lennon's buffoonery would sometimes deteriorate into a nonsensical (and frequently alcohol-fuelled) frenzy and soon would come the antics that would get him barred from pubs. "I just knew I'd never see him grow old," remarked Gerry Marsden with the benefit of hindsight. "Even as a young guy, there was something slightly worrying about him. It was like he was racing through life. He didn't have the look of a man who'd be happy in maturity."

Back in class, John's tutors could not help but imagine that he did very little reading. "You had the feeling that he was living off the top of his head," said Philip Hartas.[7] It was a veneer of self-confidence, rather than any heavily veiled air of learning, that enabled John Lennon to bluff his way through prolonged discussion on art. His bluff was often called by the late Arthur Ballard, an artist who might have gained national renown had he chosen not to remain a big fish in the small pool of Merseyside culture. A painting lecturer and general tutor at Liverpool College of Art for over 30 years, Ballard, who "looked for new ways forward while respecting tradition",[8] came to be both a figurehead and *éminence grise* of the regional art scene. However, he was just one of many, including Arthur Dooley, future creator of Mathew Street's "Four Lads Who Shook The World" statue, erected after The Beatles became famous, and the instigator of a spectacular punch-up with the pugnacious Ballard over elitism in art education.

Germane to this discussion, too, are Ballard's swim across the Seine for a bet, as well as his Art College seminars conducted in a nearby pub. A strategy regarded as unorthodox even now, in the early 1960s it verged on lunacy – as to a lesser degree did Arthur's defence of Lennon in the faces of those who wanted his expulsion. Ballard insisted that, if John was "a bloody nuisance and totally uninformed in every kind of way",[7] he possessed more than mere talent. "You could see in his written output the heritage of Lewis Carroll," reckoned Bill Harry. "John also reminded me of Stanley Unwin – his malapropisms, etc – but there was an Englishness about it when everyone else was copying the Americans."

Located within earshot of the bells of both the Anglican and Roman Catholic cathedrals, bohemian Liverpool was, so Harry reaffirmed, "a pallid imitation derived from what the Americans were doing". Nevertheless, it was enough like Greenwich Village, New York's vibrant beatnik district, that newshounds from the muck-raking *Sunday People* were sent there and to other supposed centres of romantic squalor on a crusade to root out what would be headlined "THE BEATNIK HORROR!". Lashing those present in Rod Murray's flat in Gambier Terrace with drinks, the journalists assured everyone that it was to be a feature on the difficulties of surviving on student grants.

It certainly was, agreed John Lennon, who didn't actually live there – although he was trying to persuade Aunt Mimi that everyone who was anyone had their own studio flat near college. Yet, as Mendips – his official address – was technically within the city limits, he didn't qualify for a maintenance grant for living expenses, anyway. While he would breathe in the atmosphere of coloured dust, palette knives and hammer-and-chisel at Gambier Terrace for weeks on end as a "hiding tenant", there was always the safety net of Mimi's home cooking and clean sheets if he needed to get his nerve back for another round of pooling loose change for a trip to the off-licence to see him and his intimates through palavers that turned afternoon into gone midnight.

Mostly, these sessions constituted dialogue for the sake of dialogue, with subjects ranging from the transmigration of souls to the symbolism of dreams to what Sartre wrote about the Soviet intervention in Hungary in 1956 and what Camus thought he meant. Then there were charades, word games, character assassinations of college staff, free-association poetry, séances and shy making soliloquys about the participants' lives, their souls and their aspirations, replete with asides about the masterpieces they were going to paint, the avant-garde films they were going to direct, the ground-breaking novels they were going to get published and the marvellous music they were going to compose...

As their nicotine-stained fingers scribbled, the hacks from *The Sunday People* steered such discussions towards more pragmatic matters, smiling in sympathy when – so Rod Murray remembered – John told them that "he had to go home and scrounge food off his relatives". Inwardly, however, they were feeling dubious about the assignment. The situation wasn't up to scratch – or, to be precise, down to scratch. Murray's room, in which they were sipping coffee, was mildly untidy but quite clean and agreeably decorated. One so-called beatnik flatmate had just come home from an honest day's toil in a suit, while a female tenant had said she had no qualms about inviting her parents around for a candlelit dinner.

Nevertheless, with others eager to get their pictures in the paper, John Lennon obeyed an instruction to dress down and make the place more higgledy-piggledy, chucking some household waste about to make it more photogenic. You want the readers to think you're poor, starving students, don't you?

On 24 July 1960, two million people read *The Sunday People*'s beatnik piece, which was printed alongside a photograph, the first Britain at large saw of John Lennon.[9] With sideburns now past his earlobes and sporting sunglasses, Lennon had pride of place, lolling about on the littered floor amongst Bill Harry, Rod Murray and other self-conscious "beatniks". He looked as if he probably slept in his vest.

A paragraph beginning, "They revel in filth…" consolidated further received wisdom about students for middle-class fathers in slippers, baggy trousers and "quiet" cardigans brandishing patriotic pokers in breakfast rooms whilst deploring the impending abolition of National Service – especially on reading of how one beatnik from Leeds had avoided it "by posing as a psychiatric case". These stalwart heads of families would welcome a return to the days when a sound thrashing would have turned these layabouts from the road to hell, along with every other wastrel across the country living on the grants paid for by the taxes on their elders and betters, and attempting – so it said here – "to seek happiness through meditation". What's meditation when it's at home?

The Sunday People's investigation only served to confirm what had been already guessed about what was described in its pages as "not really orgies – but they do get very naughty", as well as the sordid scenes of the fish-and-chip paper in the fireplaces, the overflowing ashtrays, the peeling wallpaper, the drunk lying face-down in a puddle of vomit on the stairwell and the fresh avalanche of plaster that the door-knocker's rapping thunder had dislodged in the hallway. Outside, rubbish sogged behind the railings of the inner city's crumbling town houses, holding each other up like the drunk and his pals rolling homewards after chucking-out time.

"An awful lot of the stuff in that article was either blatant untruths or so distorted," protested Rod Murray. "All right, we did do silly things. Everybody does when they're young, don't they? I don't think we were quite that odd. Or that bad."[7]

From THE BEATNIK HORROR! surfaced the enduring legend that John Lennon slept in a coffin at Gambier Terrace, although he actually roughed it there only for brief spells, until it made abrupt sense to look homeward again to Mendips, where the sugar was in its bowl, the milk in its jug and the cups unchipped on their saucers and set on an embroidered tablecloth. There he would make short work of the meal

Aunt Mimi prepared for him as he watched a cowboy film on television prior to soaking himself in the hot, scented water of the aqua-coloured bath before going to sleep in his own little room again.

3 "His One Saving Grace Was That Stuart Liked Him"

There was a new mood at college – for a while. It was pleasing for both Aunt Mimi and his tutors to note how industriously a suspiciously subdued Lennon was applying himself to at least aspects of his coursework. John's yardstick of "cool" was now as much Amedeo Modigliani as Elvis Presley or Gene Vincent. The Italian painter's post-Impressionist portraits of fragile females with long necks were perceived as masterpieces. Nevertheless, the Modigliani personality cult hinged more on the hand-to-mouth existence of this gifted but neurotic and improvident bloke whose noble visage effused melancholy and poor health (like Gene Vincent's). These traits were aggravated in part by a proneness to alcoholic blackouts. In 1920, he promoted one of such depth that he never regained consciousness. This was followed immediately by the suicide of his young wife, who had loved him to distraction.

Lennon's new wonderment at Modigliani was down to a new best friend, Stuart Sutcliffe, a gifted painter whose lecture notebooks were as conscientiously full as Lennon's were empty. Indeed, when written or practical assessment was pending, John would cadge assistance from Stuart – and Cynthia – just as he would a Woodbine. "Lennon's no hero of mine," glowered Johnny Byrne, now a TV scriptwriter but then one of Liverpool's arch-beatniks. "His one saving grace was that Stuart – who I respected enormously – liked him, and Stuart knew Lennon in a way that perhaps no one else did at the time."

It was certainly through Sutcliffe that what Paul McCartney would describe as the hitherto self-suppressed "closet intellectual" surfaced in

John. "John debunked a lot of intellectual analysis," judged Stuart's sister Pauline, "particularly when people found in his output roots in all sorts of literary and artistic figures that he would claim never to have been familiar with."

So it was that Lennon shook off enough ingrained indolence to manage at least his transfer from lettering to painting, and actually even to do a bit of painting. Largely because of Sutcliffe too, he became less disinterested in the theory of art to the extent that lectures were often approached as venues for either illicit relaxation or exercising his wit at the tutors' expense.

There will remain division over whether Stuart was gifted – even brilliant – in absolute terms or whether he was just a minor talent peripheral to the fairy tale of John, Paul, George and Ringo, after his purchase of one of these new-fangled electric bass guitars enabled him to be in Lennon's group from 1960 until just the wrong side of the 'Love Me Do' watershed.

Sutcliffe might not have been much of a bass player, and his earliest output as a Liverpool art student, if technically astounding, leaned on the ideas of others, most conspicuously the kitchen-sink realism of John Bratby, Edward Middleditch and other post-war Angry Young Men, themselves derivative of Van Gogh. Nevertheless, in the final months of his life, Sutcliffe produced abstracts that had little obvious precedent. We can speculate forever about whether he'd have gone on to be another Picasso, a designer of Christmas cards, a teacher or on The Beatles' payroll again. According to Astrid Kirchherr, German dress designer, photographer and Sutcliffe's fiancée, "Stuart was a genius and would have been a very, very great writer and painter."[7] Well, to paraphrase Mandy Rice Davies, she would say that, wouldn't she? A more objective view of his work is that of John Willett, a respected art critic and organiser of a Sutcliffe retrospective at Liverpool's Walker Gallery in 1964, who held that it was "a good deal more than merely 'promising'".[10]

In a contemporaneous newspaper article entitled "The Arts In Liverpool,"[11] Willett noted, "the embryonic and still-unconscious relationship between the visual arts, jazz and the rock groups. We shall become more aware of this when the late Stuart Sutcliffe's pictures are shown here in May."

The concept of a firm link between rock 'n' roll and art-college coursework was exemplified by The Beatles' conscious musical progression, and this itself was traceable to Sutcliffe. "Because of his influence," attests Pauline Sutcliffe, "they became more self-consciously 'arty' – not just in the way they looked and sounded but the whole package. After Stuart's death, they achieved something quite extraordinary, in the sense of developing pop music as an art form whilst retaining mass appeal." What cannot be denied is that, with Astrid Kirchherr, Stuart anticipated much of the look – including the gimmick haircuts – adopted by the Moptopped Mersey Marvels before their emergence as pop stars.

It's intriguing to note how many other important British acts from every phase of the mid-1960s beat boom contained members who may once have aspired to pursuing a career in fine art with music merely an extramural pursuit in which personal popularity and financial gain were irrelevant. Off-the-cuff examples are The Rolling Stones, The Yardbirds, The Kinks, The Rockin' Berries, The Animals, The Pretty Things, The Bonzo Dog Band, The Move and Pink Floyd, while Roxy Music, The Portsmouth Sinfonia, Deaf School, The Sex Pistols and Ian Dury And The Blockheads were among those that informed pop undercurrents in the following decade. Culture has been too quick to forget that, after the coming of Beatlemania, many such dabblers let themselves be sucked into a vortex of events, places and circumstances that hadn't belonged to speculation before record-industry talent scouts began to scour the country for, if not *the* New Beatles, then *a* New Beatles.

The Old Beatles' primary artistic emphasis dwelt in sound, but visuals were a good second, whether the Midwich Cuckoo uniformity that first brought them to global attention or the hiring of illustrious pop artist Peter Blake for 1967's *Sgt Pepper's* montage – on which Stuart's image was touchingly included, among more fabled celebrities.

By that time, the Fab Four's long shadow had already furnished Stuart Sutcliffe's posthumous career with its best and worst start. In 1964, the first major retrospective of his work – the one at the Walker – was attended by coach loads of Beatle fans with only the vaguest notion of what they'd come to see. They may have shared the *Liverpool Daily Post* reviewer's opinion of it being an "impressive and moving experience",[11] but to them Stuart was less a legitimate artist than "the fifth Beatle" – auburn-haired when the others were dark – and The One Who Died.

The most authoritative Beatle annals pinpoint a punch-up after a booking at Seaforth's Lathom Hall on either 30 January, 4 February or 6 February 1961 as the ultimate cause of Stuart Sutcliffe's death just over a year later. 2001, however, saw the publication of *The Beatles Shadow: Stuart Sutcliffe & His Lonely Hearts Band*, Pauline Sutcliffe's subjective rewrite of the tie-in biography to the *Backbeat* biopic movie of 1994. The lady now claimed that John and Stuart's mere scuffle in the movie was actually a full-blooded assault that climaxed with Sutcliffe sustaining a kick in the head, which "was what eventually led to Stuart's death". In parenthesis, Pauline also theorises that Stuart and John had oral sex on a bunkbed during The Beatles' first trip to Germany but, if it happened, she didn't witness it. Indeed, her source of this story was Geoffrey Giuliano's *Lennon In America*, and Giuliano was guessing too.

The *Backbeat* book blamed drugs for Stuart's demise, while the film accused some thugs who set upon him and knocked him unconscious outside some Liverpool pub on an unseasonably warm winter's evening in 1959. This incident – portrayed in the opening scene – is worth extrapolating at length, not for its historical accuracy but as an encapsulation of the personal dynamic between the two pals.

We're deep in Liverpool's dockland.

"Kiss me, honey-honey, kiss me..." The amplified song stabs the night air outside a Tetley's pub. Full and noisy, it's a Victorian monstrosity that retains a shabby pre-war grandeur. Through a nicotine haze, we see its sight-reading resident band – piano, sax, bass and drums played by aged semi-pros who always sound as if they're winding up for the night. At the microphone, the "Featured Popular Vocalist" is a pert little madam giving it all she's got. In her imagination, she's Shirley Bassey at the London Palladium. Her exhortation to seduction does not interrupt the chattering tumult of mostly middle-aged drinkers, shutting off – however briefly – the dingier realities of lives led in a huddled land of few illusions.

"Thrill me, honey-honey, thrill me…"

Perhaps making some sort of Art Statement by being in such a place where you'd be least likely to find them, two teenage bohemians, barely old enough to quaff a cherryade on the premises, are dissolving their usual Walter Mitty fantasies in low-life reality. Instead of Ban The Bomb duffle-coats, they're sham-tough in leather jackets, drainpipe jeans and teddy-boy quiffs. One of them looks like a young John Lennon mainly because he is a young John Lennon, while a watered-down James Dean – the Hollywood actor who was the prototype rock 'n' roll rebel – is Stuart Sutcliffe, sketching on the pad that never leaves his side.

At another table, conversation is petering out for Nello, Gral, Spak and Nigel, brawny Player's Navy Cut seamen all. The past ten minutes have been spent knocking back the Tetley's and dragging on cigarettes whilst nodding in guffawing appreciation of Nigel's lying account of how he'd got the bra off Marie-Christine, a hoity-toity Irish-Catholic barmaid who'd never give any of them a second glance. You can see in his leer that Nigel had stowed plenty of ale on board since opening time. Looking around, it seems that all of the judies worth being seen with are spoken for. There is, therefore, nothing for it but the frustrated strategy of a nasty piece of work who wants to make everything else nasty too.

Those skinny lads over there. They'll do. What's more, they don't belong. Everybody else here thinks that Elvis Presley is a nancy boy with his girly haircut – just like theirs. If one of them so much as glances in Nigel's direction, the action will be him. Seconds crawl by as he watches them like a lynx.

Stuart and John consider themselves right desperadoes. En route from the city centre to Injun territory, what a time they had that afternoon. John asked a particularly crabby tobacconist for "20 Players vagina, please." Next, they were thrown out of some desolate amusement arcade for potting the prizes rather than the ducks in the shooting gallery. Ending up in this tavern, they are surfacing as an unscheduled addition to the cabaret.

"Don't care even if I blow my top…"

Their mocking parroting of each line is turning a few heads. The girl's getting the giggles. Tired of waiting, Nigel decides he'll be a lion of justice, striking a blow against these disturbers of decent entertainment for decent folk. He stubs out his cigarette and nudges Nello, who is concluding a debate about Everton's chances of relegation. Bold with beer and the promise of exultant brutality, Nello and the rest scrape back their chairs with Gunfight At The OK Corral *deliberation and follow their leader over to the trouble. Nigel has already weighed things up. He'll concentrate on the weedier one. The other one with the loudest mouth looks as if he might be able to take care of himself.*

Nigel shapes up in front of Stuart, legs apart, thumbs hooked in his belt. Stuart is too involved in the drawing to raise his head.

"Hey, you! You don't like this number?"

"Ask him. It's his sister."

Stuart hands Nigel over to John, who is better at outfacing hard cases. He's the sort that people laugh at rather than beat up. Yet this new situation will not yield vintage Lennon.

There's nothing yet to justify picking a fight, even if the girl's no more his sister than Brigitte Bardot. A second line of attack comes swiftly into play as Nigel alights on Stuart's discarded picture. It's of the female singer, nude. "What's this?"

"Nothing," shrugs Stuart. Then, foolishly, "What do you think it is?"

"I think it's filth!" Nigel shouts as a sudden campaign plan stirs in his mind.

John, hopeful of transforming the slit-eyed and deadly seriousness into light banter, says, "That's art, not filth."

"Art, eh?" chuckles Gral in a manner that is not unfriendly. Maybe the danger will pass.

Nigel isn't going to let it. "Call that art?" he sneers. "What else?"

At last one of the crew cottons on. "Says it's his sister," says Nello, copying Nigel's fathomless gaze at Stuart.

"That's not his sister."

"No?"

The prattle immediately surrounding them drops to half its volume. In this corner of the pub, Nigel has taken over as the star turn. This is the thrill divine, and there isn't a second to be lost.

"That's my fuckin' wife!"

The two boys – and that's all they are – realise that nothing will stop Nigel and his thugs, types who half-kill you to impress girls. Well, if it's inevitable, John's going to stick a pin in first.

"She never is! She wouldn't throw herself away on crap like you. You're too fuckin' ugly!"

"Right!"

It's time to go. Oblivious to everything but the need to escape, John and Stuart are off like greyhounds. Indeed, they make most of their exit on all fours, scrambling through forests of under-the-table limbs. In the drink-slopping uproar above, their pursuers become a cursing search party. Although too shrill for a couple of bars, the singer is a trouper beyond her years and the show goes on.

"But honey-honey, don't stop."

The boys blunder through a sudden side door, then across a yard and over a wall into a back alley. It stinks of piss. Taking grinning stock, it seems like any one of a few such close shaves they've known since falling in with each other at art college. They're feeling lucky – but today isn't their lucky day. From hostile shadows emerge a sauntering phalanx, glistening with malicious glee.

His throat constricting, his skin crawling and his heart pounding like that of a hunted beast – which he is – Lennon forces a shaky smile. "OK, fellows. A joke's a joke."

"Here's another joke," *Nigel snarls.* "See if you get a laugh out of this." *But before the punchline comes, the victims flee in two directions. Neither gets very far. Within yards, Stuart is seized by the shoulders, swivelled around and brought down with a knee in the balls. Meanwhile, Gral has John by the collar and hurls him against the wall. In a frenzy of terror, John lets fly a wild jab that sinks into Gral's stomach and crumples him into a heap, gasping for breath.*

If it had been any other bloke but Stuart, John would probably have scarpered. There's no point in getting hurt too, is there? As it is, he wades in to even up hopeless odds. Stuart is squirming around on the cobbles to amused jeers as he tries to shield his head and genitalia from steel-capped boots. With no pause for careful thought, John lands some indiscriminate punches and even manages to grab Nigel's belt and pull with despairing triumph before losing his grip via a sock in the mouth from Spak.

Stuart is yelling in panic and blood cascades from his face, but that isn't enough. On and on it goes, even after one kick catches him just above the left ear and he loses consciousness. Finally, it stops being fun and he's rolled over into a pile of garbage.

When he comes to, there's no tranquil numbness but an ache of needle-sharp piquancy, quivering in the very centre of his brain. Cracked and rusted cathedral bells crank into reluctant and unintended motion, emitting stark tolls of angry, dischordant clanging. Through a force-field of distortion and pain, he picks up the fading clack of footsteps and John bawling in impotent rage, "I'll get you! I'll get the lot of you! I'm gonna bring a mob down here and beat the crap out of you! I'm gonna get you all!"

The unendurable noise in Stuart's skull vanishes, as mysteriously as it will when it recurs in later years, and the shuddering agony subsides to simply the mother of all headaches. John's features swim into grisly focus in the yellow light of a street lamp. He'll have a fat lip by morning.

"You OK?"

"How do I look?"

"Put it this way: you'll get better. They'll always be ugly."

In an Andy Capp cartoon in *The Daily Mirror*, Capp – a beer-swilling, womanising Geordie – is dissecting the character of his best friend, Chalky, over a venomous pint. A chap on the next barstool adds a disobliging comment of his own about Chalky. Capp's response is not grim agreement but an uppercut that sends the other sprawling: "That's my mate you're talking about!" The amity between Stuart Sutcliffe and John Lennon embraced territory just as forbidden and often inexplicable to outsiders. How else can be explained abrupt reconciliations after hours of verbal and emotional baiting, a tacit implication in a seemingly innocuous remark sparking off a slammed front door and jokes side-splitting to nobody else?

If Lennon and Sutcliffe weren't exactly David and Jonathan, June Furlong, one of the life models at Liverpool's Regional College of

Art, believed that she'd "never seen two teenagers as close as those two". Moreover, their friendship provoked in George and, especially, Paul an apprehension akin to that of a child viewing another sibling as a barrier to prolonged intimacy with an admired elder brother, and for a similar reason Lennon was to be dismayed, initially, when Sutcliffe and Astrid Kirchherr became an item – although this might have been simple jealousy because he fancied her himself.

What is indisputable is that, during the turbulent adolescence that prefaced a turbulent manhood, hardly anyone – as Johnny Byrne deduced – knew Lennon as intimately as Stuart. Nonetheless, the Sutcliffe saga prior to his 1959 encounter with John is, arguably, as interesting as the over-exposed story of his chum. Born on 23 June 1940 in Edinburgh, Stuart had been the first issue of a union that had stunned his father's relations. Charles Sutcliffe had wed a Roman Catholic, Millie Cronin, at a time when papism was still on a par with fascism in many quarters of Scotland. It was, however, the dissolution of a previous marriage that caused the couple to flee to England for several years before returning to Edinburgh for the arrival of Stuart and, in 1942, his sister Joyce. Within a year, however, the fever of mobilisation found them in Huyton, near the Merseyside shipyard, where marine engineer Charles had been posted. The family would never live in Scotland again, and Stuart, Joyce and a second daughter, Pauline, would each catch and hold a Lancashire drawl.

At Prescot Grammar School, Stuart discovered that he could duplicate any known two-dimensional form and had the naïve beginnings of a personal style, as well as a fancy that he'd like to make his way as some sort of visual artist. Nevertheless, although Arthur Ballard drank socially with Mr Sutcliffe, for all Arthur's capacity for holding down the beer, painting wasn't a man's trade, somehow, to Stuart's father. As Millie predicted, "Daddy was shocked. We'd hoped he'd become a doctor. 'My son a painter!' said Daddy. 'I'll never live it down.'"[12]

Stuart held out against his father – who was, in any case, almost permanently away at sea – and enrolled at the Art College a year below normal admittance age, surfacing as a *Wunderkind*. "He could have become a sculptor just as effortlessly as he became a painter," maintained

Philip Hartas, while Arthur Ballard, now Stuart's and Lennon's general tutor, had "met other gifted students, but few, if any, had that particular kind of spark that was genius".

Stuart's abundant output there was the culmination of much painstaking preparation. Bill Harry was immortalised in a Van Gogh-type portrait by Stuart. "First he did about 40 sketches," recalled the subject, "and then he started the painting proper on a piece of board, and he completed it in one afternoon. I was surprised at how easily it came to him. It just sort of flowed."

One of Stuart's course essays, "The Function Of A Door", betrays his preference for working by himself rather than in the chattier ambience of class: "I find in the silence of isolation the element in which all great things fashion themselves." Other philosophical confidences in his writings would coincide with the enlightening nectar that The Beatles would hear from the lips of the Maharishi Mahesh Yogi ten years later.

Ahead of his time sartorially, too, Sutcliffe was notable for combining aspects of the beatnik (such as a transient, wispy beard) with seedy flash "cat" clothes. "James Dean was his hero," said Ballard, "and he looked like him, too." He distanced himself further from others by his taste in music, as Rod Murray recalled: "He was the first to bring rock 'n' roll records into college, even when most people still thought pop was rubbish."

This was a point in Stuart's favour, as far as John Lennon was concerned when, with deceptive casualness, they entered each other's orbits through the auspices of Bill Harry. By early 1959, Bill had been editor and main (some would say sole) contributor to some short-lived and narrowly circulated magazines, one of which was for Frank Hessy's music store, "which Hessy crippled," said Bill, "with the terrible name of *Frank Comments*." Undaunted, Harry's next plan was more ambitious: he was going to write a book about Liverpool. Stuart could illustrate it and John could throw in a few of his funny poems. The project had been motivated through Bill being "very annoyed and frustrated that, whenever I had to go to the cinema, it was all American films. The best comics were supposedly American comics, too, but I personally liked the *Eagle* and things. I was staunchly liking British things, and in particular a Liverpool thing. I said, 'Why can't we do something about Liverpool?'"

An informal working party convened in a students' pub, Ye Cracke in Rice Street, to mull over Bill's latest wheeze. It was a cordial discussion, which ultimately led nowhere, but Stuart and John's friendship began in the bar's smoky recesses. Neither had any inkling then of the extent to which their lives – and deaths – would interweave.

Although they were the same age, John was in the academic year below Stuart. Because of this and their greatly contrasting standpoints over coursework, many college lecturers were surprised later that they even knew each other, let alone became the best of mates. "Stuart was a totally different character in the sense that he was a very reflective chap," maintained Philip Hartas. "He would fall into quiet moods and he'd be thinking a lot or he'd go off and he'd come back in, that sort of thing. There were things going on in his head, and he wasn't living at the tempo that Lennon was living at."[7]

While the differences between Stuart and John consolidated their friendship, so equally did all that they had in common. For instance, they both needed spectacles and neither had an omnipresent father as a guiding (or restraining) force. Each found vague enchantment in the *idea* of aping self-destructive Modigliani – starving in a garret apartment, burning his furniture against the cold of a Parisian winter and going to an early grave for his art. However, a less uncomfortable option might have been the happy(ish) ending in *The Horse's Mouth*, a light film comedy – based loosely on a Joyce Cary novel – that the pair saw at the Jacey Cinema in Clayton Square in 1958. Starring Alec Guinness and with kitchen-sink sets designed by John Bratby, the movie was about an obsessive artist, a social liability who might have been Modigliani's frightfully refined English cousin. He's frightful to live with too, but his friends stick by him. In a way, this antedated what one college contemporary was to say of Lennon: "He was a terrible fellow, really, but I liked him."

John had learned at least as much about self-immolation from his drunken exploits with more footloose lads from college than from his discussions about Modigliani with Stuart. Furthermore, unlike Modigliani, *The Horse's Mouth* character and, indeed, Sutcliffe, John was basically lazy. Yet, with Stuart showing him how, he grew less cautious about the marks he made on the canvas. "It was Stuart who nurtured an interest in John to want to know more about things than he knew," said Arthur Ballard. "In other words, he was educating him. Lennon wouldn't have known a Dada from a donkey. He was just so ignorant."[7]

Conversely, Stuart was often content to be a passive listener as John, angry or cynically amused by everything, held forth during their wanderings along street and corridor, giving his lightning-bright imagination its ranting, arm-waving head.

Occasionally, Stuart would let slip a seemingly uncontroversial comment, which might spark off a sudden and inexplicable spasm of rage in John. He'd take a long time to calm down. Then again, Lennon would mock his comrade for no tangible reason at all. "Hanging's too good for it" was his view of one of Stuart's early abstracts.

"I can imagine John taking the mickey out of Stuart mercilessly in private," reflected Bill Harry. "He'd try it on, and if you stood up to it, fine. If you put up with it, he'd keep on." Although Stuart struck back occasionally, nothing John said or did could belittle him in Stuart's eyes, and vice versa. Outlines dissolved and contents merged. They started to dress similarly and copy each other's mannerisms; John, for instance, took to flicking his cigarette away just like Stuart always did. Without purposely snubbing anybody, they evolved a restricted code that few outsiders could crack. Ballard would cite Stuart as source of "a lot of that goofy kind of...Dadaist sort of humour. It's entirely Stuart's influence on John Lennon that introduced that Dada element."[6]

In turn, Sutcliffe's fascination with Lennon extended to spectating during his rehearsals with George Harrison and Paul McCartney whenever the college's Life Room was vacant. Alternatively, John, Stuart and the other two might sit at one of the kidney shaped tables for hours in the local Jacaranda coffee bar, a convenient stone's throw away. The café was owned by Allan Williams, who began acting in a quasi-managerial capacity for Johnny And The Moondogs not long after one of Stuart's canvases, "Summer Painting", won a junior prize at the second of John Moores' biannual exhibitions at the Walker and was subsequently bought by the son of Moores himself, founder of the Littlewoods Pools empire and Merseyside's foremost philanthropist.

This gave Sutcliffe the wherewithal to make the down-payment on his Hofner President bass at Hessy's. With John, Stuart also originated a more attention-grabbing name, The Silver Beetles, although John added that it should be spelled Beatles, as in beat music.

What they needed more, however, was the drummer that had been lacking since the last days of The Quarry Men. Early in 1960, they found one in Tommy Moore – although it was assumed that, with his heart in jazz, 26-year-old Tommy would suffice only until the arrival of someone more suitable for an outfit derided as "posers" by certain personnel in fellow local bands Cass And The Cassanovas, Rory Storm And The Hurricanes, Derry And The Seniors and other more workman-like city outfits. John and Paul's pretensions as composers caused comment, too, because neither a teenager in a dance hall nor the BBC Light Programme's director would be interested in their home-made songs.

Nevertheless, The Silver Beetles were developing into a more credible attraction than The Quarry Men, having moved up from youth clubs and Students' Union supports to welfare institutes, far-flung suburban palais, Lancashire village halls, working men's clubs and, indeed, any venue that had embraced regular "beat" sessions.

Moreover, Lennon had spat out the nicely spoken Lancashire plum in his singing as well as in his speaking and now had a baritone that was bashed about and lived-in – in other words, the voice of a great rock 'n' roll vocalist. By European *bel canto* standards, the adult John Lennon couldn't sing – not "real singing", as sonorous as Roy Orbison's supple purity or Elvis Presley when he tried hymns. Lennon's voice had lost all vowel purity and nicety of intonation, probably because he had been endeavouring consciously to sound like the classic rockers he admired while it was either still breaking or just freshly broken. As Gene Pitney's polished tenor would be warped to an electric-drill-like whine – albeit an oddly appealing one – so John's uncertain treble had been corrupted for all time by, say, hot-potato-in-the-mouth Presley, the hollered arrogance of Jerry Lee Lewis, neo-hysterical Little Richard and Gene Vincent, "The Screaming End".

John's voice grew more strangled as he broke sweat and his adolescent spots rose through the lacto-calomine lotion and turned red. He was probably nothing without the PA system, but when he became intense, every sound he dredged up was like a brush-stroke on a painting. Backing off until the microphone was at arm's length, just a sandpapery quiver during a dragged-out note could be as loaded as a roar with it halfway down his throat.

Yet The Silver Beatles failed to feature among the local fare advertised low on the bill when, on 3 May 1960, Gene Vincent headlined a three-hour extravaganza at Liverpool Boxing Stadium, promoted by Allan Williams and celebrated pop Svengali Larry Parnes. The principal studs in the latter's stable of male performers were Tommy Steele, Marty Wilde and Billy Fury, while he also handled the equally charismatic Vince Eager, formerly Roy Taylor of The Vagabonds.

Roy/Vince had been on the bill of a 1960 UK tour by Eddie Cochran, a multi-talented Presley type from Oklahoma, which ended in a road accident on 17 April between the Bristol Hippodrome and Heathrow Airport. "Larry Parnes rang to say that I ought to get down to the hospital in Bath, where Eddie was on the danger list," recalled Eager. "There, the surgeon told me that Eddie was unlikely to survive. I was extremely upset, but when I emerged from the hospital, there was Parnes with the press and half his bloody pop stars, ready for a photo opportunity. I just drove off and refused to speak to Larry, who even before Eddie died had told the newspapers (a) about the 'irony' of Eddie's latest release, 'Three Steps To Heaven' – which was in fact the B-side then – and (b) that I was off to fly back to America with the coffin."

Any bonhomie of old between Parnes and Eager degenerated to probing suspicion, but Gene Vincent – also pulled from the wreckage – had insisted on honouring existing British dates, such as the one in Liverpool where Larry had ensured that Lance Fortune, Julian X and other of his lesser stars were also included. A last-minute addition to the bill, Gerry Marsden's ensemble – now rechristened Gerry And The Pacemakers – arrived in the first division of regional popularity.

In the Jacaranda after the show, Parnes thought aloud about a further, less ambitious joint venture with Allan Williams. He wanted, he explained, an all-purpose backing outfit for use by certain of his singers. Names he kept mentioning were Marty Wilde – then sagging on the ropes but bound to have another big hit soon – and Billy Fury, a Liverpudlian then on the crest of his first Top Ten breakthrough.

As ordinary Ronald Wycherley, Fury had first met Parnes in Marty Wilde's dressing room at Birkenhead's Essoldo Theatre in 1958. Ronald had recovered recently from rheumatic fever but, enthralled by his prominent cheekbones and restless eyes, Larry gave him his familiar stage alias and levered him into the package show that night. The proverbial overnight sensation, Fury was then dressed by Parnes in gold lamé and his metamorphosis from a nobody to a teen idol was set in motion. Billy/Ronnie rarely spoke to fans, as at that time he was apparently self-conscious about his "wacker" accent, which to anyone south of Birmingham sounded simultaneously alien and common then.

Nevertheless, Fury was more comfortable as an English Elvis than either Tommy Steele or Cliff Richard, who had both entered the 1960s by following the wholesome all-round-entertainer path. Nonetheless, Richard's backing ensemble, The Shadows, were respected generally as Britain's top instrumental act – although not by John Lennon, who affected to despise the showbiz polish and now-period charm of their big smiles and intricately synchronised footwork. Larry Parnes told Allan Williams that Billy Fury was looking for an outfit who could rival The Shadows as he did Cliff, and that Larry would bring Billy along if Allan could hurriedly assemble some Liverpool groups for him to see.

Although John Lennon was also present in the Jacaranda that night, he couldn't summon the courage to approach the Great Man, but two nights later he asked Williams if The Silver Beatles could audition for the job. Allan assented, but he pointed out that they'd be up against Cliff Roberts and his Rockers, Derry And The Seniors, Cass And The Cassanovas, Gerry And The Pacemakers, you name 'em – the very upper crust of Liverpool pop.

That morning, John fiddled with his hair prior to donning the current group-costume of jeans, short-sleeved black shirt, two-tone tennis shoes and apposite mock-silver pendant. Then he and the other Silver Beatles – minus a latecoming Tommy Moore – joined the midday queue of hopefuls at the Wyvern Social Club, with its essence of disinfectant and faint whiff of last night's alcohol, tobacco and food.

Although some of the other groups wore sewing-machined tat, worn and torn with frayed cuffs and indelible stains born of sweat and spillage, The Silver Beatles felt grubby beside those with starched-white handkerchiefs protruding smartly from the top pockets of their matching bespoke suits cut by city centre tailors.

George tried to locate the source of a buzz from an amplifier while John paced up and down, smoking furiously and cursing the still-absent Moore. Abruptly he stopped midstep, having decided to take up a post near the door through which he reckoned Billy and Larry would enter. It was as if he'd forgotten the emergency of the situation as he kept muttering to himself what he was going to say and the cool way he'd say it.

John and everyone else were brought up sharp when Allan Williams shepherded Billy – head down, collar up – and Larry Parnes across the dance area to wooden seats in its most acoustically sympathetic spot. During a break in the subsequent proceedings, John Lennon was among those approaching Billy Fury for an autograph. Paul, George and Stuart had never seen him this way before, so spellbound and humble. It was as he was enacting a parody of hero-worship, but it was too obvious that he wasn't. "Thanks, Billy – if it's all right to call you that," he grinned after Fury signed the proffered scrap of paper. "I...um...I'm John. I sing with a group!"

"Keep singin', man," replied Billy with a – possibly insincere – grin, "don't let it die." That was how a true star behaved.

Perhaps John had half an idea that, if Fury and Parnes didn't like The Silver Beatles, he was going to somehow ingratiate himself with them, join the payroll to fix Billy's drinks, light his cigarettes, laugh at his jokes. Maybe he'd be taken on as a clapper boy. Clapper boy? Gene Vincent used to have these two who just...well, clapped their hands, sang backing vocals and generally leapt around to get everyone raving.

After this rapt interlude, John resumed his hard-man persona as if nothing had happened, and then it was The Silver Beatles' turn to show what they could do. Unable to wait any longer for Tommy Moore, Lennon implored Johnny Hutchinson of the Cassanovas to step in until the interruption of Tommy's eventual arrival and the consequent delay while he settled behind the kit.

Yet The Silver Beatles gained the day, insofar as Parnes scribbled on his notepad, "Silver Beetles [*sic*] – very good. Keep for future work." Less than a fortnight later, John, Paul, George, Stuart and Tommy were off on a string of eight one-nighters in Scotland, backing not Billy Fury but Johnny Gentle, a Parnes luminary less likely to give Cliff Richard cause for nervous backwards glances. A year younger than Lennon, Gentle had once been John Askew, a merchant seaman who sang semi-professionally before he was spotted and rechristened by Parnes. Beginning with 1959's 'Boys And Girls Were Meant For Each Other', this square-jawed hunk's 45s all missed the UK chart, but he was often seen on British television pop series such as *Oh Boy!* and *Drumbeat* and was, therefore, guaranteed a period of well-paid one-nighters with pick-up groups who'd mastered mutually familiar rock 'n' roll standards and the simpler sides of Johnny's four singles.

Travelling to Scotland with Gentle, as each Silver Beatle's small wage dwindled the spurious thrill of "going professional" manifested itself in John purportedly assisting Johnny with the composition of a song entitled 'I've Just Fallen For Someone'. Lennon was to be uncredited, however, when the number was issued by Parlophone in 1963, when Gentle had assumed another *nom du théâtre*, 'Darren Young', and when it was recorded by Adam Faith on his eponymous debut album two years earlier.

This creative diversion was atypical of the prevalent mood of stoic cynicism during the trek around Scotland, particularly following an engagement noted for Tommy Moore drumming with his head in bandages, the sole casualty of an accident that left their van crumpled into a stationary car that afternoon. He had also become a prime target of Lennon's poking of ruthless fun, especially now that George had started to stick up for himself. Moreover, via shameless manoeuvring, John eased himself between the sheets of the only single bed available at one bed and breakfast while Tommy and anyone else out of favour spent as comfortable a night as was feasible in sleeping bags on the floor.

Well before they steamed back to Liverpool, a disgusted Moore – with only £2 left to show for his pains – had had enough of washing in streams, shaving in public-convenience hand basins, staring across a wayside café's formica tabletop as that loathsome Lennon tunnelled into a greasy but obviously satisfying chips-with-everything fry-up – and especially the van, that mobile fusion of lunatic asylum and death cell.

A beat group without a drummer was no use to anyone. Into the bargain, Britain's take on traditional jazz was now midway through a golden age, bracketed by Chris Barber's million-selling version of Sidney Bechet's 'Petite Fleur' in 1959 and Chris and his band framing Ottilie Patterson's ebullient singing over the closing credits of the 1962 movie *It's Trad, Dad*. This trend had spread across the English Channel, where The Dutch Swing College Band, Germany's Old Merrytale Jazz Band and other pre-eminent outfits on the continent had absorbed their music from British 'dads' like Barber, Kenny Ball and Acker Bilk rather than its US originators.

Trad-jazz bands were therefore more numerous than they'd ever been when John, Paul and George were Quarry Men, and so were the places in which they could play. In the Cavern, for instance, Liverpool's main jazz stronghold, there were specific designations about what should and shouldn't be heard there. Watching enthusiasts were likely to know more about the music than many of the entertainers, and it hadn't been unknown for purists to express their displeasure with slow handclapping and a shower of pennies cascading onto the stage if, say, a trad outfit deviated from prescribed New Orleans precedent by including saxophones.

While Cavern manager Ray McFall could understand that efforts to expand a given act's work spectrum must involve a degree of hyperbole and opportunism, he believed that he was entirely justified in making substantial deductions to the already minuscule fees of any young group who, having misrepresented themselves as maybe "a jump-blues outfit" to procure an interval slot there, committed the cardinal sins of amplification and creation of music in which the jazz content was negligible. The Cavern had put up with skiffle in the past, but what could not be tolerated was lowbrow rock 'n' roll. It was, he scowled, detrimental to the club's reputation.

4 *"Aggressive Restraint, A Brando Type"*

Bruno Koschmider owned the Kaiserkeller and the Indra – night clubs off the Reeperbahn ("Rope Street") in the heart of Hamburg's Grosse Freiheit ("Great Freedom"), where a red-light district had developed since the pillaging French had passed through in 1814. He had been one of the first German impresarios to put action over debate with regard to *Englander* pop. The entertainment in the Kaiserkeller had been mostly coin-operated, but a German group had been hired for the evening when, on an visit to Hamburg in spring 1960, professional interest found Allan Williams seated at one of the club's tables. When the music got under way, he moaned quietly to his companion, Lord Woodbine, another figure whose association with The Beatles eventually made him better known than he might have otherwise been.

As plain Harold Phillips, Woodbine arrived from Trinidad in 1948 to settle in an area of central Liverpool where Scouse Bohemia intermingled with a Scouse Harlem. Ennobling himself with a lordship named after the cheap cigarettes he chain-smoked, he was established quickly as "one of a great line of Liverpool characters," smiled Bill Harry, "full of cheek and audacity, but fun to know." Among his many occupations were builder and decorator, calypso singer and barman in the rougher parts of Toxteth, where he defused any unrest by brandishing a cutlass.

Woodbine was a reassuring presence at Allan Williams' side in the Kaiserkeller, where the native combo were actually quite proficient in a complacent kind of way, but Williams – abetted by Woodbine – was soon spieling in top gear about the marvellous Liverpool outfits he could procure for the fellow in charge. Outside the USA, whose rock 'n' rollers Bruno Koschmider couldn't afford, Allan's groups were rated as the finest by no less than Larry Parnes, manager of Billy Fury, who was the English Elvis as surely as The Old Merrytale Jazz Band were Germany's "answer" to bands led by "trad dads" like Monty Sunshine and Chris Barber.

The parley ended, nonetheless, on a sour note when it transpired that Allan's tape of the acts under discussion had been rendered a cacaphonous mess, possibly through demagnetisation somewhere *en route*.

Yet, following Williams and Woodbine's deflated departure, Bruno had to sample British pop for himself. Not in Liverpool, however, but Soho, the closest London came to having a red-light area. Specifically, he was looking for the 2 I's coffee bar, where this Larry Parnes person had "discovered" Tommy Steele and Marty Wilde. Familiar smells of multi-mega-tar tobacco, real coffee and Greek and Italian restaurants were lacing the evening air when, down Old Compton Street, he found what he'd been assured was still the epicentre of British pop.

The coffee bar was small, smaller than the Indra, and there was an immediate tell-tale sign of it having known better days in a yellowing photo display in the window of Tommy, Marty, Cliff, Adam and others who probably hadn't been near the place since they'd scented chart success. Nevertheless, Koschmider snatched a ragbag of London-based players – including singing guitarists Tony Sheridan and Ricky Richards, the *Shake It Daddy* man – to be reassembled as the Kaiserkeller's house band, named The Jets and put to work six nights a week on the club's rickety stage for an exploratory period.

On their opening night, the Englishmen's devil-may-care exuberance – pleasing themselves rather than the customers – brought them safely into harbour. "We had a Midas touch," said Sheridan with quiet pride. "There was no question of failure. It was nothing like we'd ever experienced in England. Our repertoire was about 50 per cent rocked-up skiffle, 50 per cent rock 'n' roll." This combination embraced a wide spectrum, from weepy 'Nobody's Child' to torrid workouts of Ray Charles' 'What'd I Say', which sometimes finished with Tony's collapse after up to 30 minutes of trading heys and yeahs with an enraptured crowd left wanting more.

However, by the late summer, the Kaiserkeller needed a comparable draw to The Jets, who were now administering their powerful elixir at a rival establishment, the Top Ten. Bruno remembered and made contact with Allan Williams, who sent Derry and the Seniors. Within days, the Kaiserkeller was thriving again and Koschmider's thoughts turned to his sleazier Indra. With few customers for its gartered erotica most evenings, it could be only more profitable to put on pop there too.

Koschmider then requested another Derry And The Seniors from his man in Liverpool, who wondered about the group now trading as just plain Beatles. The Scottish expedition with Johnny Gentle hadn't elevated the band from being a kind of pop equivalent of a stock chorus girl to instant West End stardom; on the contrary, they'd hit rock bottom as accompanists to the cavortings of Janice, a Mancunian stripper at the New Cabaret Artistes club, a fly-by-night dive run under the aegis of Williams and Woodbine.

This booking passed without incident, but there was trouble when, in June 1960, The Beatles gained a mercifully brief weekly residency at the corporation-owned Grosvenor Ballroom in Liscard, a suburb of Wallasey at the mouth of the Mersey, on the opposite bank to Liverpool. Although the group weren't mentioned in no less than two local journals' *exposés*, The Beatles played against prolonged outbreaks of hooliganism involving assault, actual bodily harm and criminal damage. These and other disturbances enhanced the district's notoriety as a scene of rowdyism, with teenagers pouring in to join the fun from as far away as Runcorn, nearly 30km (20 miles) downriver.

The venue degenerated into fist-flying roughhouses whenever delegations from enemy gangs attended. When someone was concussed by a projectile one Saturday night, a mass reprisal against his supposed assailants concluded with a broken nose and sprained wrist for one of the "bouncers" – security officers employed by promoter Les Dodd. More serious was the stabbing of a boy on a Beatles night at another of Dodd's concerns, the Institute in nearby Neston. The injured boy was rushed to hospital for treatment, requiring 24 stitches.

The musicians weren't safe, either. The drummer in one of the other groups was scragged behind his kit by "fans" who rolled him on the floor and ran off with his sticks. As for The Beatles, their own conduct – especially that of Lennon – did not defuse unrest. Yet despite purported instances of unpunctuality, slovenly stage attire and arriving a player short or with only half their equipment, they became a reliable draw. "For today's teenagers, the most basic musical standards are acceptable," one anonymous parish councillor was quoted, "as long as the song is recognisable as rock 'n' roll or fresh from the Top 20 pops. I don't object to how or what these groups play as long as it's within the bounds of propriety and that they can make a go of the 'National Anthem' at the end if hall regulations require it – which they seldom do these days."[13]

Among the Wallasey Corporation's listed complaints were smashed windows, defaced lavatory walls, countless dents to the pinewood floor by stiletto heels and – beggaring belief – persons unknown removing the piano from one of the auditoriums and abandoning it on a distant railway bridge, where it remained for almost a fortnight while two borough councils debated responsibility for locating its owner. Closer to home, a wrought-iron gate was lifted from its hinges and dumped in Grosvenor Street, causing burst tyres to the car of an elderly gentleman, who lost his spectacles in an altercation after he remonstrated with watching youths whom he suspected were responsible.

Less specific grievances from residents were the noise from motorcycles and hordes of rowdies taunting and threatening passers-by. Moreover, neighbourhood gardens were used as receptacles for cigarette butts and broken liquor bottles, while the sexton of Trinity Church, at the junction of Grosvenor Street and Manor Road, reported the finding of used condoms and discarded underwear in the long grass around the graveyard.

Les Dodd, too, acknowledged that matters were getting out of hand now that he was taking more than 300 admissions every Saturday. Yet, while these "big-beat" sessions were profitable, they had become, he agreed, a magnet for disorder beyond someone merely letting off a fire extinguisher on the way out. Therefore, he said, he was reverting to his old policy of admitting only the over 20s and keeping the music to a strict tempo – no jiving, no rock 'n' roll and definitely no teenagers.

On being told of the loss of the Grosvenor nights one afternoon in the Jacaranda, Lennon shook a frustrated fist in the direction of London, which was only maybe four hours away on the train but might as well have been on Mars. A showcase engagement in the capital was the key to going onwards and upwards. Like that clichéd movie sequence of dates being ripped off a calendar to a background of clips, a slow dazzle would preface the final Grosvenor-type bookings, then package tours with big names...sessions on the BBC Light Programme's *Saturday Club*...recording contracts...Number Ones...*Sunday Night At The London Palladium* on ITV...

Then John's reverie was brought up short. The fly in the ointment was that no one could get a booking in London until they got a booking in London. Confused? So was John. If a band made contact with an agency there, they'd be told that a representative would turn up the next time they played in London. The band would then explain that they hadn't got anything coming up in London because every time they rang a London agency, they were informed that someone would go and see them next time they played in London. At this point, the agent would say he was sorry but he couldn't do anything until they landed a booking in London.

Lennon had also heard reports that Rory Storm And The Hurricanes were going down an apposite storm during their weeks at a Butlin's holiday camp in north Wales. All the future seemed to hold for The Beatles was the trivial round of recurring and diminishing local engagements. It was likely that the battle to stay afloat would force them back to the youth clubs from whence they'd come, particularly as they hadn't yet recruited a full-time drummer since the exit of Tommy Moore.

For every door that opened, two closed – but hire-purchase debts were among principal reasons why certain Beatles couldn't really quit the group, no matter what, even when, at one of the Grosvenor evenings, of the £45 in net takings only £10 had been split between three acts.

Out-of-town trips weren't a consideration, either, mainly because there were so many new outfits being formed that the jobs went almost always to locals. Why bring in outsiders when your own can do the job just as well for a fraction of the cost?

Another worry was the continuing trad-jazz craze. The Tony Osborne Sound's 'Saturday Jump' was the opening and closing theme to *Saturday*

Club and females were fainting to such as Bilk, Barber, Ball, Humphrey Lyttelton and The Temperance Seven, even if it was as much to do with the boozy atmosphere generated as the personalities and the sounds they made – ie plinking banjos, endless tootling by front-line horns and a Louis Armstrong impersonator singing like he'd been gargling with iron filings, all set off by barrister wigs and legal gowns, Roman togas, Confederate Army uniforms or some other ridiculous take on the striped waistcoats and bowler hats that Bilk and his Paramount Jazz Band wore.

So The Beatles loitered in city centre pubs and cafés with other rock 'n' rollers in the same boat, small-talking, borrowing equipment, comparing notes, gossiping, giving away secrets. Out would pour lies about how close they were to their first single coming out and how they were a sure-fire certainty to support Screaming Lord Sutch when his never-ending string of one-nighters next reached the North, carrying on as if these possibilities were still on the cards long after the trail had gone cold, if they ever existed in the first place.

On top of that, there was a rumour that a girl was expecting Stuart Sutcliffe's child and was pressing him to do the decent thing voluntarily upon pain of her brothers manhandling him to the registry office. A spell outside The Beatles' usual orbit might have appeared a fine notion to Stuart, despite Arthur Ballard seething about his star pupil abandoning his art course for John Lennon's beat group.

It was small wonder, therefore, that the lads were open to an offer of work in Germany, on the proviso that they could enlist a drummer. At the Casbah, a teenage haunt where they'd played as Quarry Men, they understood that proprietor Mona Best's handsomely saturnine son, Pete, was beating the skins with the club's resident quartet, The Blackjacks. With the information that The Blackjacks were about to disband, there was no harm in The Beatles asking if he fancied a trip to Hamburg. Pete packed his case with Mona's full approval, but 19-year-old John had to jump the highest hurdle of parental opposition. Nevertheless, tight-lipped Mimi washed her hands of the whole business, although she would not acknowledge – as her son did – that his Art College studies were over.

On 17 August 1960, John breathed foreign air for the first time when the night ferry docked at the Hook of Holland and Lord Woodbine took over at the wheel of an overloaded minibus carrying the five Beatles, Allan Williams, his wife and brother-in-law – who was to snap a much-syndicated photograph of the passengers, minus Lennon, too comfortable in a prime seat – at the Arnhem War Memorial.

Williams and Woodbine's eyes were bloodshot with nigh-on two solid days' driving when youths and adults climbed down from the minibus outside the Kaiserkeller, which was plusher than any palais they'd played on Merseyside. However, after Bruno took charge of his human freight, he conducted them around the dingy Indra and then to three small, windowless rooms adjoining a toilet in a cinema over the road. This was where The Beatles would sleep. Even Woodbine and Lennon were too nonplussed to joke about Stalag 13, Red Cross parcels and forming an escape committee.

After a couple of hours of convalescent sloth, The Beatles rose to give their first ever performance outside the United Kingdom. How could they have imagined then that, six years later, they'd be giving a scream-rent concert at the now-demolished Ernst-Merck-Halle – a Hamburg equivalent of the London Palladium – to which they'd be driven in state in a fleet of Mercedes with *Polizei* outriders?

In 1960, however, nearly all newcomers from Britain wished that they were in hell rather than Hamburg at first, but they couldn't wait to get back there when their sojourn was over. There might have been better ways of breaking a group in, but The Beatles didn't know of any. Being on the road and staying in bed-and-breakfast establishments for eight days in Scotland was one thing, but being up each other's armpits in the dungeons in which they lived when working for Koschmider was another. All of them – including middle-class Lennon – discovered within themselves instincts that they hadn't known existed for living together in their foul quarters, which soon became fouler with the remains of junk food, empty beer bottles, overflowing makeshift ashtrays and general sock-smelling frowstiness.

Musically, too, John, Paul, George, Stuart and Pete came to know each other in an almost extra-sensory way whilst ascertaining how to "read" an audience. Thus at the Indra – and, a few weeks later, at the plusher Kaiserkeller – John's runaway tongue unfurled and the sailors, gangsters, prostitutes and tourists on nights out and teenagers who'd stumbled in from the street laughed with him and even took a chance on the dance floor as they got used to the newcomers' ragged dissimilarity to the contrived splendour of television pop singers. The five scruffy Liverpudlians had good and bad nights, of course, but there were moments when they were truly tearing it up, the most wailing combo on the planet.

After hours, they had been guided around the city's diversions by members of both The Seniors and, nearing the end of their Top Ten run, The Jets. Ricky Richards had accompanied John Lennon to the Musikhaushummel shop for the handing-over of crumpled deutschmarks for a short-armed Rickenbacker Model 1996 guitar.[14] Later, on a flying visit to Hamburg in 1961, Richards was to join The Beatles onstage, borrowing John's expensive instrument to give 'em his 'I Go Ape' and 'C'mon Everybody' party pieces.

While the band fraternised with dyed-in-the-wool rock 'n' rollers like Richards, as well as the Kaiserkeller's formidable team of waiter-*cum*-bouncers, the fact that the five Beatles who'd arrived in Hamburg were ex-grammar school and, therefore, supposedly of Britain's academic elite might have been a subliminal lure for Hamburg's existentialist crowd – the "Exis" – of which Jurgen Vollmer, Klaus Voorman and Astrid Kirchherr were leading lights. This was in spite of George Harrison's confidence to a scribbling journalist in 1967 that he thought The Beatles, overall, were "academic failures". And indeed, when the need arose, Sutcliffe, Lennon and McCartney were capable of inserting into conversations long words – in English, mind, but long words all the same – plus studentish vernacular, along with mention of the likes of Modigliani and Danish philosopher Soren Kierkegaard. With Harrison, they'd once been involved in a fusion of poetry and rock with Sussex beat poet Royston Ellis, who'd judged them to be "more of the bohemian ilk than other young northerners of the time". To a certain degree, Stuart, John and Paul – and, indeed, Pete and George – played up to it. In one incident, they dumbfounded a member of another outfit in the dressing room by pretending to be reading Russian poetry to each other, each intoning and murmuring appreciatively in mock seriousness.

Perhaps via some complex inner debate, this general arty aura enabled Hamburg's young aesthetes – who, bragged Vollmer, "spoke pretty well English that we had learned at school"[15] – to give in to a self-conscious conviviality as they tuned into the epic vulgarity taking place on stages in the Kaiserkeller, the Top Ten and elsewhere in the Reeperbahn mire. Some detected a strength of personality in John that was lacking in the rest. "Lennon, the obvious leader, was like a typical rocker," estimated Jurgen Vollmer, "cool, no gestures except for pushing his body slightly in rhythm to the music. Aggressive restraint, a Brando type."[7] Yet Lennon wasn't all sullen magnetism, as he had few qualms about using coarse language in heated moments on the boards and would attack, say, 'Hound Dog' with the blood-curdling dementia of one in the throes of a fit.

The bass player to Lennon's left, however, was no one's idea of a genius entertainer. That, however, didn't matter to Astrid Kirchherr, because during one Kaiserkeller evening she and he had crossed the boundary between inferred companionship and declared love. However odd a choice this Englishman, there were no old-fashioned looks *chez* Kirchherr after Astrid and Stuart began to share the same bed.

Ken Horton, an old schoolfriend of Stuart's, would receive written details of the moment when Stuart proposed to "my too-wonderful little angel. I'm her church and she's the bells that ring!"[7] John, a more volatile pal, thought that there were bats in his belfry, and, therefore, so did Paul, George and Pete. As self-appointed guardian of Stuart's moral welfare, Lennon dictated the party line: Astrid is a great-looking bird, granted, but fancy tying yourself down when great-looking birds are available in every corner of the Grosse Freiheit.

The subtext, of course, was that Astrid had loosened John's bond with Stuart. These days, just the subtlest inflexion in Sutcliffe's voice would send Lennon into a paroxysm of virulent bad temper, especially when Astrid was around. When she wasn't, he'd ease up, happy to have Stuart's undivided attention once again. Yet, present or absent, Astrid was often in direct line of fire when Lennon exercised an unappealing tendency – that he would never curb – to blurt out what his mind hadn't formulated in simple terms.

The astounding boorishness that would explode like shrapnel all around the Kaiserkeller could be funnelled to more concentrated effect in less public situations. Still stereotyping Germans after all these weeks, an aside like "Rudolph Hess asked me to tell you he was quoted out of context" would issue from the side of Lennon's mouth when simply ordering a lager from a barmaid. At first, Astrid couldn't imagine why she'd been singled out for worse and more relentless treatment. She'd answer back, but just as disconcerting as his tirades were John's intermittent retreats, as if to a prepared position.

To see the two people he cared about most rearing up at each other cut Stuart like a sharp knife. As if watching a tennis match, his eyes would dart from bride-to-be to best friend as harmless jesting swung in seconds to open trading of insults. He couldn't even fight for the woman he worshipped in this, the severest test ever of the mutual and reciprocal loyalty that was the bedrock of his relationship with John. As Lennon stormed off after another excruciating round with Astrid, Stuart would empty his lungs with a whoosh and begin the case for the defence – as John would do for him were the position reversed. Whether beside herself with rage or weak with relief, Astrid would receive the old placatory reassurance that John was a fine fellow when you got to know him.

Astrid's assumption that Lennon loathed her, however understandable, was actually false. She was just the sort of bird he'd have liked for himself – closer to a well-mannered Brigitte Bardot than Cynthia – but he felt that she was out of his league. Indeed, it was inconceivable initially that a girl like that was going out with Stu. Maybe he – John – wasn't so much in a lower league as a different one. If he'd been brave enough to chuck Cynthia and Stuart hadn't been interested, John might have sniffed around Astrid himself. As it was, there were long, dangerous moments, even at the height of antagonism, but like many so-called extroverts he covered a sensitivity with respect to women by brutalising himself – in his case, by coming on as the rough, untamed Scouser.

He was childish and a right bastard to boot, but both Astrid and her mother found it hard to hide a fascination with Lennon, whom both perceived to be probably the most seethingly angry person in the world. On visits to her home in the prim suburb of Altona, he would scan the bookshelves and Astrid's record rack, making few exceptions in a string of derisive comments about every author – Cocteau, Sartre, Genet ("all that Left Bank shower"[7]), Poe, Wilde, Nietzsche, de Sade – and composers like Wagner and Stravinsky, whose works he may or may not have heard.

One day, however, the tempest dropped and he stopped fighting the situation. His manner towards Astrid became not genial, exactly, but brusquely urbane. The exchange of a civil word or two gave way every so often to what might be construed as a compliment. Although his lips never moved upwards, his eyes began to smile almost gently upon her. She was Stuart's and, if she was his, he'd feel the same way about her. Suddenly, he was pleased for Stuart. He'd done all right there.

Of course, he wouldn't have been the John Lennon of popular acclaim if he'd moderated the barbed invective, but with Astrid, at least, it was delivered with much the same lurking affection that he also reserved for Stuart. Gradually, Astrid grasped the social contradiction of rudeness and bonhomie that was Lennon. This paradox in his nature was exemplified during a memorable first encounter in Hamburg with Frank Allen, one of Middlesex's Cliff Bennett And The Rebel Rousers. "Ah yes. It's Frank, isn't it?" acknowledged John after being introduced, "I've talked to other people in the club and it seems that, next to Cliff, you're the most popular member in the band. I don't know why. Your harmonies are fucking ridiculous."[16]

The concordat between Stuart, John and Astrid did not lessen the growing antipathy towards Sutcliffe shown by the rest of the outfit, long-faced from the start about his lackadaisical bass playing. Paul's summary was that "he'd fallen madly in love with [Astrid], and it peeved us like mad that she hadn't fallen in love with any of us: this great blonde chick that we'd never seen the likes of. Stu was really mad on her. We all fancied her a bit but it was, kind of, 'Hands off, I'm serious.'"[7]

Romantic entanglements aside, as the weeks slipped by, Paul, John, Stuart and George stretched out the 15 or so numbers they'd cobbled together with the newly recruited Pete until the monotony of duplicating them over and over again caused the group to insert even the most obscure material that could be dug from their common unconscious. Few

Lennon–McCartney items were unveiled then, but a typical waiter/bouncer's memory was of the two composing in the bandroom during intervals between sets rather than joining the others at the bar.

Yet the scenes in the Kaiserkeller dressing room and the cinema dormitory weren't always how susceptible fans might have imagined – John and Paul running through their latest opus with Pete slapping a rhythmic idea on a table, George tuning his guitar, Stuart sketching in the corner. I'm not sure how many people know this, but connections between pop music and sex are much more distinct than those between pop music and higher artistic expression. Indeed, the strongest motive for most red-blooded lads to be in beat groups was the increased opportunities it presented to fraternise with girls.

In Europe's premier erotic playground, 'fraternising' embraced more than the awkward fumblings that Lennon had known with the demure damsels he'd pursued when a gawky church youth-clubber. Such moments soon belonged to a previous existence.

The younger Beatles might have half-imagined – as he did – that John knew it all, but a visit to the Hippo Bar, where women grappled in mud, or the shocking Street of Windows down Herbertstrasse soon made him realise that sex was in its infancy on Merseyside as he looked the whores up and down like a farmer at a cattle auction. "You couldn't see into it," said Ricky Richards of the latter establishment, "because of great big iron doors either end like the entrance to a concentration camp."

If you liked it plain and simple, sundry orthodox corruptions – street-corner hookers, peep shows, bordellos – were to the Reeperbahn as steel to Sheffield but, as the flow-chart of immorality unfolded further, a veritable Pandora's box of kinky proclivities would open, too, and be celebrated rather than submerged as they were for the tired businessmen – fearful of identification – who indulged their fantasies in the clandestine brothels of Soho.

Before British pop musicians became commonplace on the Reeperbahn, there was usually no question of financial transaction as there would have been for unlovely old rascals purchasing fleeting respite from sexual loneliness. Now, with neither Aunt Mimi nor faithful Cynthia looking, John Lennon became quite accustomed to casual and unchallenging procurement of sexual gratification from almost any one of the girls ringing the stage apron, tits bouncing, to better ogle him and the others with unmaidenly eagerness. All he had to do was let one of his infrequent smiles rest on the front row, and then on a specific girl – maybe a pocket Venus like Astrid – for a split-second that lasted 1,000 years.

In gregarious mood, one such as Lennon would be sighted, rum and cola within reach, surrounded by a bevy of sisters-in-shame aspiring to an orgasm at his thrust in a convenient alcove via a knee-trembler that could be over in seconds or stretched out like toffee, depending on how much effort it took for his legs to give way – or how much time he thought he had. Sometimes, a group might have to fill in with, say, an instrumental until its flushed vocalist – now an expert at dressing while running – panted onstage, zipping himself up.

However, amatory pushovers could come home to roost later in an appointment at the appropriate hospital department for, say, a Wassermann test for syphilis, because a lot of the females involved weren't too fussy about whom they obliged when showtime was over, as long as he was British and in a beat group. "It was funny to witness tearful goodbyes," chuckled the late Colin Manley of The Remo Four, "only to see someone's sweetheart holding hands with a member of the next group to arrive fresh from England."[15] When cognisant of the situation, it became easy to transgress the unwritten machisimo rules lodged in Liverpool, as eager young lads learned not to spoil a no-strings dalliance by getting sulky with a woman who needed someone who didn't care any more than she did. Indeed, on departure, musicians might proffer their bedmate of the previous few weeks to a new arrival as an Eskimo might invite a house guest to "laugh" with his wife.

The Reeperbahn was also a narcotic ghetto as well as a sexual one, and, alas, it's true that British pop musicians there partook of drugs not available over the counter in pharmacies. Cocaine was mentioned in 'I Get A Kick Out Of You' and amphetamines were the subject of Bo Diddley's 'Pills' long before pop stars and drugs became as Tweedledum to Tweedledee in late-1960s newspaper headlines, and "getting high" was used as a reference by such disparate and often doomed heroes as Charlie Parker, Johnny Cash, Keith Richards, John Lennon, Eric Clapton,

Jimi Hendrix, Janis Joplin, Peter Green, Lou Reed, Syd Barrett, Gram Parsons, Phil Lynott and Boy George – plus certain members of the 1960 edition of The Beatles, whose "cool" was enhanced by promoting a drug habit deemed necessary to keep the Dracula hours of their profession rather than combat domestic exhaustion in the manner of the tablet-swallowing housewife in The Rolling Stones' 'Mother's Little Helper'.

The most common sources of artificial energy in the Grosse Freiheit were beer and the amphetamine – "speed" – content of Preludin (phenmetrazine) and, to a smaller degree, Captigun, a brand of suppressants for dieters. Unlike comparatively harmless pick-me-ups such as caffeine-based Pro-Plus – legal in Britain and favoured by sixth formers and undergraduates for all-night assaults on coursework – Preludin and Captigun had been outlawed in 1957 in the UK and were, professedly, available only on prescription in Germany. Nevertheless, unauthorised caches could be procured with ease. It was no hanging matter if you were caught with "Prello", anyway; most police officers in the Reeperbahn couldn't be bothered with the paperwork.

Some of the students with whom The Beatles fraternised dosed themselves with more Preludin than that recommended by doctors, leaving them feeling worse than dog-tired unless they got hold of more. Supplies came to be stocked, too, for the use of employees in nearly all late-night Hamburg premises that featured jazz or rock 'n' roll in order to ensure that the final session in the grey of morning by a given resident act would be as energetic as the first at dusk. Behind the bar in one such establishment appeared a photograph autographed, "John Lennon, King of Prello." Ricky Richards, however, insisted, "You didn't need drugs in Hamburg. The whole place was a buzz." Even when you had to be onstage for four and a half labour-intensive hours Monday to Friday, six on Saturday and Sunday.

It hadn't been immediate but, while pouring an increasingly gargantuan quantity of amphetamines and alcohol into himself, John Lennon became the life and soul of the party (more so than he'd been at college) as whatever little was left of his ingrained Woolton gentility flowed out of him as the liquor flowed in – and flowed out again as toilet-talk about knickers and tits. He was determined that nothing was going to show him up for the nicely brought-up *Mittelstand* boy he was. His voice got louder, his jokes got cruder, his eyes got brighter and his face got redder before he staggered off to puke. The grid of a drain fogging in and out of focus might have been the last image to penetrate his brain before he slumped into the whirling pits and woke up with a worse hangover than ever before.

Lennon's off-duty rampaging gave foundation to many of the embellished tales that would unfold in later trips to Hamburg, such as when he halted a poker game with Gerry Marsden and other Liverpudlians to pour a malevolent glass of water over the slumbering drummer of The Graduates, a group of South Africans. His victim's reciprocation in kind moments later prompted the devil in John to advise him that, if he swallowed the insult, his tough-guy veneer would be cracked forever. Leaping to his feet, he seized hold of an empty bottle and brought it down on the Boer's head. The latter's pride smarted more than his cranium, but further blows were not exchanged owing to a misapprehension that the rest of the players at the table were going to swoop unquestioningly to a fellow Scouser's defence. Had he known how sickened they were by John's behaviour, he might not have been so hasty in slinking back to a damp bed with as much dignity as he could muster.

There were other occasions just as lamentable. Golden rain squirted from Lennon's bladder onto the wimples of three promenading nuns, and foul-mouthed "sermons" were preached by him from the same balcony. While he was a popular leader rather than a follower, even his customary Rosencrantz and Guildenstern, Paul and George, cried off at the last fence during an attempt to mug a pie-eyed sailor who'd just stood them a meal. John was also full of *sieg heils* and "You zhink you play games mit der Master Race!" and so forth, goosestepping with a Hitler salute and a finger across his upper lip.

Another apocryphal story to do the rounds in Hamburg was that, one evening at the Kaiserkeller, some local Al Capone tugged at John's trousers while he was onstage and requested 'Shakin' All Over'. Lennon cracked back, "*Donner und Blitzen*! You're the *Schweinhund* that bayoneted my uncle!" There was no answer to that – not in words anyway – and Bruno Koschmider was suddenly an abject, frightened man, wringing his hands.

It was "all a terrible misunderstanding, Herr Albrecht...never forgive myself". In a way, John was in more danger then than he'd be after the famous "We're more popular than Christ" incident in 1966.

Whether this yarn was true or false, as 1960 drew to its close, it wasn't all smiles anyway with Koschmider, who had grown rather leery of The Beatles of late. "*Ist gut,*" he'd exclaim – with a scowl that said it wasn't – after interrogating them about a tale he'd been told about them planning to defect to the hated Top Ten. The Jets' contract there was about to expire and the retinue set to scatter like rats disturbed in a granary, with Tony Sheridan opting to stay on with no fixed backing unit, using instead whoever happened to be around – such as The Beatles.

Acting swiftly, Bruno gave the Liverpudlians a month's notice while withdrawing whatever immunity he'd sorted out with the police concerning the youngest Beatle's nightly violation of a curfew forbidding those under 18 from frequenting Grosse Freiheit clubland after midnight. George Harrison's deportation was arranged by late November.

As for the others, who had decided to muddle on without Harrison, Bruno looked into the middle distance and intimated that an open-all-night city crawling with human predators might not be safe for them if they dared to commence the Top Ten residency. *A propos* nothing in particular, he mentioned a Danish prostitute who had incurred the recent wrath of another club owner and whose corpse was discovered floating on the Weser in Neinberg by the River Police. The coroner had recorded an open verdict.

The two underlings flanking Bruno shook their heads and sucked on their teeth to feign sadness rather than anger at the sin that required such a harsh rebuke. You could tell from the thrust of their cruel and battered faces – cauliflower ears, Neanderthal foreheads, noses as flat as door knockers – that, when schoolboys, many of the Kaiserkeller's waiter/bouncers had been known for their persecution of the helpless. Still grinning with sheer glee at the pain of others, they were at Koschmider's beck and call if he decided that a degree of correction was required for any erring British musicians.

At a distance from safety measurable less in the miles from England than how they were going to get back there, while serving their notice at the Kaiserkeller, The Beatles pondered whether the journey might begin in an ambulance or a hearse. Violence, however, proved unnecessary – within a fortnight of George's removal, Bruno had Pete Best and Paul McCartney handcuffed, bundled into a *Peterwagon* (Black Maria) and, after questioning, ordered out of the Fatherland on a trumped-up charge of arson.

So then there were two and both were forbidden to seek employment as freshly unearthed paperwork revealed that The Beatles had had no work permits for their months at the Kaiserkeller. While Stuart remained in the house of his betrothed, John had little choice but to go home.

He dumped his luggage in the hallway of Mendips and tramped straight upstairs with a mumbled "Never again". To Mimi, he looked just like a refugee from the war-torn Europe of the 1940s. Yet he seemed fundamentally undamaged the next morning, as he lay propped up in bed, stuffed with his favourite "cowboy's breakfast" of bacon and beans and basking in winter sunshine and the sound of a faraway pneumatic drill.

The way he told it, time that hung heavy between one night onstage and the next had been spent just resting and practising guitar. On days off, he'd seen the sights, boated on the lake and visited the zoo, art galleries, museums and a couple of folk fayres. The way John told it, the only thing he'd missed was doing brass rubbings in Hamburg's older churches.

Mimi wasn't impressed. Uncle George had served three wartime years in the army, and she had gleaned that travellers' tales about the fleshpots of Germany were hard fact. Nevertheless, she imagined that she knew her John well enough to understand that his hand in any off-duty frolics had been a duty rather than a pleasure. At any rate, you should have seen the way he and Cynthia fell into each other's arms – love's young dream!

John had written to Cynthia most days while overseas and, after over three months apart, she arrived on the doorstep to coo over her unshaven, bleary eyed Heathcliff. One long kiss vaporised all the endless centuries of anguish. Later, in more private surroundings, John led the unbuttoning, buckle-searching, finger-sliding way. He was a man now, rough, earthy and confident. Cynthia couldn't ask how or why, but she may have guessed what he'd been up to from signals that penetrated the tacit vow of silence that has persisted among bands of roving minstrels for as long as *omertà* has among the Mafia.

Stray mutterings about amorous adventures in Germany were unsettling for anyone's steady girlfriend, particularly if she had to keep up a just-good-friends farce to protect the "available" image of groups that had set their sights higher than local jive-hives. Frank exchanges over tablecloth or counterpane brought near to the surface both her noisome home truths about him and his disobliging comparisons of her with unforgotten *frauleins* so self-possessed that they weren't bothered about anything as tedious as the girl he'd left behind at home.

Nevertheless, John told Cynthia that sex had been on tap in Hamburg but didn't go into detail. Finally, she came to understand that, if you're truly in love, it's better that secrets remain concealed. It meant that she also had to fool herself that John had been, like he said, so weary each night after playing at the Kaiserkeller that all he wanted to do was sleep.

In any case, the group's future was more important than what might or might not have happened abroad. They had turned into a hard act to follow. It was there for all to see on the first post-Hamburg date back at the Casbah, promoted via Mona Best's posters – boasting the "Return Of The Fabulous Beatles" – and via word-of-mouth. The full house remained spellbound until the final chord, and there was a long moment of shell-shocked hush before clapping crescendoed to a bombardment of whistling, cheering, stamping pandemonium.

Something that John, especially, had picked up from watching the likes of Derry Wilkie, Tony Sheridan and Ricky Richards was microphone technique and how to capitalise on, rather than shrink from, any inabilities to pitch a high note without cracking. The transformation was most apparent when he pitched into ravers such as 'Money' and 'Dizzy Miss Lizzy', ad-libbing huskily almost like a jazzer, pop-eyed and workmanlike but sounding world-weary, cynical and knowing beyond his years – which he was after Germany. They all were.

5 "Which Way Are We Going, Boys?"

Pulling out all the stops and unfettered by slickness, The Beatles continued to dole out nonchalantly incendiary performances that their lengthy sojourn in Germany had wrought. Well before the first encore at the Casbah, all there had homed in on the new sensation's primaeval rowdiness and contagious backbeat. Half the time you couldn't hear much more than thump-thump-thump, but even in days before onstage monitors and graphic equalisers, when vocal balance was achieved by simply moving back and forth on the microphone, the three-part harmonies of John, Paul and George had been hard won but perfected in readiness for what lay ahead for them, if not for Stuart and Pete.

It might have defied Elvis Presley to have stolen the show from the post-Hamburg Beatles – although that might not be as outrageous a statement as it seems, as the King had caught the overall drift of an era dominated by boys next door with well-scrubbed good looks (Bobby Vinton, Bobby Vee, Bobby Rydell *et al*) with Italianesque ballads, lightweight tunes with saccharine lyrics and infrequent self-mocking rockers. He was now getting on with "quality" stuff, as did his idol Dean Martin, one of Frank Sinatra's Rat Pack, who put in a back-slapping representation on a demobbed Presley's homecoming television spectacular from Miami, one of his last appearances before vanishing into the wings for nigh-on eight years.

Theoretically, as a solo entertainer Presley was answerable only to himself, in contrast to the five Beatles, who, in close proximity to each other in Hamburg, offstage as well as on, had initiated explorations of territory beyond the public intimacies of on-mic comments and momentary eye contact. This was epitomised by Stuart and Paul attempting to score catty points off each other – now not even having the grace to do so behind John's back. The tacit implication in a seemingly innocuous remark from either might spark off the other's hastily unplugged guitar and a slammed backstage firedoor.

Yet Lennon too was prone to antagonising Stuart just to see his hackles rise, and Stuart in turn articulated what the others would deny even if they inwardly concurred: that John's running commentary that had filled every unforgiving minute in Hamburg could be intensely irritating. Why wouldn't he shut his mouth for a bit? You'd fall asleep within earshot of his twittering, sometimes, and yawn and stretch to it too.

As there was no let up either in the general underminings and sly machinations that make all pop groups what they are, Sutcliffe was now shilly-shallying about whether to quit the group and resume his career as a painter. With John sitting on the fence, flare-ups between Stuart and Paul – and, to a smaller extent, Stuart and George – had increased in frequency after the bass player's return to England in mid-January 1961. John was pleased, but, to the rest, his reappearance was akin to that of the proverbial bad penny now that they'd got used to Paul's more agile bass playing. "Stuart wasn't sharing the same commitment to The Beatles as the others were," agreed his younger sister, "he was absent from rehearsals, and he didn't practise the bass. If you're in a group that wants to go places, you're not going to be very happy with a member who isn't as serious about it."

Stuart kept other options open by applying immediately for both a visa to re-enter the Fatherland and for a new course back at the Art College. Each represented an attempt to "settle down". Either way, it did not bode well for The Beatles – especially as John, for all the occasional sport that tormenting his best friend provided, had now issued the naked threat: if he goes, I go.

For Stuart, however, it made no odds now if he was a Beatle or not as he counted the minutes to Astrid's impending fortnight in Liverpool the following month. Proud beyond words, he showed her off round college where even some of the lecturers were impressed. Yet a little humility might have helped Stuart at the interview to re-join what he called "the old jeans-and-sweater gang with a pencil and sketchbook".[7] Art history lecturer Nicholas Horsfield, one of his referees, "lost patience with him. Perhaps 'aggressive' is the wrong word – but he didn't go about it in the way one usually goes about getting a recommendation."[7]

That finished him with Liverpool anyway. Stuart didn't even stick around long enough to honour existing Beatles engagements, and he and Astrid fell into each other's arms amid the gusting engine steam at Hamburg-Hauptbahnhof station. Through her, Stuart became the first Beatle to emulate the brushed-forward Exi *Pilzenkopf* – "mushroom head" – haircut, commonplace in Germany, even if a male so greaselessly coiffured in Britain would be branded a nancy boy. When Sutcliffe rejoined the group for a second Hamburg season in April at the Top Ten, John's howl of derision led him to betray Astrid by restoring his hair fleetingly to its original brilliantined pompadour. Yet, before the night was out, it was back the way she liked it.

For Sutcliffe, stretches onstage were now going by as total blurs like some run-of-the-mill job he'd done for years. Every note sounded the same, a mere vibration hovering over a backbeat that an idiot couldn't lose. Emitting an almost palpable air of self-loathing, he'd slouch on to unacknowledged applause, and glazed listlessness would set in by the first chorus. His mind would drift off further than ever before from the task in hand. Astrid's presence in the audience would split his concentration, and, to the further chagrin of his fellow musicians, he thought nothing about abandoning the bass mid-set to go over and speak to her.

He couldn't envisage being a Beatle for much longer as he was now going to recommence his studies at Hamburg's State School Of Art. After not so much an interview as a discussion in the assistant director's office, it had been agreed that he was to be exempted from the foundation course, and was to go directly into a master class supervised by no less than Eduardo Paolozzi, regarded as an heir to Arp, Tzara, Braque, Bacon and other gurus of contemporary art.

Before Sutcliffe had marshalled his thoughts and told John, McCartney and Harrison's sniping at his musicianship and overall indolent attitude towards the group became, alternately, more subtle and less courteous. As well as cold looks and cold shoulders, the various protagonists had cottoned on to badgering each other with trivia and irritating old wounds. "Bet Stuart makes a hash of it!" Harrison once shouted to all and sundry when Sutcliffe was about to deliver his solo vocal outing, 'Love Me Tender'.

Most of the other music the customers heard from The Beatles too were items – both up and down tempo – from the annals of classic rock, the current Top 20 – and US smashes from what used to be called the "race" or "sepia" charts, but obtainable easily enough in Britain.

It was replicated in moderately crude fashion, partly because the massed bowed strings on, say, The Shirelles' 'Will You Love Me Tomorrow' would prove difficult to even approximate on electric guitars. Indeed, if anything, smooth edges had been roughed up rather than *vice versa* when they'd chanced their arm back at the Grosvenor on Christmas Eve 1960.

On the day after Boxing Day, they'd not so much dipped a toe as plunged head first into new depths at the Town Hall in Litherland – with John half shouting the opening shot, and a cigarette dangling from Paul's lower lip. There wasn't an obvious stage act, and they did all-out rock like other local outfits, but the idea was to keep 'Money', 'C'mon Everybody', 'Little Queenie' and all the rest of them almost open-ended while the lead vocalist – usually John or Paul – covered a waterfront from full-blooded screech to whispery and intimate, and then back again as he piled on the pressure.

The Beatles played their guts out that night, and were a howling success. Yet it seemed silly for them – for any provincial group – to feel then that there was any kind of future, what with so many others nearer the core of the British music industry, battling likewise for record contracts and just encores.

Furthermore, even if you were able to break through nationally, you had to accept a second-hand and, arguably, counterfeit status to North American stars such as, say, New Yorker Brian Hyland, Tommy Roe from Atlanta, Georgia and others from places as outlandish and unreachable. Following the climax of classic rock and the establishment of the "Bobby" regime, the hit parades of North America and, by implication, everywhere else became even more constipated with fly-by-night dance crazes, inconsequential but maddeningly catchy one-shot novelties and further assembly-line youths with doe-eyes, hair-spray and bashful half-smiles. Their looks were commensurate with merchandise like Roe's 'Piddle De Pat' and, even harder to live down, Hyland's 'Itsy Bitsy Teenie Weenie Yellow Polka Dot Bikini'.

A domestic case study is that of Surrey-born Jimmy Justice, who, in July 1962, was to be booked for the Cavern, which had gone over almost completely to mainstream pop while The Beatles were in the midst of their first residency in Hamburg. If not as insipidly handsome as any of the predominant Bobbies, Justice was one of a mass of UK heart-throbs in the early 1960s who took their cue from North America. At the height of his fame in 1962, he breached the Top 20 with a hat trick of two US covers and one by a jobbing English tunesmith. Therefore, the Cavern was full when Jimmy appeared there, direct from a tour of Scandinavia, with his backing combo, the Jury – containing musicians from nearby Blackpool. They were supported by up-and-coming local heroes, Billy Kramer And The Coasters. Tony Sanders, the Coasters' drummer, noticed Jimmy and Billy chatting in the dressing room: "Kramer looked every inch a star, but Jimmy Justice didn't, although he was then the big event and Billy was a nobody."[17]

Yet the girls screamed loudest at Jimmy Justice that night. Before the year was out, he'd figure too in the *New Musical Express* readers' popularity poll – in which London's Helen Shapiro would emerge as the kingdom's top female singer. Her reworkings of US hits may be seen now as on a par with (and, in the case of Dionne Warwick's 'Walk On By', superior to) templates by such talents as Connie Francis, Brenda Lee, Carole King, Mary Wells, Skeeter Davis, you name 'em – and anyone with the nerve to even attempt 'Are You Lonesome Tonight' in 1962 while the Elvis Presley treatment was fresh in his fans' memories, deserved attention. Nevertheless, like Jimmy Justice, she was to leave the Top 50 forever by 1964 as a solo artist in an age of groups.

When the beat boom was two years away, however, it was sufficient for the act destined to spearhead it to be on a par with Rory, Gerry and other of Liverpool's most popular rock 'n' rollers – and for Pete Best's mum to co-ordinate the operation from the telephone in the hallway at Hayman's Green. She was now general runaround and bottle washer, conducting negotiations on The Beatles' behalf with this quizzical landlord or that disinterested social secretary – just like Rory Storm's mother, Violet Caldwell, did for him and The Hurricanes.

It was thanks largely to Mona's dogged efforts that The Beatles became fixtures at the Cavern. Otherwise, their stock-in-trade were regular one-nighters at the Casbah, Aintree Institute, the Cassanova Club and like venues that were pocking every vicinity of the city. If finding these guitar combos and their followers personally objectionable, it made sense for some middle-aged entrepreneurs to turn a hard-nosed penny by ripping the insides out of disused warehouses, mucking out cellars or extending licensed premises to make room for a stage and an – invariably standing – audience.

The same scenario was being repeated in other northern cities – as exemplified by Halifax, cradling a scene that was as self-contained as that in Liverpool. Indeed, there are parallels with the Cavern in that the opening of the Plebians Jazz Club in 1961 was motivated too by quasi-evangelical zeal to further the cause of jazz – mostly trad – regardless of financial gain. Then pop crept in and eventually took over the subterranean club in its ravine of town centre warehouses.

Halifax was to spawn no 1960s hitmakers – and seemingly impossible visions of breaking free of parochial fetters appeared before, say, Dave Berry, Jimmy Crawford, Joe Cocker and other entertainers who "coming from out-of-the-way Sheffield, are shackled before they start". Thus spake *Top Stars Special*, created in 1960 as a supplement to the *Sheffield Star*. This daddy of all pop gazettes, which covered local music, predated by a year the first independent newspaper of its kind, the celebrated *Mersey Beat*, brainchild of Bill Harry, John Lennon's college chum.

Among *Mersey Beat*'s aims was the fostering of Liverpool musicians' self expression beyond just hammering out 'Dizzy Miss Lizzy' down the Cavern. As well as John Lennon's Goonish early prose, the bi-weekly journal was responsible for innovations later adopted by the national music press – including the first "gig guide" and photographs taken on location or onstage rather than posed studio shots.

Bill's account of the journal's origin is worth quoting at length: "Since I was a kid, I'd been putting together magazines. I was planning a new one called *Storyville And 52nd Street*, divided between trad and modern jazz. Yet I remember walking down from the college one lunchtime, and thinking why do a jazz thing when there's John's band, Cass And The Cassanovas, Rory Storm And The Hurricanes and all the other groups I'd got to know?

"Soon I began making notes of what was happening locally because people didn't seem to be aware of it. Bob Wooler, the Cavern's MC, and I got together and worked out that there were over 300 groups in Liverpool of every variety – not just four-man guitars-bass-and-drums outfits, but duos, trios, octets, all girl bands and all black vocal. Incredible!

"One group might have known about a couple of venues or promoters – while another would know of different ones, but no one knew how many there were in the whole city. Every youth club, town hall, even ice rinks and swimming pools had rock 'n' roll on. Some outfits were playing seven nights a week, three or four gigs a night!

"The word got round what I was up to, and a civil servant called Jim Anderson lent me 50 quid to start *Mersey Beat*. The first issue was out on July 6th 1961. I did all the distribution myself. First, I went to the three main wholesalers – including WH Smith – who took some. Then I arranged for all the different venues to take copies. Next, I went to see the managers of the music stores.

"One of the things I was trying to do with *Mersey Beat* was get the musicians to express themselves, and bring a flavour of their world across to the readers, what it was like on the road, playing the gigs and so on – because I was always interested in dragging the potential out of creative people. That's why I used to have John writing his 'Beatcomber' columns – the first published examples of his prose – members of groups who were cartoonists...Stuart Leithwood of The Koobas was one. We had illustrations by The Remo Four too. The Roadrunners did little pantomimes for Christmas."

That each of the first pressings of *Mersey Beat* sold out within a morning demonstrated the strength of demand for venue information and news coverage as well as other activities, professional and otherwise, of a veritable host of key personalities who were as much stars in Liverpool as Cliff Richard, Helen Shapiro and Jimmy Justice were in the charts.

Nevertheless, *Mersey Beat*'s plea, "London Take A Look Up North" on 15 February 1962, was to be unheeded in the first instance.

During the previous unseasonably cold summer, its second issue had made a lot of a Beatles record date that had taken place in Germany. Among their duties at the Top Ten was backing Tony Sheridan, who'd become the city's undisputed rock 'n' roll king – and he remains the name that trips most readily off the tongue whenever British musicians in Hamburg are discussed. "I was an ingredient in the pudding," the man himself would concede. "I don't think that I was any more important than anyone else – except that I was a bit more experienced. That was my plus point."

Learning the tricks of the trade from one now nicknamed "The Teacher", Gerry And The Pacemakers had preceded The Beatles at the Top Ten – where their front man's fretboard skills had been fine-tuned through paying acute attention to Sheridan. Indeed, Gerry – and John Lennon – were to share the same high-chested guitar stance with Tony.

John and three other Beatles – Pete, Paul and George – were hired by Bert Kaempfert, freelance producer for Polydor, Deutsche Grammonphon's pop subsidiary, to accompany Sheridan on half his debut album, *My Bonnie* – including the title song which, as a spin-off single, was to enter the German chart briefly. The remaining tracks were taped with other UK musicians in Hamburg.

"Bert had been trying rock 'n' roll with young Germans," Tony explained, "but it had sounded ludicrous. He was impressed by what he thought was our authenticity. It's a shame no one taped any of the Top Ten gigs. I was doing most of the lead guitar – though if John, say, took a solo, it was halfway good because it came out of the rawness of him. George was young, inexperienced and a bit over-awed by the whole thing – but very keen to learn. Because the drummer wasn't that good, rhythm guitars had to compensate for the lack of a strong beat. Bert made no comment about this and was quite happy to leave it the way it was when we recorded."

In a perhaps wrong-headed attempt to capture the *au naturel* power they and Tony generated on the boards, The Beatles were hastened to a session mere hours after the last major sixth of the night at the Top Ten had reverberated so that their adrenalin could be pumped more profitably onto a spool of tape, a phonographic equivalent of bottling lightning – albeit adulterated by the clinical exactitudes of the studio.

All the numbers were punched out in three takes at most, and there was time in hand for Kaempfert to lend critical ears to items from The Beatles' repertoire without Tony. He was impressed particularly with their arrangement of the ragtime standard 'Ain't She Sweet' – with John on lead vocal – and 'Cry For A Shadow', a Harrison–Lennon instrumental.

Neither would be issued outside Germany until they had acquired historical interest. After fate had taken The Beatles' hand, Bert would recall that, "It was obvious to me that they were enormously talented, but no one then – including the boys themselves – knew how to use that talent or where it would lead them."[15]

Never mind, even being a backing group on a foreign disc was a yardstick of achievement for The Beatles back home – and, after so beginning their commercial discography, Lennon would assume Sheridan's lead vocal when it was incorporated into the act when, describing themselves for a while as "Polydor Recording Artists", he, Paul, George and Pete recommenced an itinerary in and around Liverpool. The spectrum of work had broadened – and they'd always have Hamburg – but there was a creeping sense of marking time. They'd taken their impact on Merseyside to its limit, but no one understood how to advance to the step between consolidation of a regional following and the threshold of the Big Time. "Which way are we going, fellows?" Lennon would shout when spirits were low.

"To the top, Johnny!" was the Pavlov's Dog response.

"What top?"

"To the toppermost of the poppermost!"

Progress to that goal had been slight since 'My Bonnie'. As well as venues where they'd gone down well before, there were forays to such disparate locations as the Merseyside Civil Service Club and New Brighton's grand Tower Ballroom, the most capacious seaside dancehall in the northwest outside Blackpool. There were two evenings at the Three Coins in Manchester, and a ghastly loss-making one-shot odyssey with amplifiers on laps in the van to Aldershot, the first ever engagement in the south.

Far closer to home, on the day of a booking 30km (20 miles) up the coast in Southport, heavy rain had persisted well into the evening; there was something good on the television and the local paper was on strike. This meant that a poster outside – with "No Weirdies, Beatniks or Coloureds admitted" along the bottom – was the sum total of the advertising. John didn't bother to tune up properly, and soon gave up making a show of it after taking the stage in front of a miniscule crowd. He also kicked off 'Three Cool Cats' before George had finished announcing it, causing the younger player to sulk all the way home.

On aggregate, an individual Beatle's income was a fraction of that of a dustman, even after they won the first readers' poll in *Mersey Beat*. Unless a bigger stroke than this was pulled, the group was soon likely to be figuratively twitching and thrashing like an aged dray-horse that'd collapsed in its shafts, lugging coal to the docks. A Beatles bash in Liverpool, see, was as commonplace as a whist-drive. They were in peril of being overtaken by newer groups like The Undertakers, Carl Vincent's Counts and Billy Kramer And The Coasters – and some not so new. The Big Three, for instance, had risen like a phoenix from the ashes of Cass And The Cassanovas.

You'd see John Lennon and one or two of the others mooching about the town centre, calculating what the one-shilling-and-sixpence they had between them could do. A plate of beans on toast washed down with a cup of liquid smoke? It was as if they'd never got drunk with Ricky Richards, made a record with Tony Sheridan, played Aldershot – only 65km (40 miles) west of the Eldorado that was London – or invoked sporadic screams from girls in the Top Ten for a particularly bravura 'Roll Over Beethoven'. Down in the dumps because of a letter from the HP firm threatening to repossess his amplifier, John looked up from filling in all the "Os" on the front page of yesterday's *Daily Sketch* to speak half-seriously of packing it in. Hessy's was always buying back instruments and equipment that they'd sold a couple of years before to a bunch of young sprogs with the world at their feet.

Stuart had sold his bass to Klaus Voorman, and had written from Hamburg to say that he'd sent off for an application form and prospectus from a teacher training college in Leicester. "Going to Germany was a bit like a student taking a year out to do VSO," reckoned sister Pauline. "It was presented like that to his mother – that he'd come back to do his post-graduate work and settle down. No one could predict that he'd fall for a German girl and base himself in Germany. The paradox was he did in Germany what he didn't do in England – complete his studies, become responsible, drop the pop, and start to make some sort of career in Art. I don't think he particularly wanted to do the teacher training course at all. It was only to placate his mum."

For much the same reason, John started thinking aloud to his aunt that a steady job, a mortgage, maybe wedding bells might be worth considering as The Beatles were on a road that was obscure, a dusty, wearisome road that didn't look as if it led anywhere important – but there was always a chance that it might.

You only had to be in the right place at the right time, hadn't you? Look at The Jaybirds – a Nottingham group who'd worked at the Top Ten too – who were actually under contract to Embassy, admittedly, a label of no great merit – but, hey, what about Cliff Bennett and his Rebel Rousers who had had a proper single out on an EMI label – Parlophone – earlier this year? Some of the other acts with whom he'd compared notes in Hamburg and elsewhere were going places too, and it disturbed John that the fish weren't biting for his Beatles as well.

Aunt Mimi often reminded him that it wasn't too late to make a proper go of it as a commercial artist. Recently, she'd undergone a descent down the worn, slippery stairwell to the Black Hole of Calcutta that was a Beatles lunchtime session in the Cavern, fighting a desire to flee the enveloping fug of mould, perspiration and cheap perfume, not to mention the prickly heat that grew by the minute as more jabbering teenagers joined the massed humanity bobbing up and down before a wooden stage beneath bare light bulbs.

Minutes after her arrival, John and the rest of those dreadful fellows sauntered on – and he was smoking! – to hit all their instruments at once to a staccato "Right!". Mimi clapped her hands to her ears with a moan of agony. What first struck her in every sense was the deafening din, and how dissimilar it was to anything pop she'd ever seen on television. Cliff Richard had indulged in a little scripted playfulness on *Sunday Night At*

The London Palladium. This was fine, but John was belching into the microphone, and saying things like the f-word. Indeed, she was more profoundly shocked by his language than she was by the "music".

Nonetheless, she restrained herself – or was prevented – from wriggling through to the front to drag John off the stage and out. Instead, Mimi contented herself instead with trying to glare him out of countenance, but then Paul stepped up for a sentimental ballad, something she actually recognised. Moreover, his pleasant-enough warbling stayed in key, and a *claque* screamed when he finished. Amongst them when John waved George Harrison forward to sing Buddy Holly's 'Crying Waiting Hoping', a jocose, middle-aged woman was clapping and cheering as voraciously as everyone else.

When the sweatbath was over, this person – who turned out to be George's mother – was there already when Mimi decided to confront John with this latest and most heinous folly the minute that he stumbled into what might be described as a changing room.

"Weren't they great!?" enthused Mrs Harrison.

Mimi was glad someone thought so. If that was entertainment, let's have a great deal less entertainment, said she.

More insidiously, John drove his mystified aunt nervous for weeks by dirgeing "A-wimoweh a-wimoweh a-wimoweh a-wimoweh..." round the house, *sotto voce* like a mantra. It was the background chant of 'The Lion Sleeps Tonight', a song that milkmen were whistling as incessantly towards the end of 1961.

Surprisingly, the British cover version, albeit using a different title – by The Karl Denver Trio – had risen higher in the Top 20 than the US template by The Tokens. That there were further signs of resistance to the dominance of North American pop was one reason for The Beatles, in optimistic moments, to at least pretend that they'd ascertained from a buzz in the air that they were almost there.

Another was that they'd acquired someone with more clout than Mona Best. If he wasn't a born manager, Brian Epstein was as determined as her to do whatever willingness and energy would do to push The Beatles further up the ladder of success, all the way up if the time came. Unlike others of his age – 27 – he didn't behave as if all he liked about pop was the money it could generate. Neither was he intending to sell The Beatles like tins of beans – with no money back if they tasted funny.

He was also too much of a gentleman to stand outside on the pavement and bark the show to passers-by. Neither would he demean himself by, say, sitting with the back of the chair against the stage, holding up the central microphone on the end of a broomstick as Cynthia Powell had done in the first flush of wonderment at John, when once a mic-stand hadn't been available.

This Mr Epstein had been lost in wonder too. The group had been vaguely aware of him as a privately educated Jewish businessman who had followed his father into the family firm, which had grown since the turn of the century into a prominent Merseyside department chain, specialising in electrical goods and furniture. By 1961, Brian was a bored and frustrated sales manager at the city centre branch of NEMS – North End Music Stores – and heir apparent to the prominent firm that had sprung from a grandparent's small suburban shop.

In a hidden history of pop, the true *éminences grises* and some of the figureheads are Jewish if you consider how many were the movers and shakers of rock as businessmen, composers of 'Hound Dog', 'Twist and Shout' and so many more standards – and chart contenders, notably Abe Zimmerman's boy, Robert, the most famous Jew since Charlton Heston. That's Bob Dylan to you, mate, just as Liverpool's own late Frankie Vaughan's surname was actually Abelson. Furthermore, Lou Reed is also Lewis Rabinowitz; Carole King is Carole Klein, and Doc Pomus is Jerome Solon Felder, though his songwriting partner, Mort Shuman – like Phil Spector, Paul Simon, Leonard Cohen and Graham Gouldman, hit composer and founder member of 10cc (three-quarters Jewish) – stuck with his given surname in the teeth of the anti-Semitism that still lingered in the psyche of even the most vehement foes of the Nazis. As late as 1966, Brian Epstein was to complain that because he was a Jew, he'd not been included on the Queen's birthday honours lists as his Beatles had been.

By coincidence, NEMS's young Mr Epstein had been attending a seminar in record retailing management in Hamburg the same month that his future clients were working at the Top Ten, but The Beatles first impinged on his consciousness via *Mersey Beat*. "At NEMS, Brian Epstein took a dozen," confirmed Bill Harry, "but he rang me, astonished, to say they'd all gone just like that, and ordered a gross of the next issue – which had on the front cover a picture and the complete story of The Beatles recording in Germany. He couldn't believe it when those sold out virtually in a day – so he asked me to come and have a sherry in his office to tell him what was happening. He was avid for information, and asked if he could write a record review column.

"He knew all about The Beatles months before a reputed guy came into NEMS and asked for 'My Bonnie', and Brian asked me to fix for him to go down the Cavern to see them."

Epstein didn't feel quite so out-of-place in the Cavern as Aunt Mimi, but he went through a brief phase of dressing down from his usual conservative suit, shirt-and-tie and sensible shoes to go there and to other venues where he was observed looking round so frequently to assess how well The Beatles were going down that observers guessed he had a vested interest. Funny, no one had ever noticed him around them before.

Much has been written about Brian's homosexuality – often the butt of unpleasant jibes by John over the years[18] – and his erotic attraction to The Beatles, particularly Lennon. Yet in his first autobiography, *Beatle!*, Pete Best states that Brian propositioned him one evening in 1962, "but there had been nothing nasty about it, nothing obscene, nothing dirty. It was a very gentle approach."

When the group – then without Pete – took a fortnight's break from a hectic schedule between 27 April and 11 May 1963, Brian – godfather to John and Cynthia's new-born son, Julian – persuaded Lennon to join him for a 12-day break in Spain. Paul McCartney's notion about the acceptance of such an invitation from a known homosexual was "John, not being stupid, saw his opportunity to impress upon Mr Epstein who was the boss of the group. He wanted Brian to know who he should listen to. There was never any hint that he was gay."[19]

Some within The Beatles' circle, however, imagined that the two holidaymakers had an affair – which John denied emphatically at the time, to the point of a drunken attack on Bob Wooler for a remark about "the honeymoon". Brian too insisted "It is simply not true," when asked about the matter by Don Short of the *Daily Mirror*. In any case, as it was with Pete Best, Epstein "wouldn't have done anything to frighten John off," stressed Brian's personal assistant, Wendy Hanson. "John was a womaniser – and Brian was a very sensitive person. He'd never push himself on anyone."[19]

Nevertheless, ever the iconoclast, Lennon, routinely unfaithful as both a boyfriend and husband, may have decided to experiment for much the same reason as French sex symbol Serge Gainsbourg, who admitted in print that, yes, he'd once had a homosexual experience, "so as not to remain ignorant".[20] In a 1983 memoir, *In My Life*, Lennon's childhood pal and fellow Quarry Man Pete Shotton wrote that John himself had confessed that there had been a half-hearted attempt at non-penetrative sex on one occasion in Spain, perhaps lending credence to Lennon's rationalisation that, "Well, it was almost a love affair, but not quite. It was never consummated – but it was a pretty intense relationship."[21] This was also implied in 1991's *The Hours And Times*, a 60-minute celluloid dramatisation of the trip – with Lennon played by Ian Hart, the same actor who portrayed him in *Backbeat*.

After the Spanish jaunt, however, there was no other indication that what passed between John Lennon and Brian Epstein was anything beyond friendship and business.

Who cares anyway? Back in 1961, Brian's first task had been to transform the four louts into what a respectable London agent or record mogul in those naive times expected a good pop group to be. As he'd been a leading light in school plays, and had once spent not quite a year as a student at the Royal Academy of Dramatic Art, Brian was only too glad to give a few pointers with regard to presentation and professional conduct.

Some thought him too old to understand what made teenagers tick, but he'd kept abreast of popular culture, partly via *Mersey Beat*, and partly via a continued interest in the gossip and goings-on within showbusiness proper. If his membership of Equity had lapsed, he still subscribed to *The Stage* and had glanced occasionally at *Melody Maker* and the *New Musical Express* – which he was now studying as a stockbroker might the Dow Jones index.

Brian had decided from the onset that The Beatles needed a smarter, more corporate image. Despite John's forceful arguments to the contrary, he visualised them, he said, in stylish but not too way-out suits plus all the accoutrements. He'd pay for these just as he'd paid off all outstanding HP debts on their equipment.

There were shows of resistance too when he insisted that they played to a fixed programme with no patter that embraced swearing – meaning anything stronger than "bloody" or "crap", then the vilest oaths cinema censorship would permit. Neither was John to insert rude words in songs as instanced by "All my life, I've been waiting/Tonight there'll be no masturbating" in Buddy Holly's 'Oh Boy!'. Luckily, they were intending to drop that number anyway.

The Beatles had to be taught to bow when they'd finished a song, and smile in a gentlemanly way. They had to rest that smile not on individuals but on the general populace. Had they ever come across the term "back projection"?

In short, Epstein wanted to instil into them poise, and charm, not to mention clear diction during continuity. However, John wouldn't take any such tutorials seriously, and kept staring at Brian in a disconcerting and penetrating manner, full of Brooding Intensity that promised nothing but mockery.

A Professor Higgins job on Lennon proved, therefore, to be too Herculean an effort. After he changed the subject when Brian pondered whether the group ought to dispense with stage dialogue altogether, bar "Thank you very much" and "Goodnight", there was no choice in the death but to let him cuss, sneer, tell off-colour jokes, spit out chewing-gum, give front row scrubbers the eye, and generally be just the sort of exhibitionist yob that Brian had been brought up to despise.

Yet some of what his manager had tried to do had rubbed off after a superficial fashion – or maybe John had become so desperate to Make It that he was prepared to mellow out as required to achieve the desired end. When that was done, and he was a showbusiness treasure like Cliff Richard, he could revert to type – or whatever the type had become.

Lennon couldn't bring himself to be extravagant with praise, but, for all the fussing around with suits and bowing, he acknowledged how

Epstein kept his cool in any kind of difficulty more effectively than Allan Williams or Mona Best might have done, even when in the midst of some tightwad of a promoter and his shirtsleeved hitmen – who were shouting and swearing that the contract wasn't worth the paper it was written on, and The Beatles were in breach of it anyway. Not raising a bland voice, Brian's reasoned contentions would be riven with phrases like "If you'll pardon my correction" and "Excuse me, but five minutes ago, you said something about…" that wore them out, and made them pay the agreed fee – which was, nonetheless, still small enough for the lads to piss it away at the nearest pub within the hour.

These days, "the lads" was tending to mean just John, George and Paul, now that Pete's mother wasn't around as much anymore, cramping everyone's style, and Pete himself was becoming a being apart from the other three, a Tony Curtis among the *Pilzenkopfs*, a non-partaker of Preludin and a swain whose intentions towards his girlfriend, Kathy, were honourable.

At least Stuart Sutcliffe had jumped before he was pushed. Casting The Beatles aside as adolescent foolishness, he'd since got his hair cut "almost respectable". He told sister Pauline ruefully, "I think I must be growing up." The emotional and physical cost of being a Beatle and then making up for lost time as a painter, however, incited fears for his health as dizzy spells, convulsions, chronic indigestion and other maladies he'd been suffering for some time became more persistent.

Correspondence with John was in aptly glum existentialist vein, dwelling at length about how pointless everything was, and upon esoteric issues in which Lennon assumed the role of "John the Baptist" and Sutcliffe that of "Jesus Christ". The most quoted and evocative lines from these letters came to be John's poetic "I can't remember anything without a sadness/So deep that it hardly becomes known to me/So deep that its tears leave me a spectator of my own stupidity."[22] Picking at these oblique lines for meaning, they are reminiscent of "True lowliness of heart/Which takes the humbler part/And o'er its own shortcomings weeps with loathing" from 'Come Down O Love Divine', a Whitsuntide hymn that both boys from church-going upbringings would have been familiar with.

Inspired perhaps by these dialogues, Stuart began an ultimately unfinished autobiography-*cum*-novel entitled *Spotlight On Johnny*. Describing himself in the third person (as "Nhoke"), Stuart disclosed that "when he stood up, he complained of a blackout and tremendous headaches". As this was happening in real life, he consulted German doctors who recommended treatments that could only retard rather than arrest the progress of what he could only refer to as "the illness".

Some can take amphetamines every day without paying a price, but Stuart Sutcliffe couldn't. The rocky road to his fatal cerebral haemorrhage was signposted by classic drug withdrawal symptoms. As well as the ailments he'd mentioned to Pauline and John, there were panic attacks, irritability, hyperactivity and long wakeful periods in bed. More sinister was muttered trepidation building to Hitlerian scream; muzzy eyesight as a harbinger of temporary loss of vision; swaying and staring vacantly as a prelude to a convulsive fit; nightmare hallucinations ("the horrors") and other disturbances that reduced Sutcliffe to a pathetic isolate.

He'd be seen sitting with Astrid at a Grosse Freiheit club's most secluded table, lost in melancholy and paranoia, his fingers pressed against his forehead, and his lips pressed together as if holding back pain. When his eyes weren't screwed shut, she'd notice that their twinkle had gone, and a burned-out look was emphasised by purple-black blotches beneath them, like mascara that had trickled and dried.

To those back home who could not see the sickness he radiated, the only indication that anything was amiss was in letters that flitted too fitfully from topic to unrelated topic, and were riven with unfathomable but disturbing sentences like, "Actually, I'm an acute migraine worker accompanied by my bloodiness so you can try and catch me from there."[7] His handwriting had become noticeably larger and more spidery, deteriorating to near-illegibility like Captain Scott's log as its writer died by inches in the Antarctic blizzards.

On Tuesday, 10 April 1962, death took Stuart Sutcliffe without effort on the stroke of 4:45pm. In the ambulance, Astrid's face was his last vision before he passed over.

A Dr Peter Hommelhoff, Director of Medicine in a Hamburg hospital, who'd examined Sutcliffe the previous June, had concluded that the patient's poor state of health was the legacy of too much alcohol – and, especially, amphetamine – and "cerebral paralysis due to bleeding into the right ventricle of the brain" was noted in the post-mortem report as an apparent confirmation of Hommelhoff's diagnosis rather than any purported blow to the head by John Lennon or anyone else.

John learned of Stuart's death directly from Astrid when he arrived in Hamburg the day before The Beatles opened at a new venue, the Star-Club, soon to be the most famous landmark in the Grosse Freiheit. The terrible news struck home, and Lennon struggled not to lose his cool. He strained his wits for some hilariously appalling remark to show how unaffected he was. He ought to combust with laughter or at least shrug his shoulders indifferently, not turn an eyelash. At the end of that briefest of pauses, he could manage neither of these pretences. For once at a loss for words, he buried himself in Astrid's embrace.

The next day, however, he stood apart from the bear-hugging outbursts when he, Astrid, Paul and Pete greeted Millie, Stuart's mother at Hamburg-Fuhlsbuttel Airport. He seemed too calm to her – like a detached spectator with no interest or stake in the tragedy. Since yesterday, he'd made up his mind to be the hard man again: too tough to cry.

Within hours, The Beatles were pitching into their first number at the Star-Club with all their customary verve. However, when all the stupid songs about fast cars and girls were over, John could no longer not believe it. During the expected after-hours carousing, he was as free with his uncouth tongue as he was with pouring a gargantuan quantity of booze and pills into himself. He appeared to be quite himself again, but, now and then, he fell silent as shards of disjointed memories pierced an already over-stimulated mind. So often they were of trivialities – Stuart flicking away a cigarette end along a college corridor, buying his Hofner "President" bass at Hessy's, catching his eye momentarily during that first night at the Indra… What amounted to an unspoken wake for Stuart ended with a now-forgotten altercation with somebody or other that you could hear all over some six-in-the-morning bar.

Beneath it all, John Lennon was a shaken and downcast man, feeling his anguish all the more sharply for realising how many functions his best pal could no longer fulfil for him: careers adviser, father confessor, straight man in their double act, healer of some of the psychic wounds of his childhood, and someone he could bounce his ideas off and be rewarded with honest, constructive answers. There would never be another like Stuart. Would there?

Stuart Sutcliffe, the boy who'd had everything it took, was buried in Grave No 552 in the 1939 section of Huyton parish cemetery after a service in St Gabriel's Church where he'd once borne the processional cross as head chorister. Owing to work commitments, The Beatles had been unable to attend. They'd last seen him in February 1962 during his last visit home. He was emaciated and corpse-grey in the face, but in other ways, he was still the Stu they remembered.

"Wearing your mum's suit then?" Paul had quipped when he turned up at a Beatles bash in a lapel-less outfit, buttoning up to the throat – one of Astrid's creations. Stuart laughed too – but not at himself. A lot of the lads watching The Beatles had their hair combed like the *Pilzenkopfs* John, George and Paul were now sporting. He'd bet even money that it wouldn't be too long before they'd be copying The Beatles' lapel-less, high-buttoned stage costumes too.

6 "I Don't Know – What Do You Think?"

More than half of John Lennon's life was over when The Beatles made their next escape attempt from the Merseyside–Hamburg treadmill. Acting swiftly, their new manager had laid on with a trowel NEMS's position as a major retailer in the northwest to cajole Decca recording manager Dick Rowe to try out his group on New Year's Day 1962 over the edge of the world in London.

After scoring a Number One with 'Broken Wings' by The Stargazers in 1953, this Mr Rowe had become recognised as a leading producer and talent spotter of the UK record industry. Later 1950s singers who also thrived under his wing as Decca's head of A&R (Artists and Repertoire) included Tommy Steele, Anthony Newley and Billy Fury. For a while, he left Decca to work for Top Rank for whom he procured a chart entrant in John Leyton, albeit, via independent console boffin Joe Meek. When the label folded, he returned to Decca to minister to further smashes such as Jet Harris and Tony Meehan's 'Diamonds' of 1963. However, for all his Top Ten triumphs, Rowe has earned a historical footnote as The Man Who Turned Down The Beatles on the grounds that "groups with guitars are on the way out".[22]

Rowe had delegated the task of auditioning The Beatles to Mike Smith, his second-in-command, intimating that it was probably a waste of time, but you never know.

Listening to the results today, the overall impression is that The Beatles weren't at their best when, for a man who was half an hour late, they ran through numbers predetermined by Brian to demonstrate their prowess as "all-round entertainers". Paul seems too eager to please, while John's lead vocals have about them an unnatural politeness. All in all, it's rather solemn. As an illustration of how solemn, it's George who comes across as having the most "personality", a prime consideration in an age when groups had to have a token "leader" – though the concept of "George Harrison And The Beatles" flashed only fleetingly across Mike Smith's mind.

Neither did Dick Rowe think that these Liverpudlians were all that brilliant. They could find his way around their instruments, but were merely competent singers, and their sound conjured up back-of-beyond youth clubs with soft drinks, ping-pong and a presiding vicar who, like Rowe, was yet unaware of Merseybeat's distant thunder. Outfits like The Beatles could be found in virtually every town in the country.[23] Only last month, he'd snapped the tape machine off before the end of something similar by The Zircons – Spalding's winners of a pan-Lincolnshire "battle of the bands"-type contest in 1961, if you're wondering where you'd heard the name.

Decca wasn't the only company to reject The Zircons – and The Beatles. Pye, Philips and three of EMI's four labels did on receiving a second-generation copy of the Decca tape: all John, Paul, George and Pete had to offer apart from the faded second-hand celebrity of 'My Bonnie'. Each label never failed to apologise in writing for any delay in replying, excusing itself with the backlog of similar packages that arrived every week. The general feeling was that, while Mr Epstein's boys did have talent, there were sufficient guitar outfits under contract already. The tape was, therefore, being returned with best wishes for future success and blah blah blah.

A despondent mood was encapsulated by Lennon sparking earnest discussion about soliciting budget labels like Embassy and Top Six, where bargain-bin acts were hired to crank out workman-like xeroxes of other people's hits, sometimes squeezing half-a-dozen such tracks onto an EP – extended play – disc. "Can you tell the difference between these and the original sounds?" was Embassy's rhetorical question on one such tacky sleeve. Indeed, you could – but only the occasional misjudged timbre of the lead vocals or a butter-fingered riff made such merchandise so-bad-it's-good.

Now that the honeymoon was over, Brian was one scapegoat for The Beatles' marking time. Another was the Bests, whose house was, nevertheless, still used as an assembly point. That Mona no longer held The Beatles in the palm of her hand was manifested in the way the others started treating Pete – whose isolation became more and more perceptible. Now and then, he'd find himself straining his ears to catch murmured intrigue when, say, Harrison and McCartney, speaking in low voices, froze him with the inadvertent malevolence of their glances – or when McCartney and Lennon tinkered on secretive guitars in a backstage alcove.

While John was handsome after a funfair bumper-car operator fashion, it was hardly Pete's fault that he was the darling of the ladies for his more conventional good looks as well as an unobtrusive content in posing no deliberate threat to the front line except when he was required to surrender the kit to Paul in order to sing and demonstrate Joey Dee And The Starliters' 'Peppermint Twist'. He did so with all the endearingly flustered poise of an otherwise desk-bound head of accounts dancing with some voluptuous typist at the office party. In the watching throng, he'd see his mother, Kathy, and brother Rory, their eyes shining with pride, but there was no such encouragement from George, Paul and John these days.

Amicability was in short supply generally as the encircling professional and personal gloom thickened. As they hadn't become stars overnight, The Beatles were less a bunch of mates out on what amounted to a subsidised booze-up than one more deadbeat group, lurching from gig to gig. At the same venues time and time again – even the Casbah, for God's sake, until it closed in June 1962 – they could be bought for fees that (on Merseyside anyway) were often static at best. Promoters, then as now, took little account of inflation.

The music was becoming static too. Why bother with anything new when praise indeed was information that the show a customer missed was just like the one he saw the time before? No one was getting any younger; performing onstage was The Beatles' only saleable trade, and they were travelling the same long-road-with-no-turning as olde-time rockers like Gene Vincent and Screaming Lord Sutch with no choice but to go right on doing it, just to break even.

One of the only perks of the job was exemplified supposedly by the witnessed aftermath of a booking at the Aintree Institute, where John was holding court outside to two girls, one squawking, "Oooo, 'e's lovely!" and the other conspicuous for a huge bosom and a turned-up nose. After a while, Lennon forwent even cursory chivalry by seizing both by the arm and manoeuvring them into the darkness.

Being central figure in a gleesome threesome, however, wasn't sufficient material reward for a night's work. John and the others started focussing more sharply and unfairly on painfully committed Brian, who, admittedly, had been responsible for one or two major blunders already whilst learning his craft – such as the choice of songs for the Decca date – and would be responsible for many more to come. His principal failing then was that he was a salesman rather than an uninhibited hustler. He was also honest and painstaking to the point of arousing suspicion from an industry that was blighted more than most by time-serving incompetence, fake sincerity, backstabbing and the contradiction of excessive thrift and heedless expenditure.

There was no one else but Brian for The Beatles to blame for the apparent petering out of interest, apart from each other. Besides, bickering helped pass the time. Yet, thanks to their learner manager dialling his finger to a stub, The Beatles were leading what the economist would call a "full life" in a way. A list that had once signified a week's work became a day's. A lunchtime session at the Cavern might be followed by a few hours convalescent sloth until an early evening session at the same venue. Before onlookers realised that they'd left the building, The Beatles' van would be halfway down the street on a dash to a town hall over the river in Birkenhead.

As for Hamburg, the latest visit in April had found them supporting and socialising with Fats Domino, Gene Vincent, Little Richard and other visiting heroes of their school days that, unlike the Top Ten, the Star-Club could afford. George Harrison hit it off immediately with Billy Preston, Little Richard's 15-year-old organist, but Lennon had made up his mind to exercise an observed disrespect towards the ineffable Richard himself. Calling him "Grandad" and telling him to shut up was the least of it, but John was as diligent as everyone else in making myriad private observations of his old idol's performance for incorporation into his own.

The previous month, Epstein had negotiated both an engagement in Stroud, a market town almost as far south as Aldershot – and Pete, George, Paul and John's first BBC radio broadcast – three numbers on *Teenagers' Turn* from Manchester's Playhouse. Even this was no indication that The Beatles were anything more than a classic local group, despite an enthusiastic response – embracing screams – from the studio audience during the show, that translated to a stylised mobbing outside.

Reaction had been similar when Birmingham's Denny Laine And The Diplomats had made their debut on the ITV magazine *Midlands At Six* – and, as it had been when The Beatles' visited Decca, nothing had come of EMI convening the outfit at its Abbey Road complex in London's St John's Wood to tape a few demos.

On the outer fringes of the capital, The Dave Clark Five ruled Tottenham's Royal Ballroom as The Beatles did the Cavern. "It was pandemonium," gasped their singing organist, Mike Smith, "crash barriers and all that. The police station opposite used to get leave cancelled whenever we were on." Everyone had a great time on Dave Clark Five nights at the Royal, but not great enough to buy in chart-busting quantities any of the three singles the Five had released by 1962.

As it was with Clark in the Five, Pete Best was the recipient of most of the fuss from fans on rare occasions like *Teenagers' Turn*. However, he proved to be ostensibly the least promising member of The Beatles when George Martin, still recording manager of Parlophone, summoned them to Abbey Road on Wednesday 6 June 1962. Accustomed to on-stage inconsistencies of tempo caused by the mood of the hour, drummers were most prone to behind-the-scenes substitution in the studio. Though he was sound enough behind the kit in concert, rumours abounded later that even Dave Clark didn't actually rattle the traps on his own discs.

"The reasons were purely financial," elucidated ex-Johnny Kidd sticksman Clem Cattini, the first dyed-in-the-wool rock 'n' roller to emerge as a familiar figure on the capital's recording scene. "You were expected to finish four tracks – two singles – in three hours. A group might take a week to do two titles, not because they were incapable, but because sessions are a different mode of thinking to being on the road. You can't get away with so much. You need more discipline."

Having someone like Cattini ghost his drumming, would, therefore, have been no slight on Pete Best, but the mere suggestion that it would be necessary was sufficient to compound the doubts, justified and otherwise, that the others had about him, and precipitate his heartless sacking a few weeks later.

How different would Pete's life – and the cultural history of the world – have been if Brian Epstein hadn't come into the life of George Martin when The Beatles were midway through their seven weeks at the Star-Club? What Brian had decided would be a final assault on the record industry had ended in a victory of sorts during an appointment with George Martin in EMI's Manchester Square offices. What Martin had heard of this Mr Epstein's group wasn't particularly enthralling, but it would do no harm, he supposed, to see how they shaped up in the studio.

If he hadn't, we can safely say that, at the very least, the chances of Martin receiving a knighthood decades later would have been the same as those of Wally Ridley, Norrie Paramor and John Burgess, EMI label chiefs of the same vintage, all good men and true but, like George, possessing simple proficiency rather than genius. Certainly, it's unlikely that Martin would have been the subject of such a six-CD celebration to his half-century in the business – *Fifty Years In Recording* – as he'd be in 2001.

At the height of the trad-jazz craze, he'd scored his first Number One with The Temperance Seven's 'You're Driving Me Crazy', a camp 1961 recreation of a 1920s dance tune, complete with stiff-upper-lip vocal refrain. Before that, however, Parlophone had been responsible for few smashes compared to rival labels. It thrived mostly on dance bands, choirs, children's favourites – epitomised by Mandy Miller's 'Nellie The Elephant' – film themes, televisual spin-offs and easy-listening outings, some attributed to The George Martin Orchestra: releases that sold well enough without actually penetrating the Top 20.

Those that did were usually short-lived novelties such as 'Robin Hood' by Dick James, Charlie Drake's 'My Boomerang Won't Come Back' and 1962's 'Right Said Fred' from Bernard Cribbins, some under the supervision of George Martin – while perhaps the biggest feather in his lieutenant, Ron Richards' cap had been overseeing an Ella Fitzgerald session.

If Martin and Richards emerged subsequently as among the least dogmatic of the British record business's backroom boys, they were both long steeped in the unbending formality and cold professionalism of ordained working hours with no extra time or favours done, and the Musicians' Union springing to the defence of any pedant who yelled a malicious "Time's up!" in the middle of a take.

The Beatles were to challenge this by running over into the small hours and creating what George Harrison was to describe as "new meanings on old equipment". Before their arrival, however, Martin and Richards' provisioning of Parlophone with some sort of equivalent to whatever chart contenders rivals had snared had been barely more than cursory – with Ron drawing the short straw for such discoveries as Shane Fenton And The Fentones, guitarist Judd Proctor, Paul Raven (later, Gary Glitter) and The Clyde Valley Stompers. As usual, Richards was also directed to take charge of the recording debut of the pop group booked for 6 June, but an intrigued Martin assumed responsibility after looking in to check progress.

Before the Great Man grinned cheerfully and waved goodbye to them as they commenced the long drive back to Liverpool, The Beatles had been less round eyed at learning of his hand in 'Robin Hood', 'Right Said Fred' *et al* than Martin's serving as console midwife to a forthcoming album by the team of BBC television's satirical *That Was The Week That Was* series as well as The Goons, together and apart. By coincidence, the last solo Goon to scurry into the hit parade with a disc specifically designed to be funny was Peter Sellers in 1965 with his cod-Shakespearean recitation of The Beatles' 'A Hard Day's Night'.

One of Sellers's lesser film comedies, 1969's *The Magic Christian*, was to co-star Ringo Starr, once of Rory Storm's Hurricanes, who had replaced Pete Best in The Beatles in August 1962, cheating him unknowingly of his "inheritance" in the 11th hour. The new recruit wasn't the most versatile drummer in Liverpool, but he was a Pete Best for girls to adore more as a brother than dream lover, and bright enough not to ask too many questions yet. Even after the shared experience of the Kaiserkeller, Starr hadn't felt he'd known The Beatles well enough to invite them to his 21st birthday party. Nevertheless, they became closer during subsequent Hamburg seasons and on the Merseyside circuit. Despite his hangdog appearance, Ringo turned out to be blessed with a ready wit that was as guileless as John's was cruel. "Ringo was a star in his own right in Liverpool," asserted John. "Whatever that spark is in Ringo, we all know it, but we can't put our finger on it. Whether it's acting, singing or drumming, I don't know. There's something in him that's projectable."[21]

The new recruit was, however, the least significant participant in September when The Beatles recorded their maiden Parlophone single, 'Love Me Do'. EMI's executive body were to be in two minds about it during their weekly scheduling conference where, before committing themselves, the more obsequious underlings tried to gauge the opinion of each label's head of A&R. Thus after the customary "I don't know – what do you think?" discussion, it was decided that 'Love Me Do' would be cast adrift on the vinyl oceans in the first week of October.

7 "Pinching Our Arrangements Down To The Last Note"

John's euphoria at this latest development had been undercut by a grave domestic complication. Pregnancy wasn't what happened to nice girls like Cynthia, but one afternoon in the summer, she'd announced that her period was a week overdue – and she'd been sick in the morning, though that might have been through stomach-knotted anxiety. That her waist measured one inch bigger may have been nothing either, but her wrists, armpits and ankles felt peculiar.

She was seeing prams and pregnant women everywhere, in the streets, in public parks and on television. In an episode of *Dr Kildare* – the *ER* of its day – there'd been an unmarried mother. Her boyfriend smiled like John. The screen couple had separated and the baby was adopted – but perhaps there'd be a delightful romantic scene with John proposing on one knee, and promising to love Cynthia forever. Gruff pragmatism ruled, however, and she may have been left with the impression that, if the lyrics to some of The Beatles' numbers – about mister moonlight and words of love – were anything to go by, John and she were being conned out of something.

John's courtship of Cynthia had been fraught much of the time, but that was when they'd been closest because, as far as John – torn between resentment and panic – was concerned, the minute they left the registry office on 23 August 1962, they were already over somehow. The heart, the essence of what they had been, was wrapped up by the time they arrived at the reception – at which Aunt Mimi was pointedly absent – in an unlicensed restaurant. Yet, while marriage wouldn't blinker his roving eye, Cynthia at least felt hopeful during that hiatus between the wedding celebrations – interrupted by a Beatles booking that evening at some ballroom in Chester – and the issue of 'Love Me Do'.

Initially, the sales territory of the record was limited to loyal Liverpool – where it went straight in at Number One in *Mersey Beat* – until scattered airplay began humbly with a solitary spin crackling from Radio Luxembourg between the National Anthem that concluded the evening's viewing on BBC television and the pre-dawn shipping forecast on the Home Service.

Next, 'Love Me Do' slipped into the *NME* list at Number 21 on 8 December, and hovered on the edge of the Top 20 until just after Christmas, outselling on aggregate the latest by Chris Montez – the most recent US Bobby – and an expedient revival of 'Love Me Tender' by Richard "Dr Kildare" Chamberlain. At Number One was Frank Ifield, a new pretender to Cliff Richard's crown, with an exhumation of a 1949 country-and-western million seller, 'Lovesick Blues'. He'd headlined over The Beatles earlier that month on a mismatched bill at Peterborough's Embassy Cinema.

The local paper reported that they'd "made far too much noise".[24] Adding insult to injury as 'Love Me Do' continued to lose its tenuous grasp on the British charts, The Beatles were back at the Star-Club, supporting Johnny And The Hurricanes, a saxophone-dominated combo from Ohio, nearly all of whose hits – and there hadn't been any of late – were rocked-up treatments of old chestnuts.

Yet, all told, The Beatles had done well for first-timers, but who would assume that they wouldn't be back doing Liverpool-Hamburg piecework by this time next year, even as Brian Epstein negotiated their maiden national tour, low on the bill to Helen Shapiro?

However, the rip-tide of Merseybeat that was to overwhelm Helen, Johnny And The Hurricanes and Frank Ifield swept closer as the new year got under way. Ifield would be performing in venues where current chart standing had no meaning within 18 months of *Mersey Beat*'s announcement in January 1963 of the impending release of a second Beatles single, 'Please Please Me'. Hinged loosely on 'Please', a Bing Crosby ballad from the 1930s – which Frank Ifield had sung at Peterborough – it had been written mostly by John, and conceived initially in the style of Roy Orbison, a US balladeer typecast as a merchant of melancholy.

Similarly, 'Love Me Do', had been as dirge-like in embryo, presented as, recalled Lennon, "a slower number like Billy Fury's 'Halfway To Paradise', but George Martin suggested we do it faster. I'm glad we did." He was also to confess later, "We all owe a great deal of our success to George, especially for his patient guidance of our enthusiasm in the right direction."[25]

Martin's efforts "represented the highest examples of recorded art from every standpoint," fashionable 1970s producer, Richard Perry would gush.[26] Yet the Knight of Parlophone's position as The Beatles' artistic enabler was earned in large part for what he *didn't* do. After the first exploratory session, he'd dismissed the notion of singling out one of the group as nominal "leader". Neither had he foisted his own compositions on them as, say, Pye's Tony Hatch would on The Searchers or Decca's Tommy Scott on Twinkle and Them, taking advantage of a young act still too much in awe perhaps of the voice calling them to order via the control-room intercom to splutter, "We'd rather not, sir."

From the beginning, Martin had involved the group in the technical side of studio methodology. He'd also been prepared to accommodate the most radical suggestions – initially, The Beatles' preference for 'Please Please Me' to the perky and "professional" non-original 'How Do You Do It', once earmarked for Adam Faith, which Martin considered ideal as a follow-up to 'Love Me Do'. On the producer's instructions, nonetheless, the arrangement of 'Please Please Me' was accelerated and simplified with tight harmonies and responses behind Lennon's lead vocal.

Even at this early stage, George Martin had discovered that John, immodest about other matters, was genuinely unconceited about his singing to the point of insisting, "I can't say I ever liked hearing myself."[27] It made him wary of compliments about such contrasting items on The Beatles' first LP, *Please Please Me*, as downbeat and sensitively handled 'Anna' to 'Twist And Shout' on which he almost ruptured his throat with a surfeit of passion.

"I could never understand his attitude," sighed Martin, "as it was one of the best voices I've heard. He was a great admirer of Elvis Presley's early records, particularly the 'Heartbreak Hotel' kind of sound, and he was always saying to me, 'Do something with my voice. Put something on it. Smother it with tomato ketchup. Make it different.' He was obsessed with tape delay – a sort of very near-echo. I used to do other things to him, and as long as it wasn't his natural voice coming through, he was reasonably happy – but he'd always want his vocals to get special treatment. However, I wanted to hear its own natural quality."[27]

The timid songbird and his new bride were living at Mendips when 'Please Please Me' was released. Children would swoop from nowhere to see John Lennon, Woolton pop star, answer the door or be collected by road manager Neil Aspinall in the van for transportation to a palais maybe six or more counties away. Wherever "the newest British group to challenge The Shadows"[28] went nowadays, it always seemed to be one week after Cliff Bennett And The Rebel Rousers and one week ahead of Johnny Kidd And The Pirates in Chatham's Invicta, Tamworth's Assembly Rooms, the El Rio in Macclesfield and like venues played by every group that expected its run of luck to fizzle out at any minute.

Nevertheless, a sea change was taking place as epitomised by the actions of a certain Peter Stringfellow, awaiting his destiny as the self-proclaimed "world's greatest disco owner". Fresh from spinning the latest sounds in Nottingham's Dungeon, he had, with his brother Geoff, opened Sheffield's Black Cat – alias St Aidan's Church Hall – where one florin (10p) would buy admission. In February 1963, the Stringfellows had caved in to repeated requests by girl fans to book The Beatles. After wringing their hands over the seemingly extortionate fee demanded by Brian Epstein, a show was pencilled in for The Black Cat but, on police advice, this was moved to the more capacious Azena to limit the danger of scream-rent riot.

Back on Merseyside, heads turned when Ringo Starr's old Ford Zodiac stopped at a zebra crossing, but no Beatle yet attracted the beginnings of a crowd, despite a quote attributed to Lennon: "Our fans like us. They know that that whenever possible, we'll meet them, talk to them and sign their autographs."[29]

Yet even dates at the Cavern soon became quite ticklish operations. While Helen Shapiro was, technically speaking, the main attraction on the current round-Britain tour, she'd been upstaged by The Beatles and, on two dates when she was indisposed, so had Danny Williams and Billie Davis – British vocalists with a backlog of hits and a current chart strike.

On the very opening night (2 February) in Bradford, 'Please Please Me' had, according to *Record Mirror* – and the *Record Retailer* trade journal – entered at Number 16 in the charts. The following week, it jumped 13 places to hold the same position for a further seven days before reaching its apogee of Number Two. It was checkmated by Frank Ifield's 'The Wayward Wind', featuring his trademark yodel. A fortnight later, it was down one place, but returned to Two on 16 March with only 'Summer Holiday' from Cliff Richard in the way. Then it was downhill all the way – 5, 7, 11, 17 and out.

The pattern was similar in the other charts – except that *Melody Maker* had 'Please Please Me' lording it over 'The Wayward Wind'. In this respect, The Beatles were the first Merseybeat act to reach Number One in Britain – as proclaimed by Bob Wooler one lunchtime at the Cavern.

With a little logical blindness and retiming of the truth, The Beatles might be said to have tied at the top with Frank Ifield, but we must add the raw information that *The Guinness Book Of Hit Singles* – the Yellow Pages of such matters – has 'Please Please Me' at Two, and confirms that the first disc by a Liverpool group to unarguably top all UK singles charts was 'How Do You Do It' from Gerry And The Pacemakers (also on Parlophone) in April 1963. Yet what was becoming supposedly discernable as the "Mersey Sound" or "Liverpool Beat", would germinate the following month when The Beatles' 'From Me To You' eased 'How Do You Do It' from the top.

Moreover, in less than a week after the Shapiro jaunt, The Beatles had supported Tommy Roe and Chris Montez on another "scream circuit" trek where these boy-next-door North Americans had been obliged to conduct themselves with studied good humour when, right from the first evening, the running order was reshuffled as crowd reaction dictated that the home-grown Beatles play last, even on the three stops where they appeared as a trio, owing to John being huddled under bedclothes at Mendips with influenza.

Yet Decca and other of EMI's rivals thought they smelt a perishable commodity. What about The Beatles and Gerry And The Pacemakers' tour in May with the long-awaited Roy Orbison – who, bar the remote Elvis, commanded the most devoted British following of any US pop star? He'd be no lamb to the slaughter like Montez and Roe. Toughened by more than a decade in the business, Roy proved still able to work that old magic without obvious effort, enough to disconcert any Merseybeat group, chart-riding and frantic, on the same bill.

All he had to do was stand his ground with his black guitar and emote the nine hits he'd racked up since 1960. Indeed, at the Adelphi Cinema in Slough, he was required to reprise 1961's 'Running Scared' midway through his preordained quarter of an hour, while the sustained and rabid cheering – rather than screaming – after his 'In Dreams' finale was such that impresario Tito Burns at the back of the hall bore witness that "after 30 minutes, we still couldn't get The Beatles on. This was the first time I'd seen a standing ovation in Slough."[30]

Thus was set the pattern for the rest of the three weeks that the sonorous Orbison came on after Gerry and preceded The Beatles onstage. Alighting on this with false hope, those with axes to grind liked to imagine that the peril from the northeast was in retreat. Indeed, to Joe Meek, Merseyside had always been following rather than setting trends as instanced by a Liverpool "answer" to Screaming Lord Sutch in a new act called The Mersey Monsters. As far as Meek could see too, "The Beatles have nothing new about their sound. Cliff Bennett And The Rebel Rousers have been doing the same thing for a year."[31]

It was business as usual, therefore, for Joe with his productions of Bennett's cover of The Shirelles' 'Everybody Loves A Lover' – a Merseybeat "standard" – and Sutch's 'Jack The Ripper', vilified in *Melody Maker* as "nauseating trash".[32] All the same, Meek paid heed to what he regarded as a passing trend via 'You've Got To Have A Gimmick Today' by The Checkmates in March 1963, and a Beatles–Frank Ifield crossover in 'I Learned To Yodel' from The Atlantics, fronted by a vocalist with the negotiable name of Jimmy *Lennon*.

Nevertheless, "What's this Liverpool outfit everyone's talking about?" was a question asked with increasing frequency by elderly executives in

London record company offices while office juniors discussed whether The Beatles had got into a rut what with their next A-side, 'From Me To You', having the same overall melodic and rhythmic thrust as 'Please Please Me'. Next, talent scouts from the capital came sniffing round Merseyside just in case the word about a "Liverpool Sound" carried any weight – especially as other Epstein clients (Billy J Kramer, The Fourmost and Cilla Black) had been tossed Lennon–McCartney songs almost as licences to print money long before the dissimilar ilk of Bernard Cribbins, Ella Fitzgerald and Celine Dion dipped into the same portfolio.

Though only amateurs then, Kramer and his Coasters, had found themselves two places behind The Beatles in *Mersey Beat*'s 1963 poll, their individuality lying in Kramer's boyish charm and pleasant croon – which, if required, could turn into a mannerly growl. Recognised as the one that mattered, Billy alone was covered by Epstein's management agreement, and The Coasters replaced by The Dakotas, a more accomplished quartet from Manchester. Under George Martin's direction, the pairing's debut 45 was a crack at The Beatles' album track, 'Do You Want To Know A Secret', the work of Lennon.[33] At the composer's suggestion, Kramer's name on the Parlophone record label was split with a non-signifying "J". John also supplied 'Bad To Me' – penned during the Spanish holiday with Epstein – Kramer And The Dakotas second hit. Seeing out 1963 in fine fashion was another Beatles-associated smash – this time by Paul McCartney – 'I'll Keep You Satisfied', as well as an instrumental Top 20 entry, 'The Cruel Sea', for the Dakotas only.

Neither Billy nor the Dakotas were able to recapture the success they enjoyed in 1963 and 1964 – and the same was true of the second string to Epstein's bow. It was almost a matter of course that, prior to Kramer, Gerry And The Pacemakers would melt into Epstein's managerial caress, even though, on a first-come-first-served basis, he did not attend to their recording career until The Beatles had left the runway with theirs. So it was that a few months after 'Love Me Do', Gerry's lot had gained an EMI contract too.

Before 'How Do You Do It' was dragged down, Gerry had joked, "How does it feel to be Brian's number two group then?" when bumping into John at NEMS. Around the same time, joint press interviews were convened in a London hotel for Marsden and Lennon as principal spokespersons for the Merseybeat movement.

Shortly after the first *Beatles Monthly* was published, a similar periodical devoted solely to Gerry And The Pacemakers was considered a worthwhile market exercise for a while. Both outfits remained on terms of fluctuating equality as Gerry's second offering, 'I Like It', wrenched 'From Me To You' from the top. After The Searchers did likewise to the latest by Elvis Presley in August, they, Gerry, The Beatles and Billy J Kramer slugged it out for hit parade supremacy for, more or less, the rest of the year.

The first signs of danger were to rear up in spring 1964 when Gerry's 'Don't Let The Sun Catch You Crying' stalled at Number Six, a true comedown by previous standards. By then, however, he was already considering – as so many of his kind were to do – pantomime, charity football matches and children's television, and was tracing Tommy Steele's scent as an "all-round entertainer". This aspiration had, I suppose, become apparent initially on 1963's *How Do You Like It* LP when the expected Merseybeat was mixed with orchestrated evergreens, notably 'You'll Never Walk Alone' – which infiltrated folklore as the Liverpool Football Club anthem.

Most other Merseybeat entertainers with the faintest tang of star quality had at least a moment of glory when London got in on the act. Having mastered individual crafts in the ranks of outfits like The Thunderbeats and The Midnighters prior to their formation in April 1963, a debut single was a long time coming, but 'Magic Potion' was issued shortly after Brian Epstein saw Beatle-like potential in The Koobas. Through him, they were to land nine dates supporting The Beatles, going down so well that a golden future was predicted by both the music press and the in-crowd that frequented the Scotch of St James, the Speakeasy and other metropolitan clubs.

The Remo Four weren't amateurs either. Connected genealogically with Jimmy Justice's Jury, Liverpool's most esteemed instrumental unit were seized likewise by Epstein and, through him, Pye, though they functioned principally as all-purpose accompanists on disc for such as Gregory Phillips and Tommy Quickly, and on nationwide package tours.

Pye also hooked the biggest non-Epstein fish in The Searchers. Their saga is a cautionary tale of how it might have been for John, Paul, George and either Pete or Ringo. As The Beatles reigned in the Cavern, so the similarly mildewed Iron Door was the fiefdom of The Searchers, following much hard graft in Hamburg where the group developed the tidy chorale and unique fretboard interaction that would influence later acts (notably The Byrds).

The Iron Door was also the location for The Searchers' after-hours taping of 11 tracks that secured them their deal with Pye in June 1963. By August, they were home and dry when an exuberant reading of The Drifters' 'Sweets For My Sweet' booted Elvis from Number One – as 'Sugar And Spice', the soundalike follow-up (composed by Tony Hatch) nearly did 'She Loves You', The Beatles' fourth 45. Yet, foreseeing only fleeting prosperity for Merseybeat, Pye was disinclined to risk promising group originals as A-sides, preferring to stampede the boys into its Marble Arch studio for *Meet The Searchers* and, less than four months later, *Sugar And Spice*. On each of these LPs, The Hit was padded with items from tunesmiths based in Denmark Street – Britain's Tin Pan Alley – and stand-bys from the stage repertoire.

With respect to the latter, while they could rock as hard as anyone, The Searchers were exceptional for less frantic versions of standards like 'Twist And Shout', preferring calm precision to then lead singer Tony Jackson risking damage to his vocal cords, Lennon-style, on what was only doggerel about an already outmoded dance.

The Searchers' approach paid dividends with lighter selections too. Like The Beatles, they were particularly adept at stealing the show from wilder co-stars by adapting songs by The Shirelles, The Ronettes and other US female vocal groups of ingenuously fragile conviction. From The Orlons' catalogue alone, 'Shimmy Shimmy' and May 1964's chart-topping 'Don't Throw Your Love Away' were conspicuous on *It's The Searchers*, their third Pye album in less than a year.

Provoked even more by EMI's infuriating success with The Beatles, a chastised but cynical Decca adopted a more scattershot approach by flinging numerous discs by beat groups from Liverpool at the public, albeit by being "excessively thrifty" over the publicity needs of all but the most consistent best-sellers. In January 1963 alone, the label made off from Liverpool with The Big Three, Beryl Marsden, new Cavern master-of-ceremonies Billy Butler, and (because their drummer was now *ex*-Beatle Pete Best) Lee Curtis And The All-Stars.

On George Harrison's recommendation, Dick Rowe signed The Rolling Stones in May. Dave Berry And The Cruisers, Surrey's Nashville Teens, Macclesfield bluesman John Mayall, Them from Belfast, The Moody Blues (a sort of Birmingham "supergroup"), Unit 4 + 2 (likewise in Cheshunt), The Applejacks from Solihull and The Zombies (pride of St Alban's) were among later acquisitions but for each such hitmaking act, there was a Beat Six, a Bobby Cristo And The Rebels, a Gonks, a Falling Leaves – and a Lee Curtis And The All-Stars.

A dependable draw both in Liverpool and Hamburg. Curtis "was delighted that he (Pete Best) joined me because he was such a personality on Merseyside. To have Pete Best drumming behind you was a tremendous attraction. I'd seen him with The Beatles and it was absolutely amazing because the girls screamed like hell for Pete to sing."[34] Nevertheless, it was the start of something small. During one of their residencies at the Star-Club, Astrid Kirchherr commiserated with Pete, but her sympathy wasn't sufficient to mitigate "continuing with a group not as popular," he sighed, "doing the same old gigs I'd done with The Beatles".[2]

Along with other companies, Decca lugged mobile recording equipment up to Liverpool to tape as many acts from the city of overlapping towns as could be crammed onto a compilation LP with a title like *This Is Merseybeat* or *At The Cavern*. Acts selected for any additional attention had, preferably, to have won their spurs in Hamburg or scored in *Mersey Beat*'s latest poll. The Big Three were advantaged further by being managed by Epstein, while The Mojos had a rich stockpile of their own songs into which other combos dipped. Others were fronted by outstanding showmen like Kingsize Taylor, Rory Storm, Derry Wilkie, Freddie Starr – and Bill "Faron" Russley who led his Flamingos through a British take on The Contours' 'Do You Love Me', the sure-fire smash that, purportedly, he'd let slip through his fingers in 1963 when he dictated its lyrics to Essex's visiting Brian Poole for the price of a double whiskey. Unable to extend much beyond being adored locally too, Beryl Marsden, rather than a lesser singer like Cilla Black, should have represented Merseyside womanhood in the 1960s charts.

The Escorts' elegant 'The One To Cry' and the arresting 'Lies' by Johnny Sandon And The Remo Four were among other undeserved flops – not to mention sterling tries at 'Fortune Teller', 'Some Other Guy', 'Twist And Shout', 'Let's Stomp' and other set-works that went down a storm on the boards by also-rans who more than bore out Bill Harry's gloomy comment to me that "the cream doesn't necessarily come to the top in this sort of business".

According to one story – probably apocryphal – the entire personnel of one picked-to-click Merseybeat outfit wound up stacking and loading auto parts in the same warehouse by autumn. That was when they saw a picture of The Merseybeats in the same issue of *Music Echo* in which some southern ponces were duplicating both the sheepdog fringes and the mid-air jump against brick-strewn wasteland patented by The Beatles on the cover of July 1963's *Twist And Shout* EP. Moaning about it to *Melody Maker* in August, John Lennon had noticed that Gerry And The Pacemakers suffered "terrible copying" too, but far more groups had been formed in The Beatles' image, "pinching our arrangements and down to the last note at that."[35] While some used insectile appellations – Termites, Moths, Grasshoppers *ad nauseum* – others would work the word *beat* into their titles – Beatstalkers, Counterbeats, Beat-Chics, Fourbeats, Beat Boys, Beat Merchants, Beathovens and so on.

Youth club combos in the sticks wore collarless suits and moptops that resembled spun dishmops whenever they shook their heads and went "oooooo", and there'd be continuity in tortuous Liverpudlian accents by either "John" or "Paul", and an unsmiling lead guitarist who, in imagination at least, played a black Rickenbacker through a Marshall amplifier, just like George Harrison, the most androgynously hirsute of the four.

Was it only last year that a Billy Fury quiff was a sure sign of a cissy? Today's pony-tailed navvy might take heed how contentious the issue of long-haired males could be then in households in which, with increasing frequency, grandmothers pleaded for calm amid blazing rows between parents and once-tractable children over the teenage noise issuing from transistor radio, Dansette record player and black and white television, not to mention the wearing of winkle pickers – "Are your feet really that shape?" – thigh-huggingly "crude" drainpipe jeans, eye-torturing ties, and haircuts. A nasty rumour was soon to be filtered round provincial Britain that Mick Jagger of The Rolling Stones, whose hair was girlier than that of The Beatles, was to undergo a sex-change operation so that he could marry one of the others.

Mersey Beat reckoned that the Stones were "a London group with the Liverpool sound" – in common with Brian Poole And The Tremeloes maybe? The latter's 'Twist And Shout' reached the UK Top Ten in 1963 – and they were chosen to launch the first edition of ITV's *Ready Steady Go*, remembered as the most atmospheric pop showcase of the decade. Next up was 'Do You Love Me' causing Decca to cancel a xerox by Kent's Bern Elliott And The Fenmen so that Brian's boys could have a clearer run and the edge over those by Faron's Flamingos (relegated to a B-side by Oriole) while the more dangerous enemy, The Dave Clark Five, just signed to Parlophone's sister label, Columbia.

London talent scouts, see, were sparing themselves a trip to England's crowded northwest by getting pop talent from different areas to steal a march on the Merseysiders. Fanning out from the Holy City, they'd discovered that numerous other acts had been rifling the same classic rock and R&B (rhythm and blues) motherlode too. Some were also coming up with originals of similar persuasion. Glaswegian beat groups, for example, had matured in a similar fashion to their Scouse counterparts through years of isolation from the main sequence of British pop. Though the high summer of Scottish rock was to be a long time coming – peaking in 1969 when Marmalade scored a UK Number One with a Beatles cover – Dean Ford and his Gaylords, the outfit from which Marmalade sprang, appeared regularly at the Picasso (Glasgow's "Cavern") where they shared the limelight with The Alex Harvey Soul Band, The Golden Crusaders, Chris McClure's Section and other performers with the strongest possible local reputation.

After leaving their scotch-and-cokes half-finished in the Picasso, some A&R representatives then crossed the Irish Sea where, say, Dickie Rock and the Miami Showband were coaxed into releasing a version of 'Boys', Ringo's solitary lead vocal on the *Please Please Me* LP, for the Pye man, as the beat boom pushed even the most up-to-date showbands – a phenomenon peculiar to Ireland – out of the picture. A few would weather the storm, but, shortly, the showband was to be an anachronism.

Like everywhere else nowadays, the republic was deemed to have a form of pop music peculiar to itself, namely "Blarney Beat" as propagated by such as The Creatures, The Four Aces, The Chosen Few and, from Dublin, Dominic Behan, brother of playwright Brendan, who was signed to Pye for a crafty 1963 single of 'Liverpool Lou', a shanty that had flowered from the same stem as 'Maggie May', 'Heave Away' and 'Row Bullies Row'.

Thus, as the close of 1963 loomed, Liverpool's leading pop executants – most of them as good as they'd ever be – were no longer as sure as they had been only a few months earlier that accident of geography would facilitate the procuring of a slot on ITV's *Thank Your Lucky Stars* next month that would kick off a week-by-week scramble into the Top Ten. Yet there were a few that were still clinging onto that as a certain hope even as the hire-purchase company carted off their equipment, following, say, desperate strategies such as the lead vocalist pooching-out his lips like Mick Jagger's – or the enlistment of a saxophonist and organist as a nod towards The Dave Clark Five, who were ahead of The Beatles for a split second early in 1964.

The Beatles, The Searchers and The Mojos had been among far-sighted Scouse musicians who had uprooted themselves to become London-based concerns. The Koobas had done likewise, following three triumphant weeks at the Star-Club in December 1963, even if Britain was no longer crying out so loudly for four-man beat groups with Beatle haircuts and assumed or genuine "wacker" accents, who could crank out 'Twist And Shout', 'Hippy Hippy Shake', 'Money' and the entire Chuck Berry songbook.

Yet, heard on Oriole's *This Is Merseybeat* centuries ago that summer, Rory Storm would insist, with his hand on his heart, that he'd never harboured any desires about becoming nationally famous – although he could have been any time he liked. Lee Curtis, however, would "envy all those people who made it. I'd loved to have made it, and I think about it every day of my life."[17]

Curtis dismayed his female following when he appeared on a *Mersey Beat* list of performers thought to be married. Heading this was John Lennon, but the image of him held by most lovestruck pubescent girls in Inverness or Penzance was born of the pages of Catherine Cookson-esque romantic chivalry and grown to man's estate as a Poor Honest Northern Lad Who'd Bettered Himself as a pop singer with an electric guitar. How many of them wondered what his penis was like (or whether he even had one)? Ignorance was bliss – and worship of an idol without vice or blemish was, I suppose, less harmful an analgesic than most to an otherwise mundane provincial existence of school, homework and youth club.

John was married, true enough, but it was to Cynthia, known then – erroneously, as events were to prove – as the shrinking violet of The Beatles' clique. The speed of events after take-off with 'Love Me Do' had not, however, overwhelmed her as she coped with marathon fan vigils outside her, John and the baby's Kensington bedsit; stifled giggles from those who'd winkled out the ex-directory number, and even an attempted kidnap of Julian. Disguises, decoy tactics and secret destinations were to be as essential as spare underwear whenever the Lennons went on holiday. On one occasion, Cynthia had to be smuggled out of a hotel in a laundry basket.

She knew nothing of John's fleeting assignations with "scrubbers", which took place in the seclusion of, say, a backstage broom cupboard, or the cursing that marinated the air after the van broke down, and Neil Aspinall's new helpmate, Malcolm "Big Mal" Evans, once a Cavern bouncer, located the problem and knew that it'd be a long and messy botch job. This he'd explain patiently just as heavy drops of rain spat on the windows and pummelled the roof, and he began tinkering under the bonnet to the necessary accompaniment of an engine spluttering like an old man coughing his guts up after a lifetime of 60 cigarettes a day. Fifteen, twenty minutes later, the downpour eased, and suddenly Lennon was glooming over Mal's shoulder, goading him with sarcastically useless suggestions.

John had been singled out as "leader" in the lyrics of 'We Love The Beatles', a 1964 single by The Vernons Girls, recruited originally from employees of the Liverpool Football Pools firm. Weeks prior to all four Beatles comprising the panel in a special edition at the Liverpool Empire, he was also token member on BBC television's *Juke Box Jury* – and the main feature of the opening edition of *Midland Beat* in October 1963 was an interview with "John Lennon of The Beatles, but otherwise the entire content is restricted to Midlands items" – for, according to editor Dennis Detheridge, "Liverpool started the ball rolling. Now the Midlands is ready to take over."

As a Birmingham pop picker might scan *Midland Beat*, so her country cousin could the pages of Torquay-based *South-West Scene* and more local sources where too were so many beat groups that amid the *Andover Advertiser*'s reports on jumble sales and winter farrowing, its "Teen Scene" section would be summarising 1964 as "the year of the groups. The Record Charts were inundated with them and so was Andover!"[36] The town was to cradle The Troggs, who were to work the country bumpkin angle in 1966: *ooo-arrr* Long John Silver-isms and media hacks quoting "I" as "oi", "us" as "we", "we" as "us", you get the idea... The only stroke they didn't pull was "be" instead of "am", "is" or "are".

Back in autumn 1963, however, Scouse was still the most alluring dialect in the kingdom, and from its slang, words like "fab", "gear" and "grotty" filtered through the pages of teenage comics and into the mouths of the most well-spoken young Britons. Yet, though every other dance floor request seemed to be for 'Twist And Shout' or, when some idiot wanted it, 'She Loves You', Horsham's Beat Merchants were typical of a strain of groups that ditched Beatle-esque winsomeness and stage suits for a motley and belligerently unkempt interpretation of "authentic" R&B when they supported The Rolling Stones, shortly after The Beatles had headlined both at *Sunday Night At The London Palladium* and, before that, at a recital for the seated young toffs and their with-it headmaster at Stowe public school in Buckinghamshire.

John, Paul, George and Ringo had also been seen in May 1963 waving a cheery goodbye during the closing credits on ventriloquist dummy Lenny The Lion's show on BBC TV's *Children's Hour*. Then there was a prime-time evening sketch involving the donning of boaters and a singalong of 1912's 'On Moonlight Bay' with comedy duo Morecambe and Wise. Whatever next? Would there unfold a Gerry-esque flow-chart of pantomime, soft-shoe shuffling and charity football after they were overtaken – as they surely would be – by a newer sensation?

Offstage, The Beatles were hanging around with the likes of Alma Cogan, bubbly singing perennial of television variety. She had been endeavouring to recoil from the lightweight, tulle-petticoated jauntiness that had made her – 'Banjo's Back In Town', 'Twenty Tiny Fingers' *et al* – by sifting through the sheet music, LPs and, if lucky, demo tapes of beat groups. The most glaring expression of this policy was to be her cover in 1964 of 'Eight Days A Week' by The Beatles who liked her well enough to accept an open invitation to the liberty hall that was her Kensington flat. She was also omnipresent on the pilot series of *Ready Steady Go* in autumn 1963 – which also featured then a besuited interlocutor in his thirties and occasional send-ups of current hits by comics of the same age. Alma developed an on-screen soft spot for near-neighbour John Lennon, once cuffing him playfully on *Ready Steady Go*, following some – possibly scripted – ad-libbing between cheeky young shaver and jovial voice-of-experience commensurate with The Beatles' apparent toeing of a winsome line of pseudo-rebellious behaviour. Well, we're all a bit wild when we're young, aren't we?

It was, however, The Beatles' spot in *The Royal Variety Show* at London's Prince of Wales Theatre that November that prompted the *Daily Express* to brief its Liverpool-born showbusiness correspondent, Derek Taylor, do a "hatchet job" about their yielding to showbusiness proper, even if Lennon raised a laugh with the larger-than-life bluntness of his "rattle yer jewellery" announcement. Taylor, however, could only praise them – and be rewarded with a post as Brian Epstein's right-hand man and ghost writer of his *Cellarful Of Noise* biography.

Though located in the same city, the distance from the pearly cleavages and bow-tied tuxedos of the Prince of Wales theatre might have been measurable in light-years from the frayed jeans, CND badges and beatnik beards in the Marquee, Studio 51 and and other R&B clubs from whence had sprung The Rolling Stones as well as The Yardbirds, Kinks and Pretty

Things – all groups to enter the charts in 1964 without much compromising their long-haired images, and by sticking to their erudite guns musically. Running in the same pack, The Downliners Sect were well placed to do likewise as they too started to sound and look alarmingly like a pop group, but they surfaced instead as patron saints to legion also-ran provincial combos like The Beat Merchants.

Taking the same cue as the Sect and The Merchants, Joe Meek wheeled in North London's Syndicats to see if they could make numbers by Howlin' Wolf, Chuck Berry and Ben E King *not* sound like The Beatles.

By 1964, the Olympic torch of both Merseybeat and Home Counties R&B had been carried to every nook and cranny *sur le continent* where 'Money', 'You'll Never Walk Alone', 'The Hippy Hippy Shake' and further set-works had been worked into the repertoires of every other domestic pop star from Johnny Halliday – a sort of Gallic Elvis – downwards after France dropped territorial defences to import British pop talent by the ton. Former solo vocalists in Italy, say, or Spain were now integrating themselves into beat groups, and a venture into Teutonic Merseybeat had been made already by Manfred Weissleder, proprietor of the Star-Club. Guided by him, four Hamburg teenagers became The Rattles, a name with the same scansion as "Beatles" and an implication that here was the German wing of the movement – especially since there'd been a cultural "twinning" of the two cities as exemplified by Bill Harry's organisation of an aeroplane trip for Cavern regulars to Hamburg in 1963.

In parenthesis, loitering at the airport with passport at the ready, Lord Woodbine occupied a last-minute spare seat. He spent most of the subsequent weekend buying up contraband to sell at inflated prices back home. On the return flight, he spread his booty amongst pliant fellow passengers, retrieving it after they'd passed through customs.

Though everyone from The Rattles to The Beatles continued to turn to US R&B as monks to the Bible, North America's domination of post-war pop was over for the time being – in Europe anyway – now that the British beat boom, spearheaded by John, Paul, George and Ringo, the "Fab Four", had set new commercial and artistic yardsticks for schoolboy groups (including my own Ace And The Crescents) engaged in shambolic garage rehearsals, but daring to dream of Beatle-sized renown.

British pop musicians in general had been moving up in highbrow circles too following Adam Faith's intelligent and eloquent showing on BBC television's inquisitorial interview programme *Face To Face* in 1960. Adam was the first from the world of pop to experience such a grilling, and, because he gave a good account of himself, he paved the way for further "articulate" pop pundits such as ex-Oxford undergraduate Paul Jones, Spencer Davis with his BA in German – and John Lennon.

However, the notion of pop music as a viable means of artistic expression wasn't taken seriously amongst prominent intellectuals until the coming of The Beatles, unless you counted the earnest fascination of Andy Warhol, Peter Blake, Eduardo Paolozzi, Richard Hamilton and other pioneers of Pop Art in Top 40 radio from the late 1950s onwards.

Initially, "quality" newspapers like *The Times* and *The Observer* were preoccupied almost exclusively with the hysteria that accompanied Beatles performances on the "scream circuit", putting condescending inverted commas around their name, followed by "the Liverpool 'pop' group" or similar explanatory phrase.

Then William S Mann – who covered classical music for *The Times* – entered the fray on 27 December 1963. The day after a prosy end-of-year cultural overview (credited to "Our Music Critic") was published, John Lennon – not revelling in pretend ignorance as usual – confessed truly that he had no idea what Mann meant by phrases like "Aeolian cadences", "sub-mediant key switches", "chains of pandiatonic clusters" and "melismas with altered vowels". Neither was John aware of a similarity between the chord progression in 'Not A Second Time' (from *With The Beatles*, the second LP) and those in the coda to Mahler's *Song Of The Earth* (*Das Lied Von Der Erde*). He was, nevertheless, vaguely flattered by Mann's laudation of Lennon and McCartney as "the outstanding composers of 1963".

Two days later, Richard Buckle of the *Sunday Times* had them as "the greatest composers since Schubert". Nor far off were a random Beatles B-side, 'Yes It Is', analysed in *Music And Musicians* magazine, and Fritz Spiegl's *Eine Kleine Beatlemusik*, a 1965 album of their hits arranged in the style of Mozart.

Although McCartney and Lennon would still be damned with such faint praise as "reasonable good 'amateur' composers, greatly assisted by the poverty of British composing standards" in the *Sunday Times* as late as 13 November 1966, the die had been cast, and the elevation of The Beatles from dealers in ephemera to attracting the sort who read the likes of Mann and Buckle as gospel, was about to become unstoppable.

In a world beyond *Times* subscribers and, indeed, Britain's entire population, penetration of North America by The Beatles seemed an impossible dream in 1963 – though they'd entered the US Hot 100 by proxy when, during a break in a British tour, Del Shannon, a US pop vocalist of similar kidney to Roy Orbison, booked a London studio and some session players for a cover of 'From Me To You', purely for the US market. It was issued on the Bigtop label, and had slipped in at Number 86 on 6 July, climbing nine places over the next fortnight.

Progress for Beatles records in their own right was negligible. The first four singles and the *Please Please Me* long-player (minus two tracks and retitled *Introducing The Beatles*) were not deemed worthy of release by Capitol – EMI's regular US outlet – as, declared Jay Livingstone, a senior executive, "We don't think The Beatles will do anything in this market", unmindful as he was of whatever was gripping a backwater like Britain.

That's why 'Love Me Do' was issued by Tollie; 'Please Please Me', 'From Me To You' and the album by Vee-Jay, a Chicago company of slightly more importance; and 'She Loves You' by Swan. Thanks in a perverse way to Del Shannon's version, 'From Me To You' crept by association to Number 116 towards the end of the summer, and that appeared to be that for The Beatles in the USA – so much so that George Harrison was able to spend three pleasurable weeks as just an English relation at married sister Louise Caldwell's home in Benton, a small Illinois mining town. "That's the only experience", reflected Louise, "any one of The Beatles had of living in the States as a normal human being. Nobody had ever heard of him."

An interview on local radio – by WFRX's Marcia Raubach, the first presenter to spin a Beatles disc on US airwaves – and even a stage appearance with The Four Vests, Benton's boss group, had the impact of a feather on concrete, and Harrison was to return to Britain with a funny story about the aftermath of his bash with the Vests when someone told him that "with the right kind of backing, you could go places". This judgement proved correct, and the next the good people of Benton saw of Mrs Caldwell's brother was on the nationally networked *Ed Sullivan Show* the following February.

8 "Kids Everywhere Go For The Same Stuff"

By the middle of 1964, news of The Beatles and everything else that was gripping young Britain had spread to the other side of the world. In every Australasian city, you'd come across many an outfit that had reinvented itself as an ersatz British beat group. There were also instances of domestic talent checkmating the originals in the charts – for example, a New Zealand ensemble, Ray Columbus and his Invaders, whose version of Lennon and McCartney's 'I Wanna Be Your Man' sold more than those by both The Beatles (on a New Zealand-only A-side) and The Rolling Stones.

On the mainland, a bunch of skiffle latecomers in Melbourne found a Mick Jagger soundalike in future accountant Rod Turnbull and bowlerised the Stones' name. What's more, The Spinning Wheels hired Roger Savage, the lately emigrated engineer of the Stones' first Decca session, and worked up a repertoire as rife with – often the same – Bo Diddley, Chuck Berry, Howlin' Wolf and Muddy Waters favourites and unoriginal "originals" as that of their role models. Most spectacularly of all, however, Sydney's Bee Gees mutated from an updated Mills Brothers into quasi-Beatles.

Over in Japan, the most renowned "answer" to the Fab Four was The Spiders while Los Shakers – Caio, Hugo, Osvaldo and Pelin – cornered Latin America. The latter outfit came closest to copying both the Look and the Sound, while The Spiders jettisoned their covers of 'Please Please Me', 'She Loves You' and so forth soon to develop an in-built and charmingly naive originality lacking in most other acts of their kind, even if lead vocalist Masaaki Sakai hadn't much notion what he was singing apart from those self-composed items that, if dependent on what was going on in Swinging London, were delivered in Japanese with an abandoned drive, all the more piquant in the light of government disapproval of pop – to be manifested in frenzied protest demonstrations about those Beatle *ketos* polluting the Budokan Hall, Tokyo's temple of martial arts, for three evenings in summer 1966.

In reciprocation, The Spiders undertook a tour of Europe. Los Shakers, however, chose to consolidate their standing at home. Yet their take on British beat was more melodic than a lot of the genuine articles. Moreover, the pronunciation of their all-English lyrics is so anonymously precise that they wouldn't have been out of place in the Star-Club or the Cavern, *circa* 1963 – just as all-American Her Majesty's Coachmen – with bowler hats their gimmick, and 'Money' their first single – would have been quite comfortable depping for The Searchers in The Iron Door, judging by their second 45, jingle-jangling 'I Don't Want To See You'.

The Coachmen rivalled the comparably Anglophile St George and his Dragons as Sacramento's boss group – and The Creatures from Maryland could have filled in for The Zombies at St Alban's Town Hall, despite an electric organ tone like someone piddling into a metal bucket. There were also familiar-sounding rings to Michigan's Flowers-Fruits-And-Pretty Things and The Merseybeats (of Kentucky!). Likewise, The Gants from Mississippi grew out their crew-cuts and wore vestments of visual and musical personality bespoken by The Beatles and, especially, The Dave Clark Five – to the extent of Xeroxing two successive Five US A-sides – with singer Sid Herring as *norf* London on these as he was Scouse on a treatment of The Beatles' 1966 B-side, 'Rain'.

Northeast to New Jersey, The Redcoats' singing drummer, John Spirit had been one of The Ran-Dells, who, in 1963, reached the US Top 20 with the novel 'Martian Hop'. Then John heard The Beatles, and formed The Redcoats with himself as Lennon and guitarist Mike Burke as McCartney. Next, they enlisted a George Martin in Steven Rappaport, producer of 'Martian Hop', and proved as capable of sounding as much like mid-1960s Beatles out-takes as a luckier regional quartet, The Knickerbockers, did with 1966's chartbusting 'Lies'.[37]

No such luck befell more hastily assembled discs by the likes of The American Beatles, The Bug Men, John And Paul, The Manchesters, The

Wackers and The Beatlettes – some of whom had no physical form beyond television and recording studios, being the work of session musicians who probably bitched during coffee breaks about this Limey unit everyone's talking about.

Of more committed entities attempting to likewise cash in on The Beatles and British beat, the usual summit of short careers was recurring parochial engagements and sporadic regional airplay for one, maybe two singles that demonstrated musical ability at odds with overweening expressive ambition until the perpetrators were able to come to terms with the world of work, the marriage bed and Vietnam, and stop yearning for the next feedback-ridden, drum-thudding evening at the local hop.

Until what has passed into myth as the "British Invasion", no UK pop act, let alone native copyists, had ever made sustained headway in North America. The most recent instance had been Billy Fury's backing group, The Tornados racing to Number One in the US Hot 100 with 1962's aetherial 'Telstar'. Also produced by Joe Meek, an attendant LP had sold well too before further US advances were checked by executive politics causing the cancellation of a coast-to-coast tour.

Yet our sceptr'd isle had become the sub-continent's – indeed, the world's – prime purveyor of pop after The Beatles' messianic descent on 7 February 1964 onto what had been called Idlewild Airport a few months earlier. It had now been renamed "Kennedy Airport" because, on the same November day in 1963 that British newspapers had announced The Beatles' forthcoming US trip, President John F Kennedy had been assassinated in Dallas, "a place not known for war". So would sing Jerry Lee Lewis in 1966's 'Lincoln Limousine', a breezy, Macgonagall-esque album filler that remains my all time fave rave of requiems to any dead celebrity – especially with its inane "Oh Lord, it would have been better if he had stayed at home" line, and another about the "20 dollar rifle" that "took the life of this great man" as Lewis leads up to the truism that "you never know who's your enemy or your friend".[38]

Jerry Lee himself received composer's royalties for "Lincoln Limousine", but the Joseph Kennedy Jnr Foundation For Mental Retardation was the beneficiary of profits from budget-priced *John Fitzgerald Kennedy: A*

Memorial Album (which included his inaugural speech in its entirety). Produced and broadcast by a New York radio station within half a day of the shooting, it shifted four million copies in less than a week.

The late JFK waded in with a second hit LP, *The Presidential Years,* after a 45, 'The Voice Of The President', nestled uneasily on juke box selection panels between Bobby ballads – and the Californian surf music that dominated the pop airwaves in North America then. Ruling the genre were The Beach Boys, who celebrated surfing and its companion sport, hot-rod racing with chugging rock 'n' roll backing overlaid with a chorale more breathtaking than that of The Beatles.

To the chagrin of the Boys and others on Capitol, John, Paul, George and Ringo were to be launched with one of the most far-reaching publicity blitzes hitherto known in the record industry. Then 'I Want To Hold Your Hand' (the first Beatles disc the company had been prepared to release) reached the US Hot 100 on 1 January 1964 – and, within months, it and repromoted 'Love Me Do', 'Please Please Me' and 'She Loves You' had all risen to Number One. Even the B-sides of the first two made the Top 40 too. However, 'From Me To You', the one that had climbed highest of all before 1964 – though that's not saying much – could only manage Number 41.

While the intruders so swamped the Hot 100, The Beach Boys' resident genius, Brian Wilson, felt both threatened and inspired artistically. "I knew immediately that everything had changed, and that if The Beach Boys were going to survive, we would really have to stay on our toes," Wilson wrote in 2001. "After seeing The Beatles perform, I felt there wasn't much we could do to compete onstage. What we could try to do was make better records than them. My father had always instilled a competitive spirit in me, and I guess The Beatles aroused it."[39]

"I do my best work when I am trying to top other songwriters and music makers," he'd remarked to a journalist in 1964. "That's probably my most compelling motive for writing new songs: the urge to overcome an inferiority feeling."[40] While 1965's *Beach Boys Party!* LP was to include three Beatles covers, "When 'Fun Fun Fun' came out the previous year," assessed New York producer Phil Spector, "Brian wasn't interested in the money, but how the song would do against The Beatles."[40]

Whatever Wilson, Spector and others in the US record business thought, sages in the media had predicated that The Beatles' North American walkover had been an antidote to both an unexciting Hot 100 and the depressing winter that followed the Kennedy tragedy. "Kids everywhere go for the same stuff and, seeing as we'd done it in England, there's no reason why we shouldn't do it in America too,"[41] had been John Lennon's more forthright judgement on why most of the UK's major groups – and many minor ones – made progress to varying extents in the unchartered United States and Canada.

After The Beatles, the New World had gone almost as crazy about The Dave Clark Five, Freddie And The Dreamers – fronted by a kind of Norman Wisdom of pop – and Herman's Hermits. The more introspective Zombies – who'd struggled to Number 11 with their solitary UK Top 20 entry, 'She's Not There' – all but topped the US Hot 100 with it. In 1965, 'Tell Her No', which faltered outside the Top 40 at home, came to rest high in the US Top Ten too, aided by The Zombies' mild-mannered, scholarly image and regular visits to the States where 'She's Coming Home' and 'I Want You Back' were less spectacular hits but hits all the same.

To adult North America, The Zombies – like the combos led by Dave Clark, Freddie and Herman – were a palatable compromise to "hairy monsters" like The Rolling Stones, The Pretty Things, Kinks and Them. In tacit acknowledgement, US immigration authorities temporarily refused visas in 1965 for more Limey longhairs wishing to propagate their degenerate filth in Uncle Sam's fair land. Nevertheless, alighting on mid-west towns, even in the graveyard hours, a British group might be greeted by hundreds of hot-eyed teenagers, a large percentage chaperoned by parents who hadn't chastised them for squandering their allowances on, say, a six dollar can of 'Beatle Breath', or 'My Boyfriend Got A Beatle Haircut' by Donna Lynn.

This first US Beatle-related 45 was not to be the last. However, as well as anthems of adoration – 'Santa Bring Me Ringo' from Christine Hunter, The Beatlettes' 'Yes You Can Hold My Hand' *ad nauseum* – there were others such as 'To Kill A Beatle', a single of unconscious presentiment by someone called Johnny Guarnier. Its lyric was from the perspective of a US teenager, insanely jealous because every other girl at high school had lost her marbles over the new sensations from England.

Less sinister in retrospect are the likes of 'Beatles You Bug Me' and 'The Beatles' Barber' directed at those posses of "manly" types – in Australasia[42] as well as the USA – who expelled much hot air planning raids on the group's hotel quarters to hack off their girly locks, knowing that such an assault would be applauded by right-thinkin' folk who also frowned on male hairstyles longer than a crewcut.

Such an attitude bolstered the integrity of British beat amongst the hippest of the hip. The Animals' hit arrangement of traditional 'House Of The Rising Sun' confirmed folk singer Bob Dylan's resolve to "go electric", and Andy Warhol sneaked backstage at the Brooklyn Fox auditorium because "I wanted to be in the presence of The Yardbirds". To a more practical end, many US music industry bigwigs, correctly anticipating further demand for UK talent, crossed the Atlantic to stake claims in the cultural diggings.

Fascination with all things British peaked most conspicuously in that 1964 week when two-thirds of the Hot 100 was British in origin, and The Beatles occupied *nine* positions in the Canadian Top Ten. So insatiable was demand for anything on which any of the Fab Four had even breathed that Tony Sheridan was brought to a wider public than he may have warranted in the normal course of events after a repromoted 'My Bonnie' sold a purported million in 1964. Other releases by Sheridan might have been of greater musical worth, but the the tracks he smashed out on that bleary eyed 1961 morning with John, Paul, George and Pete better enabled him to protract a prolific recording career up to the present day.

"For a short time, there was a bit of interest in Britain and the States," shrugged Sheridan, "even if nobody was pushing me very much. I also went to Australia at the same time as The Beatles. Then I returned to England where, for a while, I played one night stands – but I never made anywhere near the money that could be made in Germany."

Meanwhile, The Beatles' cast-out drummer had already milked his affinity to the group via a six month run of sell-out dates in North America – principally in Canada – with his Pete Best Combo. For many, Pete will always remain "the Fifth Beatle", but less plausible candidates for this ludicrous honour had already included New York disc-jockey "Murray The K" (also "the Sixth Rolling Stone") – because he almost-but-not-quite blagged his way into rooming with George Harrison during that first US visit – and Cynthia Lennon after *Confidential*, Hollywood's most scurrilous showbiz gossip magazine, assured readers that she had once been considered as the group's lead singer.

This deathless claptrap apart, there *was* a Cynthia Lennon US Fan Club that found plenty to fill the pages of a monthly newsletter. "They wrote about about what I wore to film premieres, and what I said," elucidated Cynthia to me in 1996. "They were really sweet. I was only a housewife, but a very special housewife to them until divorce divorced me from The Beatles."

As the formation of such an organisation demonstrates, the British Invasion as a phenomenon had less to do with the main participants themselves than the behaviour of the North American public, who, once convinced of something incredible, exhibited a fanaticism for it that left the British themselves, even the most passionate Beatlemaniacs, at the starting line.

Back home, however, the Fab Four's renown was such that any direct connection with them was a handy bartering tool to rake in a bit of loot. After 18 years as the most shadowy figure in John's life, Freddie Lennon, then a kitchen porter in a Surrey hotel, had reappeared with his hands open in March 1964 on the Twickenham set of *A Hard Day's Night*, The Beatles' first movie. After a short conversation with a bemused John, he left and some money was – through John – mailed to his place of work. Freddie capitalised further by selling his life story to something-for-everybody *Titbits* magazine and then recorded a self-written single, 'That's My Life' (My Love And My Home), coupled with 'The Next Time You Feel Important' (a revival of a Vera Lynn number) for Pye late in 1965 – on which he was accompanied by some former Vernons Girls and, glad of the session fee, Folkestone's Loving Kind, veterans of poorly waged spots low on the bill of round-Britain package tours on which they were never sure of sleeping in proper beds each night.

Because of its singer's talismanic surname, 'That's My Life' received a modicom of airplay and was said to be "bubbling under" the UK Top

50. Allegedly, Brian Epstein – at John's instigation – then prodded nerves to curtail further headway. Freddie was determined to tell the boy about what must surely be some mistake, and arrived at "Kenwood", the mock-Tudor mansion in nearby Weybridge in which John, Cynthia and Julian now lived. Outside a banged front door, Freddie would be at a loss to understand his son and heir's deafness to his pleas. So began a family feud that would never quite resolve itself.

Many others better qualified to board The Beatles bandwagon were finding the going rough too. The Fourmost had secured an eight month season in a 1964 variety presentation at the London Palladium – at which John Lennon was a frequent attendee. Though their *raison d'être* was centred on comedy, there was a lake of offstage tears. Guitarist Mike Millward had been diagnosed with cancer which was alleviated with radium treatment during which it was discovered that he also had leukaemia.

With the-show-must-go-on stubbornness, he wouldn't let the lads down. If a huge, scalp-revealing tuft of his hair fell out the very moment the compère spoke their name, he'd stick it back on with Sellotape. When he could no longer keep such a level-headed grip on himself, he asked bass guitarist Billy Hatton if he ought to throw in the towel. "I said yes," remembered Hatton, "and it was the hardest yes I've ever had to say."[17] In a Cheshire hospital, nothing more could be done for Mike, and he died peacefully on 7 March 1966.

The following month, A Night For Mike took place at the Grafton Rooms in Liverpool 6. "A Host Of Top Show Business Stars" was promised, but most of these consisted of those who'd missed the boat in 1963: ghosts from the recent past, still battling through 'Twist And Shout', 'Hippy Hippy Shake' and all the other anachronisms. When the *Titanic* was sinking too, its house band carried on playing even as the waters covered their heads. On a calm mid-Atlantic night, you might hear them still as a spooky drift as if through a seashore conch.

On the evening in 1965 when The Beatles performed before nearly 60,000 at New York's Shea Stadium, Rory Storm had been hip-swivelling in front of his Hurricanes in a Seaforth ballroom.

Possibly because Rory was such a flamboyant showman, there'd been no place for him in that same year's *Ferry Across The Mersey*, a belated period film starring Gerry And The Pacemakers, in which the main thrust of the plot was a Battle of the Bands contest. Among the losers were The Koobas. Adding insult to injury, their sequence ended up on the cutting room floor. This might have been a blessing in disguise because it would have drawn attention to the group's compromising origins at a time when the Merseybeat ferryboat was grounding on a mudbank. Indeed, the belated flick's evocative title theme was Gerry's UK Top Ten farewell – and a requiem for Merseybeat's passing.

In the States, Billy J Kramer's fourth single, 'Little Children', was his biggest smash there, but momentum was lost through ex-public schoolboys Chad and Jeremy's US-only cover of Billy's next single, Paul McCartney's 'From A Window'. Into the bargain, Kramer's desire to update his image was thwarted by prior commitments to pantomime and like engagements – and 1965 began with his first serious flop in 'It's Gonna Last Forever' and the co-related departure of most of the original Dakotas. Finishing eight places below composer Burt Bacharach's version, 'Trains And Boats And Planes' was Kramer's final hit.

By then, The Beatles were the only Liverpool act that could still take chart placings for granted. *Mersey Beat* was finished too, having been absorbed in March 1965 into *Music Echo* in which the Liverpool scene was confined to a solitary page commensurate with faded interest – even in the city itself – in any more quartets who shook their moptops and went "oooooo".

"It was always a struggle to keep *Mersey Beat* going," grumbled Bill Harry, "but we persevered. Eventually, we'd built up circulation to 75,000 a week and gone national. The first ever front cover of The Rolling Stones was in *Mersey Beat* in 1963. Then Brian Epstein became involved. At first, he kept things as they were – with me having complete editorial control. Then he started doing things like commissioning a gossip column by some London writer, and insisting that bog standard record company photos of whoever was Number One had to be on the cover rather than anything more atmospheric.

"The first week we did that, the same picture – of The Kinks – appeared in both *Disc* and *Record Mirror*, but Brian insisted we keep on doing it. I told him it was mad, and that I wasn't going to do any other of his stupid ideas either. Then I walked out of the office and never went back."

Whereas they had frequently graced *Mersey Beat*'s front page – and those of national music journals – The Searchers were soon to leave the UK Top 20 forever with 'Take Me For What I'm Worth' – which lent its title to their final LP of the Swinging '60s – and one with a commendably high quota of sturdy group originals. Most of these dripped from the pen of drummer Chris Curtis, whose exit in 1966 exacerbated further the *volte-face* of The Searchers' fortunes.

Yet even in the spooky era after their chart adieu, The Searchers continued delivering goods that at least *sounded* like hits – and could have been if the group's very name hadn't become a millstone round their necks. "We were groping in the dark then," shrugged Frank Allen – who'd replaced Tony Jackson in 1964 – "and we'd lost the knack of picking hits."

While The Searchers floundered, The Beatles continued to flourish – by fair means or foul. Straight in at Number One in Britain during 1964's cold, wet December, 'I Feel Fine' began with a buzz like an electric shaver: mid-range feedback. The following summer, The Kinks would approximate this at the start of 'I Need You', B-side to 'Set Me Free'. At the same time, The Who were enjoying their second hit, 'Anyway Anyhow Anywhere' – and, lubricated with feedback too would be The Yardbirds' 'Shapes Of Things' and its flip-side 'You're A Better Man Than I' in 1966. Each made a most effective melodrama of what was merely implicit in the mild gimmick had that kicked off 'I Feel Fine' – a rival group's idea that The Beatles had picked up so fast that, as was often the case, the general public assumed that they'd thought of it first.

Months before 'I Feel Fine', The Yardbirds, The Kinks and The Who had all been featuring guitar feedback on the boards as a deliberate contrivance to sustain notes, reinforce harmonics and, when necessary, create severe dissonance. This strategy had been logged by Lennon when The Kinks were low on the bill to them at Bournemouth's Gaumont Cinema on 2 August 1964. In the teeth of audience chants of "We want The Beatles!", Dave Davies, The Kinks' lead guitarist, began 'You Really Got Me', their recent chart breakthrough, by turning up his amplifier to feedback level, "and the high-pitched frequency cut right through the screams of The Beatles' fans" his brother was to write in his autobiography, X-Ray.[43] Ray Davies noticed too that John Lennon was watching from the wings.

Come Christmas and Lennon had composed 'I Feel Fine'. "That's me completely," he was to insist. "The record with the first feedback anywhere. I defy anyone to find a record – unless it's some old blues record in 1922 – that uses feedback that way. So I claim it for The Beatles before Hendrix, before The Who, before anyone – the first feedback on any record."[21]

Though John played the tricky ostinato of 'I Feel Fine' on the record, George learnt it parrot-fashion for regurgitation onstage as The Beatles travelled a world that was becoming an intrusive and frequently dangerous place; its immensity and richness lying beyond a barrier of screeching hysteria and the pitiless woomph of flash-bulbs – particularly during an exceptionally stressful world tour in 1966. The Coca-Cola tasted just the same, but they'd guess they might be in, say, Canada by Mounties patrolling the besieged hotel – or Chicago because pizza is the city's equivalent of fish and chips.

Wherever they were, John, George, Paul and Ringo dished out a routine 30 minutes-worth of unheard music through a usually inadequate sound system at what were more tribal gatherings than concerts now. Prior to each, they sometimes had to field the stock questions about haircuts and when Paul was going to marry, at press conferences where certain of the local media took umbrage that the Fab Four seemed vague about what country they were actually visiting, having long ceased to care about the glimpses they caught of the places where their blinkered lives had taken them.

The Beatles and their retinue would, however, be made to care in Manila, capital of Luzon, the largest island of the Philippine Archipelago. They'd managed two performances – to 30,000 in the afternoon, 50,000 in the evening – on 4 July 1966 at the city's Rizal Memorial Football Stadium. At the hotel, Brian Epstein received an invitation for them to be guests of honour at a party to be thrown by Imelda, wife of Philippines' autocratic President Ferdinand Marcos, at Malacanang Palace on the morning after the Rizal shows, for the families of the totalitarian government and military junta. Not appreciating that it was less a request than an order, Epstein let the weary entourage sleep on.

The following day, Beatle fans at Manila International Airport were puzzled that they could have ventured close enough to touch their idols had it not been for a jeering, jostling wall of flesh formed of the enraged dictator's creatures, assured of official leniency and even commendation no matter how they behaved towards the departing foreigners.

Open malevolence stopped just short of naked ultra-violence as the agitated Beatles hauled their own baggage up switched-off escalators, and shuffled through a customs area pulsating with pushing, shoving and snail-paced jack-in-office unpleasantness. Out on the tarmac, the party scuttled for the aeroplane where they fastened seat-belts, weak with relief. Final escape was delayed, however, when, no sooner had they unstiffened and emptied their lungs with a *whoosh*, Mal Evans and press secretary Tony Barrow were summoned back to the terminal to be questioned over some freshly unearthed red-tape.

Sent on their way by the boos and catcalls of the mob, never had arguments – particularly from John and George – against The Beatles continuation of touring made more sense.

As a post-script to this episode, when The Zombies dared eight concerts in the Philippines a few months later, "We did all these long interviews," recalled their Rod Argent, "and they asked us what we thought of The Beatles. Then all the papers the next day said 'Zombies Say Beatles Are Louts And Hooligans For Attacking Our First Lady!' We didn't know anything about all that stuff that had happened before."[44]

Hot on the heels of The Beatles' experience of The Philippines, a battering psychological rather than physical had awaited them on the North American leg through John Lennon's off-the-cuff comments about the increasing godlessness of our times during an interview with the London *Evening Standard*. When reprinted in the US teenage magazine *Datebook*, his opinions that The Beatles "are more popular than Jesus right now" and that "Christianity will go, it will vanish and shrink" were interpreted by a more general media as boastful "blasphemy" in a land that, until the British Invasion – and with Colonel Parker's manipulation of Elvis setting the sir-and-ma'am standard – had been used to a pop star being relatively devoid of independent opinion, having been put in motion by his handler as a walking digest of truth, justice and the American way.

Subliminally through the medium of teen magazines and even in some of the piffle he released on disc, he would echo stolid middle-aged dictums – your parents' word was law, don't talk dirty *et al* – and parade an apparent dearth of private vices. With the gentlest humour, he'd answer questions about his favourite *color*, preferred foodstuffs and the age at which he hoped to wed.

Lennon's nearer-the-knuckle ruminations were a particular red rag to "redneck" whites from the Deep South, caricatured as clannish, unsophisticated and anti-intellectual, thanks to incidents like the beating-up of black entertainer Nat "King" Cole in 1954 by racist extremists during his act before a mixed audience in Birmingham, Alabama. Soon to come was the firebombing of a Houston radio station by some good ol' boys who begged to differ over its radical anti-Vietnam policy. Their right-wing militancy was laced with pious fear of not so much "God" as "the Lord", "the Man In The Sky", "the Boss Of The Riders" or, if one of them had swallowed a dictionary, "The Big Architect". He was entreated as the need arose as either a homespun prairie philosopher, a sort of divine pimp – or an enforcer of redneck prejudices, which included the ongoing disapproval of long hair on men as it was written in 1 Corinthians xi 14: "Doth not nature itself teach you that, if a man have long hair, it is a shame unto him?"

It was here, in the heart of the Bible Belt, that thousands of Beatles discs were being ceremonially pulverised in a tree-grinding machine to the running commentary of a local disc jockey. Other mass protests were just as demonstrative. The group's new LP, *Revolver*, was removed from 22 southern radio playlists, and hellfire sermons preached of the fire and fury that would fall from above on any communicants who attended forthcoming Beatles concerts – though the sub-text of the casting out of this pestilence by one Memphis station was that it was as much in a kind of inverted vengeance for Brian Epstein's dim view of its exposure of a hush-hush (and subsequently scrubbed) Beatles' session at the city's Sun

Studios, where country boys like Elvis, Jerry Lee and Roy Orbison had been groomed for greener pastures.

Radio blacklisting and hostile audiences, however, were trifling problems compared to the possible in-concert slaughter of Lennon by divine wrath – or someone acting on the Almighty's behalf – even if hard-nosed US promoters considered this insufficient reason for cancellations. After all, even as 'To Kill A Beatle' had been making its deserved journey to the bargain bin, nothing had happened when two earlier death threats had been directed at The Beatles. On 20 August 1964, an anonymous telephone caller informed the management of the Convention Center in Las Vegas that a bomb had been planted somewhere in the building after the group's matinee performance at 4pm, but this was not taken seriously enough for the second show at 9pm to be nixed.

Eighteen days later, the switchboard operator at The Beatles' hotel in Montreal put through a call to Brian Epstein from someone who said that a bullet would have Ringo Starr's name on it when he perched behind his kit that evening at the city's Forum auditorium. Better safe than sorry, Epstein arranged for a detective to hunch beside the drum rostrum – to catch the slug, maybe – as Starr "played low" like Pete Best, with cymbals positioned straight up *à la* Buddy Rich. Nobody minded that his posture impaired the performance because who could hear it – or gunfire – anyway against the bedlam?

As the ripples of the "holy war" spread in August 1966, the danger was more omnipresent than ever. "The *Evening Standard* piece was by a very responsible journalist, Maureen Cleave, and the quote was put in its correct context," cried Tony Barrow. "John was making a statement on the world at that moment, and the fact that a pop group seemed to be drawing more attention than God. Certainly, there were more people going to pop concerts than attending Churches. It was lifted completely out of context and, in that respect, it was a terrible thing for a PR man to have his client say."[45]

A final attempt at damage limitation took place at a press conference hours before opening night in Chicago. There, John was trotted out to make a statement that most took as an apology. "It was the first time I had seen him really nervous at a press conference," observed Barrow, "probably because he didn't really know what to apologise for."[45] Lennon said as much to the assembled media, though adding "I'm sorry I opened my mouth…"

Engagements in the north passed without unanticipated incident, other than picketing by Ku Klux Klansmen outside Washington's DC Stadium. Below the Mason Dixon line, the anti-Beatles ferment was counterbalanced by "I love John" lapel badges outselling all associated merchandise. Nonetheless, a promise was made to Epstein from a pay phone that one or more Beatles would die on the boards at the Mid-South Coliseum in Memphis. Yet, though a firework that exploded onstage gave all four a horrified start, the show was delivered. The next morning, The Beatles slipped smoothly away into a temporary airborne respite from what was becoming an uneasy existence.

More insidious a worry had been – and was still – one German *fraulein*'s strong claim that one of The Beatles had fathered her child. That was a main reason why the group didn't work in the federal republic between 1962's final Star-Club residency and the Ernst-Merck-Halle show in 1966, despite losing out on lucrative appearances on *Beat Club*, a televisual pop showcase as vital in its fashion as *Ready Steady Go*. It was the means whereby Salisbury's Dave Dee, Dozy, Beaky, Mick And Tich became more popular in the Teutonic market as they were at home, to the extent of beating The Beatles by over 3,000 votes to win the German pop periodical *Bravo*'s Golden Otto award in 1966 – the equivalent of being Top Vocal Group in the *NME* poll.

However, for all the professional and personal problems whirling round The Beatles' protective bubble, the Hamburg stop on 26 June 1966 had been one of increasingly rarer oases of calm during their troubled trek around the globe. In a mellow mood, John doled out bite-sized chunks of unspoilt-by-fame attention to each of the old pals allowed into a backstage area that was as protected as Fort Knox. Yet for all Lennon's mateyness, Astrid Kirchherr sensed that he wanted to but couldn't invite her back into his life once more. He wanted to but couldn't rewind to 1961 and moments when…

Abruptly, there was a lull when Astrid, Lee Curtis, Bert Kaempfert *et al* fell silent and stared, wondering if John was real. After that, the atmosphere loosened up between them before he risked being confronted with Stuart Sutcliffe's spectre during a late night amble round some of the old haunts still standing down the Reeperbahn.

Then it was back to the party where a lot of the guests had decided that The Beatles had done enough showing-off for one night, and were keeping the watches of the night by joking around, yarning about what Rory Storm had said to Bruno Koschmider at the Kaiserkeller in 1960, and skirting round any old bitternesses that simmered still. It seemed so faraway now: the Indra, Lord Woodbine, Ricky Richards, the Top Ten, The Graduates, Pete Best, 'Ain't She Sweet', Johnny And The Hurricanes...

Two months later, The Beatles played their last concert – in San Francisco's Candlestick Park – and, for all their common ordeals and jubilations, the ties that bound them began to loosen. While mere sideshows to his pivotal role in The Beatles, among solo projects undertaken by John already were *In His Own Write* and *Spaniard In The Works* – two slim but best-selling volumes of verse, stories and cartoons – and he was to be seen as "Private Gripweed", a bit-part in *How I Won The War*, a movie on general release in the period between Brian Epstein's untimely death in August 1967, and December's interesting-but-boring TV spectacular, the self-produced *Magical Mystery Tour*. After that, the only direction should have been down, but Beatles discs continued to sell by the mega ton.

9 "Controlled Weirdness"

The journey to a John Lennon all but unrecognisable from the Merseyside beat merchant of 1962 had commenced weeks before the last date of the 1966 tour with a drug experience beyond, say, some speed to wire him up for the show and a "spliff" to unwind tense coils within afterwards.

Lennon had had, so he was to say, several spliffs – marijuana cigarettes – about his person when, soberly attired, he, Starr, McCartney and Harrison had been driven in a black Rolls-Royce through cheering masses to Buckingham Palace for their investiture as Members of the British Empire on 26 October 1965. "Taking the MBE was a sell-out for me," Lennon growled later, "one of the biggest jokes in the history of these islands."[2]

That the whole business was anathema to him was reflected further when he contended that, whilst waiting to be presented to the Queen at 11:10am, he and the other three had retired to a palace washroom to light up and pass round one of his spliffs. Yet Lennon's recollections may have been an attempt to beef up an image of himself as a rebel rocker – and his story was to be refuted by George Harrison, who maintained that nothing more narcotic than ordinary cigarettes were smoked. Certainly, none of the national treasures seemed noticeably under the influence of marijuana's admittedly short-lived magic when either talking to the sovereign or discussing the morning's events with the media at the Savile Theatre up the West End.

Perhaps no ordinary newshound would have noticed anyway. Not yet versed in the effects, paraphernalia and jargon of illicit drugs either, the BBC would pass The Small Faces' 'Here Comes The Nice' single – dealing with the dazzling effects of amphetamine sulphate ("speed") as it had already Bob Dylan's 'Rainy Day Women Nos 12 & 35' and its "everybody must get stoned!" chorus. 1966's 'Heroin' by The Velvet Underground, however, hadn't a hope of a solitary Light Programme spin, and the Corporation frowned on The Byrds' 'Eight Miles High', and, later, even Beatles tracks like 'Tomorrow Never Knows', 'A Day In The Life', 'Lucy In The Sky With Diamonds' and 'I Am The Walrus' as the "us and them" divide intensified with the Fab Four among celebrities advocating the legalisation of marijuana, and assisting on 'We Love You', the Rolling Stones 45 issued in the aftershock of the famous drug bust in guitarist Keith Richards' Sussex cottage.

In 1967 too, the spoof 'LS Bumble Bee' by Peter Cook and Dudley Moore was symptomatic of a general knowledge if not use of lysergic acid diethylamide 25 – LSD. To a degree, the effects of "acid" were simulated via light shows and other visual effects in renowned "underground" venues like Middle Earth in London, Amsterdam's Paradiso and New York's Fillmore East, where "bands" – not groups anymore – played on and on and on and on for hippies in a cross-legged trance and whirling dancers, their psyches boggling with paranormal sensations and surreal perceptions.

On the USA's west coast, LSD was far more prevalent than in Europe. It underpinned the music of Jefferson Airplane and The Grateful Dead, brand-leaders of the "flower-power" ethos of the Haight-Ashbury district of San Francisco, a city about to become as vital a pop Mecca as Liverpool had been – while down in Los Angeles, Brian Wilson's now acid-drenched visions were to be made tangible in *Smile*, a jettisoned masterwork – though excerpts were to serve as selling points on later Beach Boys albums.

Though Wilson studied the British opposition's output assiduously – as it did his – he had caught individual tracks on the radio but did not listen to the US pressing of *Rubber Soul* (The Beatles' last pre-LSD album) in its entirety until several weeks after its release in December 1965 – when a friend arrived at Brian's Laurel Canyon home with a copy. "When I heard *Rubber Soul* for the first time," recalled Wilson, "I was so blown out, I couldn't sleep for two nights."[40] He was particularly impressed with John's 'Girl' and Paul's 'Michelle', and overall aspects that he was to perceive as "religious, a white spiritual sound".[40]

After *Rubber Soul* had spun its little life away four times, Wilson told his wife, Marilyn, "I'm going to make the greatest rock 'n' roll album ever made."[40] Almost straightaway, he started work on what was to become *Pet Sounds*, which was to vie with 1967's *Sgt Pepper's Lonely Hearts Club Band*, the follow-up to *Revolver*, as "greatest album of all time" in turn-of-the-century assessments by broadsheet newspapers.

Brian commented during a 1995 television documentary, "We prayed for an album that would be a rival to *Rubber Soul*. It was a prayer, but there was no ego involved – and it worked. *Pet Sounds* happened immediately."[39] It wasn't up to *Rubber Soul*'s fighting weight commercially, but *Pet Sounds* was The Beach Boys' most critically acclaimed LP, causing The Beatles' nervous backwards glances – with Paul McCartney citing Wilson as "the real contender"[46] rather than The Rolling Stones.

Exacerbating the indignity of coming third to the Stones in the *New Musical Express*'s yearly chart points table – and second to Dave Dee, Dozy, Beaky, Mick And Tich in *Bravo* – the *NME*'s 1966 popularity poll had The Beatles second to The Beach Boys as World Vocal Group. "Good luck to them," grinned Ringo Starr, "We haven't been doing much lately, and it was run at a time when they had something good out."[47]

Starr was referring not only to *Pet Sounds*, but also 'Good Vibrations', Brian Wilson's chart-topping "pocket symphony".[40] This was part of *Smile*, which Brian Wilson reckoned would surpass both *Rubber Soul* and *Pet Sounds*, but the advent of *Sgt Pepper's Lonely Hearts Club Band* was among factors that caused its abandonment. "When I heard it," recalled Brian, "I knew that The Beatles had found a way to really take rock in a new direction. It scared the heck out of me."[39] It also kick-started Wilson's wretched LSD-fuelled journey across a terrible psychological desert for the next two decades.

John Lennon too had come to know acid well, and was to be The Beatles' most avid consumer. It had been part of the anything-goes – some would say "nihilistic" – spirit of Swinging London for many months before John was "spiked" by one of George Harrison's passing acquaintances in January 1966. Dick Taylor, The Pretty Things' lead guitarist, recalled, "The students above me when I lived in a flat in

Fulham in 1966 organised these lock-out nights – 'raves' you'd call them now – at the Marquee when LSD was legal. Personally, I was extremely wary of it."

"I had a good time on acid," parried the group's singer, Phil May, "but other people had problems." John Lennon did not include himself amongst them, and his reasons for continuing to take LSD were once much the same initially as those of Eric Burdon of The Animals: "I want to take a piece from every book. I want to learn from everything. That is why I originally took LSD. No, that's not right. I took it just to get stoned."[48] This was a bone of contention between Burdon and a new-found friend, Frank Zappa, leader of The Mothers Of Invention, who hissed, "The general consensus of opinion is that it's impossible to do anything creative unless you use chemicals."[49] Yet the "psychedelic" mental distortions of LSD were to transport John Lennon to untold heights of creativity – and further from 'Twist And Shout' than any Cavern dweller could have imagined.

More knowingly, again largely through George Harrison, he was now more open to the music of other cultures – what would be termed "world music" – though The Beatles weren't by any means the first pop stars to do so. Rolf Harris, for example, had woven the didgeridoo into the rich tapestry of Western pop in 1963, and Serge Gainsbourg issued *Percussions*, a 1964 LP that indicated a stark awareness of African tribal sounds. Moreover, Rosemary Squires, omnipresent on BBC radio light entertainment programmes even before Alma Cogan, listed Tibetan music among her extra-mural pastimes, becoming secretary of Britain's Tibetan Society from 1972 to 1975.

The Beatles were notable for their corresponding fascination with India. As with LSD, one individual's reaction to the sub-continent's classical tradition can be markedly different to that of another. Lennon found the droning ragas transfixing, and complementary to his more celestial acid reveries as well as his current reading of *The Golden Bough*, *Autobiography Of A Yogi* and further hardbacks of philosophic and aerie-faerie bent, purchased from the hip Indica bookshop off Piccadilly. He also bought a sitar – but, unlike George, he never got further than treating it like some fancy guitar.

John and the other Beatles' interest was gratifying news for stockists of Oriental merchandise in the West. Moreover, the most seemingly unlikely musicians latched on to it as well. Mainstream jazz drummer Buddy Rich, for instance, was to team up with tabla player Alla Rakha on a 1968 album – though, because he composed and conducted most of the written (as opposed to improvised) music, *Rich À La Rakha* was as much the work of Ravi Shankar, the master sitarist under whom George Harrison was to study.

Another catalyst in this collaboration was jazz flautist Paul Horn, a European disciple of the Maharishi Mahesh Yogi, whose international profile – like Shankar's – was to be heightened by the patronage of The Beatles, but not until later, in the watershed year of 1967, when music, passing hastily through its own "classical" period, was elevated from ephemera to Holy Writ, and the notion of pop as an egghead activity intensified. The most lasting effect was that "bands" began demanding public attention for "concept" albums and similar epics that couldn't be crammed into a ten-minute spot on a package tour with Helen Shapiro.

Instead of screaming hysteria, there was now knotted-brow "appreciation" as a working band's appeal became reliant not so much on big smiles and tight trousers as stamina to sustain lengthy extrapolations of items from both its last album and the unfamiliar successor being "laid down" during a studio block-booking of weeks and months, much of it impossible to reproduce onstage using conventional beat group instrumentation.

Naturally, The Beatles, though no longer stage performers, were at the forefront of this new attitude towards recording, notably after George Martin declared his independence of EMI in 1965 via the formation of his Associated Independent Recording (AIR) production company, taking Ron Richards with him – and then reaching his professional apotheosis through the making of *Sgt Pepper*.

As much Martin's baby in its way as The Beatles', it was judged to be a milestone of pop: "a milestone and a millstone", qualified George Harrison.[50] Many – especially in the States – listened to The Beatles' latest gramophone disc in the dark, at the wrong speeds, backwards and even normally. Every inch of the label and sleeve montage was scrutinised for concealed communiqués which would turn listeners into more aware, more creative human beings, truly at one with John, Paul, George and Ringo.

Nothing would be the same, not even the past. The "come on, come on" call and response in 'Please Please Me', for example, was, estimated a member of Clayson And The Argonauts in 1977, John Lennon's vain plea to Cynthia to menstruate and thus assuage fears about an unwanted pregnancy. Such banal argument still provides hours of enjoyable time-wasting for Beatle freaks, old and new – despite, say, a lyrical error ("two foot small" instead of "two foot tall") on 1965's 'You've Got To Hide Your Love Away' that Lennon decided should be uncorrected because "The pseuds'll love it."[51] More pointedly, his 'Glass Onion' in 1968 denied that there were ever any secret sub-texts to be found anywhere in The Beatles' *oeuvre* in the first place, whilst inserting false clues – like "the Walrus was Paul" – and misleading self-quotations, "just to confuse everybody a bit more".[51]

Perhaps 'Glass Onion' was a double-bluff – because there's no reason for the list of "uncovered" hidden meanings to ever end. The most conspicuous insertions as the Swinging '60s drew to a close were based on clues traceable to *Sgt Pepper*, which supported a widespread rumour that McCartney had perished in a road accident, and had been replaced by a *Doppelgänger*.

Very much alive in 1967, Paul, more than John, had been prime mover on an album that had been conceived as less a regular LP with about a dozen separate tracks than a continuous work with no spaces between songs. This was to be the artistic climax of EMI's liaison with The Beatles, which had heralded a new budgetary commitment towards the long-playing pop record, a product that had been, more often than not, a testament to market pragmatism rather than quality, and targeted – particularly in the USA once more – at fans so beglamoured by an artist's looks and personality to be rendered uncritical of frankly substandard, haphazardly programmed output, excused as an exhibition of "versatility", but of no cultural value. Brian Wilson was to heap further praise on *Rubber Soul* with "It was the first time in my life I remember hearing a rock album on which every song was really good."[39]

The Beatles' first LP had been padded with a brace of singles, but each that followed was a conscious musical progression, with an increasing ratio of tracks the equal of A-sides. Moreover, by the close of the decade, it had become common procedure to issue a 45 off an already successful album – as 'Something'/'Come Together' was to be from 1969's *Abbey Road*.

Nonetheless, the absence of the usual Christmas single in 1966 had made it necessary to release 'Penny Lane' coupled with 'Strawberry Fields Forever', tracks intended originally for the forthcoming *Sgt Pepper*. This was regrettable, but not disastrous – even if George Harrison was to admit, "There are some good songs on it, but it's not our best album."[50]

With its expensive and syncretic precedent, record companies found themselves underwriting albums of like persuasion (eg The Rolling Stones' *Their Satanic Majesties Request* and *Days Of Future Passed* by The Moody Blues) plus "rock operas" (The Pretty Things' *SF Sorrow*, The Kinks' *Arthur*, and The Who's *Tommy* – all, technically, song-cycles) and other *magnum opi* (John Mayall's *Bare Wires*, *The Crazy World Of Arthur Brown* LP and The Small Faces' *Ogden's Nut Gone Flake*).

Yet *Sgt Pepper* may be seen – albeit with a certain logical blindness and retiming of the truth – as not the first time such an idea had been attempted in pop. This may be a silly analogy, but perhaps all albums are concept albums in the sense that all pop songs expose a point of view.

Is being thematic the same as having a concept? Was 1965's *The Sect Sing Sing-Songs*, four repulsively amusing ditties about death by The Downliners Sect, a concept EP? What about 1963's *Little Deuce Coupe*, on which The Beach Boys string together a bunch of songs about hot-rod cars, whether lauding the record-breaking 'Spirit Of America' or weeping over 'Old Betsy', maybe one oil-change away from the breaker's yard? Certainly, in its unsubtle way, *Little Deuce Coupe* created more of a specific and recurring mood than *Sgt Pepper*.

The same is true of Joe Meek's *I Hear A New World Part One*, a narrowly circulated 1960 EP of mood music to help audio dealers demonstrate these new-fangled "stereo" gramophones in 1960 – and its cancelled *Volume 2* [*sic*] follow-up. As you might gather from titles like 'Orbit Round The Moon', 'Magnetic Field', 'Love Dance Of The Saroos' and 'Dribcots' Space Boat' – not to mention the wordless "little green men" vocals and overall electronic aetheria – it was a sound painting concerned entirely with Joe's almost child-like fascination with outer space. Part of Meek's reputation as a record producer rested for decades on *I Hear A New World* – as *Smile* still does for Brian Wilson – until all 30 minutes of the two *I Hear A New World* EPs were made available as a CD album in 1991, courtesy of reissue specialists RPM Records.

While it did contain various seques and links, plus the reprise of the title theme, *Sgt Pepper* wasn't "about" anything as *I Hear A New World*, *Little Deuce Coupe* or, more germane to this discourse, *SF Sorrow* and *Days Of Future Passed* were – and only at the beginning and near the end were you reminded of what was supposed to be Sgt Pepper's show. "It was as if we did a few tracks," said Ringo Starr, "and suddenly there was a fire, and everyone ran out of the building, but we carried on playing."[52] Yet, regardless of its diverted intention, *Sgt Pepper* is tied forever to psychedelic times past – and perhaps that's the lasting "concept". Listening to it decades later, a middle-aged hippy would almost smell the joss-sticks and see its fabled jacket being used as a working surface for rolling a spliff.

Technically, *Sgt Pepper* improved on *Revolver* as close-miked vocals floated effortlessly over layers of treated sound, and gadgetry and constant retakes disguised faults, if impinging on grit. These days, a mere ten hours – the time spent recording the four's first *LP* – was no longer considered adequate for one Beatles *track*. For example, in 1968, 'Not Guilty', a George Harrison number, ran to a marathon 100-odd takes.

A year earlier, 'Strawberry Fields Forever' and 'Penny Lane' had also travelled mile upon mile of tape, week upon week of studio time, but had been kept from Number One in the UK by Engelbert Humperdinck's schmaltzy 'Release Me', thus allowing Decca and Dick Rowe a moment of revenge. Though he'd continued to strike lucky with outfits like The Small Faces, The Animals – who'd defected from EMI – Marmalade and, for Decca's new "progressive" Deram subsidiary, The Move and Procol Harum, Dick was more at home with "real singers" like some of his pre-Beatles finds had been – and so it was that Humperdinck and Tom Jones led a counter-revolution of "decent" music when signed up by the late

Rowe in the mid-1960s before his calculated withdrawal from a business in which his critical prejudices no longer fitted.

The Beatles were to prove ultimately more sound an investment for EMI than Humperdinck and Jones put together for Decca. Accumulated since their partnership began in the late 1950s, Lennon and McCartney's ever-swelling stockpile of hit songs could – even by 1962 – fulfil EMI's contractual requirements many times over, and even allow a "Lennon–McCartney–Starkey" credit for *Rubber Soul*'s unremarkable 'What Goes On' ("resurrected with a middle eight thrown in with Paul's help to give Ringo a song" explained John[21]). With their works being covered now by everyone from international stars like Matt Monro and Peter Sellers to banjo bands and barbershop quartets, John and Paul could afford to be generous.

They and the other two had long been granted unlimited studio time, and the freedom to requisition all manner of auxiliary instrumentation and musicians – as instanced by the highly waged Mike Sammes Singers, a mixed sex aggregation – more a choir than a vocal group – whose living hinged principally on up to three studio sessions a day. Among more renowned employers were The Beverley Sisters, Tommy Steele, Cliff Richard, Anthony Newley, Matt Monro, Helen Shapiro, Tom Jones, Engelbert Humperdinck – and The Beatles, for whom the Singers were equally at ease with Lennon's psychedelic 'I Am The Walrus' as 'Goodnight', his lushly orchestrated lullaby to five-year-old Julian that was to close 1968's *The Beatles* (alias the 'White Album').

EMI smiled fondly too as John, Paul, George and Ringo, like unrestrained children in a toy shop, fiddled about with whatever weird-and-wonderful implements were either lying about their favoured Studio Two or staring at them from one of the Abbey Road complex's storerooms. In this workshop–playroom ambience, George Martin had been quite acquiescent to, perhaps, an Arabian bongo pepping up 'Don't Bother Me' on *With The Beatles*; Ringo swatting a packing case in place of snare on 'Words Of Love' from 1964's *Beatles For Sale*; and the hiring of a string quartet for 'Yesterday' the following year.

Engineers muttered darkly but said nothing out loud when console dials went into the red during *Sgt Pepper* sessions or George Martin razored a tape of Sousa marches to pieces and ordered someone to stick it back together any old how for the instrumental interlude in John's 'Being For The Benefit Of Mr Kite', the item that was to round off side one.

According to Martin, it was Lennon who first coined the term "flanger", which entered general technical vocabulary for an electronic strategy whereby two signals in a slightly out-of-time alignment were deployed as automatic double-tracking. It was used to enhance The Beatles' vocals – for example, John's on 'Lucy In The Sky With Diamonds' – but is more noticeable when applied to percussion, as in the effervescent drumming on The Small Faces' 'Itchycoo Park', Eric Burdon's 'Sky Pilot' and throughout 1968's *Strictly Personal* LP by Captain Beefheart.

The likes of The Small Faces, Burdon and Beefheart were, however, unable to attract the same financial outlay from their respective investors as The Beatles, whose *Sgt Pepper* vied with their most recent 45, 'All You Need Is Love', to top the Australian *singles* chart. Fittingly, *Sgt Pepper*'s 'A Day In The Life' epilogue was also the valedictory spin on Britain's pirate Radio London when it went off the air in August 1967.

If *Sgt Pepper* had been the station's most plugged album, the single was surely Procol Harum's 'A Whiter Shade Of Pale', which John Lennon started singing playfully as members of the group – sorry, band – trooped into the Speakeasy one evening. He remembered Procol Harum under a less abstract appellation, The Paramounts, supporting The Beatles when they last played the Hammersmith Odeon in 1964.

The selectively amiable Lennon, however, wasn't all smiles when Pink Floyd were conducted in from the adjacent studio at Abbey Road to see the masters at work. He was the only Beatle not to return the call on hearing reports of the otherworldly sounds emitting from the less sophisticated four-track lair where the Floyd were recording their first LP, *Piper At The Gates Of Dawn*. Could it be that the younger quartet were achieving what The Beatles were still chasing? After all, composer Syd Barrett – their biggest asset and biggest liability – had, with the other personnel keeping pace, gone further into the cosmos than they had on 'Astronomy Domine', and disconnected with our solar system altogether on 'Interstellar Overdrive'. Moreover, 'Gnome', 'Matilda Mother', 'Flaming' and his mock-medieval 'Scarecrow' had cornered pop's gingerbread-castle hour more effectively and instinctively than had 'Lucy In The Sky With Diamonds'.

In Abbey Road, too, The Pretty Things were completing their transition from a Home Counties R&B group to operating ambiguously with chart-directed singles and increasingly more erudite "musicianly" fancies on albums. Issued in November 1967 after much prevaricating from EMI, 'Defecting Grey' was a 45rpm medley of five pieces that paved the way for *SF Sorrow*, unquestionably the first rock opera. "What we were after," elucidated Phil May, "was an album that didn't have tracks but musically was just one piece. That's why it had a story – the only way we could give it continuity. What was also relevant was that *SF Sorrow* was made on acid."

If you want my opinion, *Sgt Pepper* – on which LSD played its part too – remains a lesser work than *SF Sorrow* and *Piper At The Gates Of Dawn*. Nevertheless, The Beatles' album, rather than The Pink Floyd debut and the relatively poor-selling Pretty Things offering, had been the more manifest trigger for countless beat groups from The Rolling Stones downwards to mutate into a "band" of self-absorbed pseudo-seers, exchanging smirks across the mixing desk at one another's cleverness. Thus *Their Satanic Majesties Request* appeared in the shops, complete with a fold-out sleeve as freighted with symbolism as *Sgt Pepper*'s. A month after 'All You Need Is Love' came 'We Love You', coupled with 'Dandelion', a piece of similar pixified scenario as 'Lucy In The Sky With Diamonds'.

Absorbing the signals as they came from a greater distance, Caio, Hugo, Osvaldo and Pelin adjusted to *Sgt Pepper*-esque psychedelia without quite getting the point, judging by 'The Shape Of A Rainbow' and 'I Remember My World', which occupied the dying minutes of a "concept" album that might be all most UK record buyers will need to experience of the latter-day Los Shakers.

Back home again, The Koobas also recorded a "work" with dialogue *et al* filling space between tracks. Taped at Abbey Road with Geoff Emerick, The Beatles' usual engineer these days, this was to be The Koobas' only long-player, released belatedly and appreciated only in retrospect despite the efforts of Brian Epstein and a more committed Tony Stratton-Smith, who became the group's manager (and occasional lyricist) in 1966.

After four years of following trends set by others, The Koobas were becoming their own men at last. Conversely, when 1967's Summer of Love climaxed on 25 June with The Beatles' satellite-linked televisual broadcast of their 'All You Need Is Love' flower-power anthem, others moved in quick. Direct from Denmark Street, 'Let's Go To San Francisco Parts 1 & 2' was spread over two sides of a single by The Flowerpot Men – who mimed it on *Top Of The Pops* and went on the road in beads, chiffony robes and like regalia, tossing chrysanthemums into the audience.

The Flowerpot Men were not among the more superficial pop newcomers who captivated John Lennon, but his taste was sufficiently broad-minded to appreciate The Monkees, four youths put together by a cabal of Californian business folk for a networked TV series based on the *Hard Day's Night*-period Beatles. Their hit records were merely part of the package of one of the most ruthless marketing strategies the entertainment business had ever known.

When The Monkees visited Britain, John was amenable enough towards them when introduced, but was to have a deep friendship – comparable to that he'd known with Stuart Sutcliffe – with one of the four's hired songwriters, Harry Nilsson, then a semi-professional who kept body and soul together as a Los Angeles bank clerk.

There remains division over the late Nilsson. Was he an inconsistent genius who defied categorisation or a tiresome *bon viveur*, content to have fulfilled only a fraction of his potential? Artistically, the second half of his career was certainly less impressive than the first. An impressive number of tracks on Nilsson's quaint *Pandemonium Puppet Show* were subject to cover versions, among them Billy J Kramer's of semi-autobiographical '1941', singing disc-jockey Kenny Everett of 'It's Been So Long', and 'Without Her' by Engelbert-ish Jack Jones. Other items from this debut LP and 1968's *Aerial Ballet* were tried later by The Turtles, Rick Nelson, Mary Hopkin, The Yardbirds, Herb Alpert, Andy Williams, Blood, Sweat And Tears, actor George Burns – and, most spectacularly, Three Dog Night – with a million-selling treatment of the latter album's 'One'.

A lot of the syndications sounded tame when up against what were more than useful demos. The most transforming ingredient was Nilsson's supple three-octave vocal daredevilry, encompassing trumpet impersonations, scat-singing and further idiosyncrasies. Despite bouts of overdone grandiloquence, neither did Brooklyn-born Harry disgrace himself on his own reshapings of such as Ike and Tina Turner's 'River Deep Mountain High' and Fred Neil's 'Everybody's Talkin'', a Grammy winning chartbuster when used in 1969's *Midnight Cowboy* movie. Thus evolved the enigma of Nilsson as the acclaimed composer whose most enduring releases were penned by others.

One of his most immediate personal characteristics was that Nilsson was prey to sudden mood shifts, commensurate with the classic "artistic temperament". A closer parallel with John Lennon was that, when he was young, his parents had separated, with Harry choosing to remain with his mother. They moved to San Bernardino, California, where, until they acquired a proper house, they made do with a mobile home where "gangs of Hell's Angels would encircle the trailer late at night and harass the people."

Later, Harry went back east to attend high school at Long Island, New York, where he emerged as a promising baseball player. More cerebral activities included painting and sculpture, and he taught himself to play the piano when captivated by Ray Charles ("he made me want to do something with music"). Finished with formal education at the age of 15 in 1956, he hitch-hiked to Los Angeles, where he worked as a cinema usher, rising to assistant manager before being made redundant when the place closed.

The priesthood was among vocations that beckoned next, but he landed a post as a night-shift computer operator with the Security First National Bank (where he was known as "Harry Nelson") whilst writing songs and hawking the results round Hollywood by day. 'Groovy Little Suzy' was accepted by Little Richard, who, stunned by the young man's vocal range and mastery of "scatting", suggested that Harry might make it as a pop star in his own right, despite an ingrained dislike of singing in public ("I just wanted to be a record person"). He ticked over with television jingles and demos for music publishers, and, backed by the cream of Hollywood session musicians, released unviable singles as 'Johnny Miles' and as 'The New Salvation Singers' (ie his voice multi-tracked up to 90 *times*).

Still semi-pro, he became recognised around Los Angeles studios as a reliable session vocalist and jobbing tunesmith. After co-writing 'Readin' Ridin And Racin" – a hot-rod opus – for The Superstocks, and 'Travellin' Man' for The New Christy Minstrels and Slim Whitman, he placed two more of his compositions with The Ronettes, and another with The Modern Folk Quartet. A liaison with these acts' producer, Phil Spector, promised much, but three songs recorded by Harry with the "Svengali Of Sound" remained unissued for ten years. Though the Spector connection opened doors, Nilsson contemplated a withdrawal from the music business altogether on experiencing The Beatles ("As soon as I heard what they were doing, I just backed off"). Now married, and promoted to computer-department supervisor, he seemed to be on the verge of "settling down".

After The Monkees had selected his 'Cuddly Toy' – later castigated for its "sexism" – for 1967's *Pisces, Aquarius, Capricorn And Jones Ltd* album, Nilsson was offered a contract by RCA and surfaced as the toast of the London In-Crowd after Derek Taylor – now publicist for The Byrds, The Beach Boys and other US acts – mailed *Pandemonium Puppet Show* to Brian Epstein with the testimonial that "he is the something The Beatles are". The group itself agreed, perhaps flattered by the spin-off 45, a medley of 11 Lennon–McCartney songs, under the umbrella title, 'You Can't Do That', which climbed the Australian Top 40.

Nicknaming him "The Fab Harry", John Lennon was prompted to nominate the new cult celebrity as his "favourite American group"[53]. John next took the initiative by telephoning Nilsson at the bank ("Hello, this is John Lennon." "Yeah, and I'm Uncle Sam."). Invited to drop by when in London, Harry was to meet Lennon in 1968 – and thus begin a lifelong amity.

Attempts to add the talented Harry to NEMS's galaxy of stars proved futile as he had decided to take care of business himself on resigning from work: "That job gave me insight. You gain a business experience that helps you understand why companies make such decisions." Besides, Brian Epstein's stake in Beatles' matters – and those of his remaining Liverpool artists – was becoming more and more detached as the expiry dates of his five-year contracts with them crept closer – as did his association with them in more absolute terms.

Brian's often severely tested loyalty to his principal charges had extended to proffering in vain his personal fortune to compensate promoters if they consented to cancel the final US tour in the light of real fear for John's life after his "We're more popular than Christ" remark. Yet once-merry rumours darkened to a certainty that, perturbed by some of the irretractable mistakes he'd made whilst learning the job, the group were at the very least to reduce Mr Epstein's cut and say in their affairs.

In an interview given to *Melody Maker* on 9 August 1967, however, he'd been "certain that they would not agree to be managed by anyone else". Television chat-show appearances – frequent these days – also assured fans that he was as much The Beatles' clear-headed mentor as he'd ever been. Indeed, on their behalf, he was in the midst of setting the wheels in motion for a *Yellow Submarine* cartoon fantasy about them as Sgt Pepper's bandsmen.

To David Frost on ITV, however, he'd spoken less of the Fab Four than the Savile Theatre, in which he'd had a controlling interest since 1965. The current Sundays At The Savile pop presentations, which sometimes mitigated the poor takings for the drama and dance productions during the week, had been Brian's brainwave. However, his preoccupation with this and other projects were but analgesics, alleviations to the pangs of despair, general insularity and an essentially guilt-ridden homosexuality. These had been symptomised by Brian's interrelated and increasing apathy towards the needs of those still on his books, even Cilla Black, his main concern after The Beatles. She was so disenchanted that she'd been on the point of leaving him until moved by both a tearful plea for her to reconsider, and a consequent swift negotiation of a weekly TV series.

Cilla was going from strength to strength, but Gerry And The Pacemakers had thrown in the towel by 1967. After unfruitful bids for solo chartbusters, Gerry bounced back to a degree as the "all-round entertainer" he'd always aspired to be. He was host of ITV's *Junior Showtime*, broadcast from Manchester, where he was in his element with his unforced Scouse backchat. Next, he secured the male lead in the West End musical *Charlie Girl*, which ran and ran after an opening night dignified by the presence of John and Ringo in the audience.

Similarly, Billy J Kramer kept the wolf from the door as a compère on children's television whilst try-trying again with '1941' and a patchwork of other diverse styles on releases that included one attributed to "William Howard Ashton". While his tenacity is to be admired, all his post-Epstein attempts to get back on his perch pointed in the same direction: the 1960s nostalgia circuit, belying the title of a 1983 single, 'You Can't Live On Memories', freighted with a reference to his former svengali.

Billy's feelings about Brian as a businessman were not indicative of any loss of personal affection. The same was true of Cilla Black, who was among the few to whom Epstein confessed his private anxieties. Another was Pattie, George Harrison's wife, who warned Brian of the dangers inherent in the over-prescribed tablets that he took to sleep, to stay awake, to calm his nerves, to lift his melancholia.

During the last month of Brian Epstein's life, another messiah had risen for The Beatles as he himself had at the Cavern eons ago in 1961. His Divine Grace the Maharishi Mahesh Yogi seemed at first glance as different from Brian as he could be. He was, he replied, a dealer "in wisdom, not money" when pressed about how his International Meditation Society was financed.

To Cilla Black, this meditation caper he propagated was akin to "somebody who goes to the loo with a big pile of papers and sits there and reads them all".[39]

She could cackle but The Beatles were serious enough about meditation to undergo the Society's initiation course, conducted by his Divine Grace at a university faculty in Bangor during the Bank Holiday weekend in August 1967. Once, it might have been the last bolt-hole anyone might have expected to find them. Yet fans and the media had were out in force at Euston railway station for what one tabloid named "The Mystical Special", the mid-afternoon train to the north Wales seaside town that was a short drive from Gerry Marsden's recently purchased home-from-home in Anglesey.

"I was there that weekend that made such a change to our lives," recalled Gerry, "and it didn't register that they were only a few miles away with the Maharishi – but I wasn't interested in all that."

Brian Epstein was interested but not convinced about all that either – and, in the end, neither, collectively, were his principal clients. Both Epstein and The Beatles' misgivings had been reinforced as much by the satirical magazine *Private Eye* dubbing the Maharishi "Veririchi Lotsamoney Yogi Bear" as the fellow's own submission that they ought to tithe part of their income into his Swiss bank account.

Brian had, nevertheless, half promised that he'd join his boys at Bangor. "That's how it used to be," Ringo would reminisce. "If someone wanted to do something, all we'd do was follow them."[52] The wives and girlfriends – John's Cynthia, Ringo's Maureen, George's Pattie and Paul's Jane Asher – were the same, as exemplified by the uniform pale-blond hairdos they were all sporting by the middle of 1967.

That's as may be, but as Ringo and Maureen's second child, Jason, had been born on 19 August – and, by sickening coincidence, Ty Brien, guitarist with Rory Storm And The Hurricanes, had died onstage that same month – the Starrs hadn't been ready to tear themselves away from their Surrey acres to a lecture by the Maharishi the following week at the Park Lane Hilton to which George and Pattie had dragged along Paul, Jane and the Lennons.

Their attendance there was traceable to the previous February, when Pattie had attended a lecture on "Spiritual Regeneration" at London's Caxton Hall. The doctrines advanced that evening were imperatively appealing, although the orator had stressed that his words were but a vague daub, and that his guru – the Maharishi – could paint a more pleasing verbal picture.

Born plain Mahesh Prasad Varma, the robed and ascetic Maharishi – "Great Soul" – had founded a British branch of the International Meditation Society in 1959 and had worked up around 10,000 initiates by the time Pattie – and George – relayed to the rest of the gang the sweet flowers from his silver-bearded lips. It seemed that, through short daily contemplations, all vices would be eradicated bit by bit until a pure state of bliss was achieved. Moreover, such washing of spiritual laundry was possible without forsaking material possessions (bar the Society's membership fee).

This seemed an excellent creed to a supertaxed Beatle as he stole into the Hilton's hushed functions room. The Great Soul so lived up to the Harrisons' spiel that, directly afterwards, George, John and Paul buttonholed him and wound up promising to join him in Bangor.

While packing, they rang others who might want to go – and boarding the Mystical Express too would be Ringo, Mick Jagger, Marianne Faithfull and Pattie's sister, Jennie. Waylaid by "What's the Maharishi like?", "Do you think you'll all be changed by next Tuesday?" and other bellowed questions, Jagger dismissed the outing straightaway as "more like a circus than the beginning of an original event".[39] Unable to shove through the mob, Cynthia Lennon missed the train – and one of the last opportunities to save her deteriorating marriage.

The rest of the party crammed eventually into the same compartment as the Maharishi. The uproar at Euston had brought home to him what a catch he'd made. Previously, he'd been unaware of The Beatles' stature, but he made a mental note to try to insert quotes from their lyrics into his talks about karma, the transmigration of souls – and the world of illusion.

For pop stars who'd lived in more of a world of illusion than most since 1963, it was perhaps too much of an adventure. Hard cash had become as unnecessary to them as eyesight to a monkfish, and, after a communal meal in a Bangor restaurant, George Harrison was the first to realise why the waiters kept hovering around the table. And it was he, too, who settled the bill with a roll of banknotes he chanced to have – as you do – in the hollow sole of his shoe.

Neither this incident nor the hard mattresses in the student hostels on the campus were as disconcerting as the press conference that Varma's public-relations agent had set up in the main hall, where most newsmongers appeared to regard The Beatles' preoccupation with meditation as flippantly as Cilla Black did. Hard to take seriously by those who thought they knew him was rough old John Lennon becoming a mystic.

One or two sick jokes circulated among the press corps on Sunday afternoon. Brian Epstein's lonely life had ended suddenly in London the previous night. Pattie Harrison's disquiet had been justified, because, as Westminster Coroner's Court would conclude, Brian had been killed by "incautious self-overdoses" after he'd become bored with a dinner party at his country home and chosen to drive back to his London flat. The doors to his bedroom were forced open the next morning and an ambulance called, but there was nothing the paramedics could do.

The expected rumours went the rounds before the day was out. The most absurd was that he'd been bumped off by a hitman connected to a New York syndicate who'd offered Brian millions for The Beatles three years earlier. The most commonly held notion, however, was that he'd committed suicide. There'd been a purported attempt late in 1966, followed by a spell – not the only one – in a London clinic in May 1967 to combat combined depression, stress and exhaustion. He was visited by Larry Parnes and John Lennon sent flowers and a note ("You know I love you. I really mean that"), which caused the tortured Brian to burst into tears.

Just over a month later, his 63-year-old father was taken by a heart attack, but Brian was unlikely to have added to his beloved and newly widowed mother's grief by doing away with himself. Moreover, in keeping with the *Melody Maker* interview, a letter he sent the previous week to Nat Weiss, The Beatles' US attorney, was quite upbeat, ending, "Be happy and look forward to the future."

As in the "happy ending" in a Victorian novel, with all the villains bested and the inheritance claimed, Brian at 32 could have retired, rich in material comforts and enjoying the fruits of his success. Money, however, can't buy you love – at least, not the love that Brian was wondering if he was losing since the armoured car had whisked his Beatles away from Candlestick Park. Suicide or accident, perhaps Brian Epstein was past caring.

Inside the college at Bangor, the Great Soul had consoled his famous devotees. Nevertheless, as twilight thickened, The Beatles brushed past the stick mics, note pads and flashbulbs as they strode from the university building into a black Rolls-Royce. For all the dicta they'd just absorbed that trivialised death, they were visibly shaken. "I knew we were in trouble then," John was to state with retrospective honesty. "I didn't really have any misconceptions about our ability to do anything other than play music, and I was scared. I thought: we've fucking had it."[5]

So it was that The Beatles became as kites in a storm and the man-in-the-street started raising quizzical eyebrows at their increasingly wayward activities – beginning with *Magical Mystery Tour*.

Nearly two years after their second film, *Help!*, The Beatles were discussing the third one they were contractually obliged to deliver to United Artists. *Yellow Submarine*, apparently, didn't count. After they'd turned their noses up at suggestions ranging from a Western to an adaptation of *The Lord Of The Rings*, Paul McCartney came up with a plan to make something up as they went along.

Like many Beatle ideas – particularly after Epstein's death – it was more intriguing conceptually than in ill-conceived practice. Less than a fortnight after the funeral, journalists were pursuing a charabanc, which, with "Magical Mystery Tour" emblazoned on the sides, was trundling through the West Country containing, reportedly, The Beatles and a supporting cast as variegated as a disaster movie's.

As well as the chaos that their very presence summoned, the 40-seater bus – now divested by a disenchanted Lennon of its too-distinctive trappings – failed to negotiate Devon's twisty country lanes, thus ruling out such potentially stimulating locations as Berry Pomeroy Castle and Widecombe Fair.

Though the bulk of *Magical Mystery Tour* was drawn from this troubled excursion, many interior sequences were shot elsewhere, mainly back in London where The Beatles also began six weeks in a darkened cutting room, wading through the formless celluloid miles of improvised dialogue and scenes that had seemed a good notion at the time. As Paul was less uncertain about the finished picture, John, George and Ringo elected to leave him to it. Unless called to give second opinions, they whiled away hours in an adjacent office with such diversions as inviting in and clowning around with "Rosie", a Soho vagrant who'd been immortalised in a recent hit by street busker Don Partridge.

A completed *Magical Mystery Tour* was premiered on BBC1 on Boxing Day for the majority of Britons still with black-and-white TVs, and repeated in colour on BBC2 on 5 January prior to general big-screen release across the Atlantic. While it wasn't *Citizen Kane*, 35 years of celluloid extremity later *Magical Mystery Tour* is less the hybrid of turn-off and tedious cultural duty it used to be than an occasionally intriguing curate's egg. Witness The Bonzo Dog Doo-Dah Band accompanying the cavortings of a stripper, and the visuals for The Beatles' own songs – which were, according to Paul McCartney's biographer, Barry Miles, "the vehicle for a number of prototype rock videos, some of which, like 'Fool On The Hill', could be shown on MTV and look as if they were freshly made".[46] Finally, when divorced from the film, the soundtrack – 'I Am The Walrus', 'Flying' and the rest of the double-EP that all but topped the UK singles chart – is still a winner.

Yet, as 1967 mutated into 1968, apart from predictable plaudits from the underground press and the *New Musical Express* – and a less foreseeable one in *The Guardian* – *Magical Mystery Tour* as a film was almost universally panned. Most common-or-garden viewers agreed too that it wasn't the most suitable viewing – especially in black and white – for a nation sleeping off its Yuletide revels. You can't help wondering too how many would have watched it to the bitter end if it had starred The Koobas or Los Shakers.

Though uneasy about it from the start, John Lennon hadn't said much at the time, passively attempting to quell media forebodings by not contradicting the others when they spoke of *Magical Mystery Tour* being full of "interesting things to look at, interesting things to hear" and "aimed at the widest possible audience" namely, "children, their grandparents, Beatle people, the lot".[54]

In other matters, however, he seemed his usual plain-speaking self, cracking back at critics with faultless logic and calm sense laced with the quirky wit they expected of him. When the group and its creatures repaired to Rishikesh, the Maharishi's *yoga-ashram* (theological college) on the Ganges, for further study in February 1968, it was John who was to perceive that his Grace was all too human, telling him so to his face after a Beatles hanger-on accumulated enough tittle-tattle to speak to Lennon about Varma's apparent clandestine and earthly scheming for the seduction of a lady student, propositioning her with the forbidden meal of chicken as other cads would with a box of chocolates. Deaf to protestations of genuine innocence after confronting the Great Soul with his infamy, Lennon announced his and Cynthia's immediate departure.

When they got back to England, rock 'n' roll revival was in the air, and The Beatles took heed with their next chart-topper, 'Lady Madonna', reminiscent of Fats Domino. After being sucked into a vortex of experiences deeper than just plain folks could ever have imagined, John had surfaced with the certain knowledge that rock 'n' roll was healing, inspirational. It had saved Lennon's soul more often and more surely than any amount of sermonising from vicar or guru.

It was on John too that the truth about their post-Epstein business affairs – a truth that he and the others had refused to avow for too long – most inflicted itself. It was he who was chief advocate of calling in Allen Klein, one of the bigger apes in the US music business jungle, to sort out the mess that was the so-called "controlled weirdness" of their multi-faceted Apple Corps, a blanket term for artistic, scientific and merchandising ventures under The Beatles' self-administered aegis when the company was launched in April 1968 – the beginning of the tax year.

Some of their pop peers diversified for fun and profit too, random examples being Chris Farlowe's military memorabilia shop in Islington on earnings from his 1966 Number One, 'Out Of Time'; Merseybeat Tony Crane's stake in a Spanish night club; Monkee Davy Jones's New York boutique; and The Troggs' Reg Presley patenting of his fog-dispersal device. The far wealthier Beatles could be more altruistic. According to eye-catching newspaper advertisements, actively encouraging people to send in tapes, a kindly welcome awaited not just those who'd nurtured a connection within the group's inner circle, but any old riff-raff who wished to solicit Apple for finance for pet projects.

When 3 Savile Row was established as Apple's permanent address, sackfuls of mail would overload its postman, pleading voices would bother its switchboard, and supplicatory feet would ascend its stone steps morning, noon and night until a burly doorman was appointed to shoo most of them away. "We had every freak in the world coming in there," groaned George Harrison.[55] Yet to loitering pavement fixture Alex Millen – an "Apple Scruff" – his fallible idols "did strengthen the belief that Joe Soap was important and, yes, you too could have something to say".[55]

With this in mind, impetuous cash was flung at such as two unprofitable shops that closed within three months; "Magic" Alex Mardas, the one who blackened the Maharishi's name in Rishikesh, who was also a so-called "electronics wizard"yet whose wondrous inventions advanced little further than him talking about them; a troupe of grasping Dutch designers, trading misleadingly as "The Fool"; poets who couldn't write poems; and film-makers who didn't make films.

While Apple Films was to produce a handful of worthy if rather specialist labours of love like *Messenger Out Of The East*, a documentary of Ravi Shankar and the land that bore him, Apple Records was the organisation's only lasting success. It was subject to a leasing deal (and Parlophone catalogue numbers) with parent company EMI, who were to refuse to release the likes of one-man-band Brute Force's 'The King Of Fuh' (containing a chorus that ran, "I'm the king of Fuh/I'm the Fuh king") and worse. Nevertheless, the founding of an ostensibly independent label reduced the number of middlemen and increased The Beatles' own quality control of product.

None of the – sometimes critically acclaimed – records that Ronnie Spector (Phil's missus), ex-Undertaker Jackie Lomax and New York soul shouter Doris Troy made for Apple would make them rich, but Welsh soprano Mary Hopkin began a three-year chart run when her 'Those Were The Days' debut knocked inaugural Apple single, The Beatles' own 'Hey Jude', from the top of the British charts – and both Billy Preston and Badfinger, a Merseyside act spotted by Mal Evans, had hits too. The Modern Jazz Quartet and classical composer John Tavener also reached a bigger audience through Apple Records.

An Anglo-American "supergroup" containing ex-Byrd Dave Crosby, Steve Stills from Buffalo Springfield and Graham Nash, late of The Hollies, were approached to sign with Apple, but as no member of Crosby, Stills And Nash could extricate himself from existing contracts, the deal fell through – as did that with another promising outfit, Fleetwood Mac. A lesser star in embryo, James Taylor, was taken on, but 20-year-old David Bowie slipped through The Beatles' fingers after a chat with Paul McCartney. So also did Freddie Garrity, front man of Freddie And The Dreamers, and The Remo Four, who mutated into one-hit wonders

Ashton, Gardner And Dyke. While a one-shot Apple single by Hot Chocolate was issued in 1969, did The Beatles commit the Dick Rowe error by auditioning and then rejecting Bamboo, a Swedish outfit that would connect genealogically with Abba?

While the record division was profitable, Lennon saw quickly that the rest of Apple was as dodgy as Rafferty's motor-car. In the kingdom of the brainless, the half-wit is king. That's how good intentions came to cradle deceit – with personality masquerading as principles, and power intrigues as crusades.

In his memoir, *As Time Goes By*,[56] Derek Taylor, an obvious choice to organise the press department, likened his two years at Apple to being "in a bizarre royal court in a strange fairy tale". Derek's urbane, sympathetic manner won many important contacts for Apple, but John Lennon's was, ostensibly, the loudest voice of reason amid the madness. The music press had been full of how "mellow" he was in his late 20s too. "It's a groove growing older," he told them.[57] He therefore gave the outward impression of a person completely in command of his faculties, an affluent and happily married family man in perfect health, smiling and laughing, with no worries.

Actually, he was deeply worried.

10 *"The Change In Him Was Like Jekyll And Hyde"*

By the end of 1968, Joe Average thought John Lennon was as mad as a hatter. In restaurants in which fame hadn't prevented The Beatles from dining, strangers on other tables would speak in low voices and glance towards him. Some insisted they could sense an aura of lunacy effusing from Lennon as others might the "evil" from the late child murderer Myra Hindley's eyes.

Was he really off his rocker? Had he – like Friedrich Nietzsche – lost his mind during an unremitting contemplation of his own genius and glory?

Previously, he had seemed to teeter on the edge of insanity – or, if you prefer, craziness – as epitomised by Merseyside polymath Adrian Henri witnessing him lying on the floor of a local pub, pretending to swim. Told by the landlady to stop, Lennon replied that he daren't because he'd be sure to drown. Some of his scrapes later in Hamburg and after he'd taken acid were on a par with this – but he seemed lucid enough in interview, and, in all respects, he appeared sane to Cynthia.

Neither of them were infatuated teenagers any more, holding hands around Liverpool. Now all such pretty fondnesses had long gone. Circumstances had obliged him to marry her – though, had he been reading Nietzsche in 1962, Lennon may have stumbled upon and agreed with the German philosopher of irrationalism's personal credo: that marriage and family are incompatible with a life of constant creativity. In other words, domesticity is the enemy of Art. Beatle John the rock 'n' roll bohemian didn't believe in wedlock, but Woolton John the nephew of Aunt Mimi went ahead with it. For him and Cynthia, therefore, there had never been much hope. He could have, but didn't make enough of their relationship.

That isn't to say he didn't care about the mother of his child – for all the confusion there had been since 1963 between Lennon the husband and father and Lennon the "available" pop star. Neither was he immune to twinges of conscience as the enormity of what he was about to do sank in – but, by mid-1968, he had no apparent option but to burn his boats as far as he was able and either instigate a new beginning or anticipate a fall from grace by destroying his former self. In the end, he did both.

To a journalist's tape recorder, he had declared his love for Yoko Ono, a Japanese–American who many still see as walking evidence of her own conjecture: "You don't need talent to be an artist."[58] As some mug with a pocketful of money, John had been introduced to her on 9 November 1966 during a preview of her *Unfinished Paintings And Objects* display at the gallery attached to the Indica bookshop. Charmed by the bewildering exhibits, he was the anonymous sponsor of Yoko's *Half Wind Show* at another London gallery, taking a benevolent interest in her activities, past and present. Because she was doing a turn there, he was among promenading onlookers at the "Fourteen Hour Technicolor Dream", a mixed-media extravaganza – all flickering strobes and ectoplasmic light projections – at Alexandra Palace on 29 April 1967.

Yoko had captured his heart during a period when, according to Barry Miles, a vulnerable John was in the throes of a nervous breakdown, informing Miles later that "I was still in a real big depression after *Pepper*. I was going through murder."[46] Yoko – who'd made the more non-committal statement that she was then "very fond"[59] of John – was a most unlikely Morgan le Fay-esque figure. If it was a *Carry On* film, you'd see an ecstasy of off-camera bodice-ripping that fateful night in May 1968 when Yoko was invited by her secret admirer to Kenwood when Cynthia was away. Just before the closing credits roll, Yoko turns a furtive key on the bedroom door and winks at the camera to maybe a melodramatic flash of lightning.

If it was a romantic novel, however, there'd have been an abrupt and inexplicably tearful reconciliation with Cynthia – followed, no doubt, by nature taking its course – but things don't happen like that in books. At least, they didn't to Cynthia.

Lennon's behaviour was to puzzle and then infuriate what was left of the Cynthia Lennon Fan Club after he left her and Julian to move into a London flat with his new love – and at this point, the story becomes as much Yoko's as John's, and the enigma of their liaison has only deepened since.

Like most of their fans, The Beatles' authorised biographer, Hunter Davies, blamed – and continues to blame – "the arrival in John's life of Yoko Ono"[22] for the end of the group. At the time, a perturbed *Beatles Monthly* had passed her off as John Lennon's "guest of honour"[60] after he brazened it out by escorting her to London's Old Vic on 18 June 1968 to catch a National Theatre adaptation of part of *In His Own Write*. *Two Virgins*, the Bed-Ins and further "happenings" were to follow swiftly.

"The change in him was like Jekyll and Hyde," sighed a still saddened and perplexed Cynthia in 1997. "John would have laughed at himself years before if he could have seen the future. Before he met Yoko, there was an item in *The Times* about her film, *Bottoms*" – myriad naked human buttocks in close-up – "and John said, 'Look at this mad Japanese artist. What will they print next?!' So his attitude then was she was a nutcase – and I agreed. I'm not a conceptual artist. When I look at things, I like to understand what I'm looking at."

For schoolgirl subscribers to *Beatles Monthly*, Yoko was destined to turn into pop's cross between Wallis Simpson and Beryl Formby, who watched her henpecked husband, George, the Lancashire music-hall entertainer, like a hawk, and ruled him with an "iron petticoat". However, in the world of Art – and music – Ono was already a Tracey Emin *du jour* via exhibitions that embraced, say, an all-white chess set and an apple with a £200 price tag, and an event in Liverpool's Bluecoat Chambers, where she'd had different paying customers picking up pieces of a jug she'd just smashed. Other escapades included wrapping Trafalgar Square statues in brown paper, the writing of *Grapefruit* – a self-help book of stultifying inanity – and, of course, *Bottoms* (remade as *Four Square*).

Yoko had also tried to make it as a pop singer, actually sending demos to Island, a record label that went in for oddball ethnic material. She had, however, found a niche in the distant reaches of the avant garde through vocal gymnastics that owed much to the free choral babbling and odd tone clusters of modern "serious" composers Schoenberg and Penderecki as well as stubbornly chromatic *seitoha* (Japanese classical music).

Moreover, in the company of free jazzers, notably Ornette Coleman, she used her voice like a front-line horn – as she did at a performance on a Sunday in March 1969 at the University of Cambridge with musicians of the same kidney as Coleman. With Lennon at her feet, back to the audience, either holding an electric guitar against a speaker – causing ear-splitting spasms of feedback – or twiddling with some electronic device to create bleeps, flurries, woofings and tweetings to complement the peep-parps from Danish saxophonist John Tchikai, the clatterings of drummer John Stevens and Yoko's screeches, wails and nanny-goat jabberings.

They were cynosures of an unnerving stare from what looked like a gigantic photograph of silent and undemonstrative students. A minority absorbed it in a knowing, nodding kind of way, whilst blocking out an impure thought in the tacit question, "How could anyone like this stuff?" Everyone onstage, even Beatle John, was an artist after all, and it became obvious that the greater the effort needed to appreciate this squiddly-bonk music, the more "artistic" it must be.

After clapping politely when the row ceased, the highlight of the night was the opportunity afterwards to babble about how "interesting" it all was, this "spontaneous music" that was an avenue to drop names like Ornette, John Cage, Edgard Varèse and Luciano Berio. Once, when so many venues had been closed shops to The Beatles because of jazz, that had been the sort of attitude John couldn't stomach: that air of pitying superiority towards those who didn't like it – or enjoyed it for what was derided as "the wrong reasons".

It was sweet, however, to have checkmated McCartney in the game of hipper-than-thou one-up manship that had persisted between them since time immemorial. Once The Beatles had moved south, Paul had held the winning hand what with living in the heart of London while John dwelt on on his Weybridge stockbroker estate. This was exemplified by Paul being in thicker with, well, Berio after sitting through his electronic avant-gardenings at London's Italian Institute on 23 February 1966.

That evening, it had been too much effort for Lennon to drive the long and gradually more hated miles from Surrey.

His hand in that crazy, far-out music at Cambridge had been one in the eye for McCartney, but nowhere as much as Lennon and Ono's *Unfinished Music No 1: Two Virgins*, not least for its sleeve photographs of the pair naked, back and front, that pledged John to Yoko more symbolically than a mere engagement ring ever could. After a macabre fashion, it paralleled the front picture of 1963's *The Freewheelin' Bob Dylan*, showing the artist in casual attire ambling down a wind-swept New York street, arm-in-arm and happily in love with his then-girlfriend. Lennon and Ono too demonstrated that they didn't look much different from anyone else, but the intention of *Two Virgins* was more to do with magnifying the gap between its makers and the common herd – or in their mind, "us two and you lot" – which would soon include Ringo, Paul and George as well.

When auditioning unsuccessfully to join The Texans – later, Rory Storm And The Hurricanes – in 1957, Harrison as a 14-year-old had played and sung Gene Vincent's arrangement of a song from the 1920s, 'Wedding Bells'. Its hookline ran, "Those wedding bells are breaking up that old gang of mine."

"The old gang of mine was over the moment I met Yoko," concurred John Lennon. Forgetting about both previous *amours* and Cynthia, he continued, "It was like when you meet your first woman, and you leave the guys at the bar and you don't play football anymore and you don't go play snooker and billiards. Maybe some guys like to continue that relationship with the boys, but once I'd found *the* woman, the boys became of no interest whatsoever, other than they were like old friends – but it so happened that the boys were well known and not just the local guys at the bar."[2]

As well as an expression of this, *Two Virgins* was also, so he and Yoko explained, an Art Statement. Joe Average was, however, too bewildered to give an Art Reply.

On a rare visit to London just before Christmas that year, I noticed the back cover – you could see their bums – in the window of One Stop Records, a small West End record store renowned for being first with the latest sounds. Inside, I pretended to thumb through the wares nearest the window whilst squinting discreetly. The previous autumn, I'd bought the edition of *International Times* (*IT*), Britain's foremost underground organ, that had first impinged on the general populace via a minor media fuss about a centre spread of Frank Zappa stark naked on the toilet, but with his modesty strategically hidden. Partly as a result of this, both *IT* and its companion journal, *Oz,* had been subject to intense and unwelcome attention from the police. *IT* was raided mostly for its for sex contact ads, and the *Oz* saga climaxed at the Old Bailey after the notorious "Schoolkids" edition (to which my teenage self contributed four articles).

That lay two years in the future of when my eyes were searching for the front of *Two Virgins* in One Stop. I'd heard that San Francisco's groovy *Rolling Stone* – not yet readily available overseas – had dared to print both sides of the sleeve. Nevertheless, it is difficult to articulate how extremely shocking that first sight of Lennon's flaccid Beatle willy was to a 17-year-old product of a strait-laced, church-going upbringing – not unlike John's own ("Sunday School and all that"[27]) – in a Hampshire country town where the 1950s didn't really end until about 1966. John Lennon, the Moptop Mersey Marvel, couldn't have done it, but, by God, he had! How could he have been so rude? Whatever did his auntie think?

When *Two Virgins* appeared, the "hippy" musical *Hair* had opened in London. Its murkily lit "nude scene" was there for all to see the very day after stage censorship was abolished in 1968's Theatres Act. This would also allow a presentation by a band from Leicester, Black Widow, that featured a bare lady prostrate beneath singer Kip Trevor's sacrificial sword amid chilling screams and abundant spilling of fake blood.

Generally speaking, however, even the most scantily clad female on the jackets of the budget label Hallmark's *Hot Hits* series of carbon-copies of then-current smashes wore more than girls did then on a summer's afternoon on Margate beach.

Yet a *Hot Hits* photo (especially the one in which a blonde in a bikini grips a phallic fishing rod) was far more erotic than *Two Virgins,* as was *Oh Calcutta!,* a post-*Hair* revue that ran at the Roundhouse in Chalk Farm, embracing nakedness in clear light – and also, incidentally, an apposite comedy sketch about schoolboys masturbating together, penned by John Lennon, whose career summary in the printed programme ran, "Born October 9, 1940. Lived. Met Yoko 1966." In London's Underground stations at the same time, a poster promoting a newly released flick, *Till Death Us Do Part* – based on the BBC comedy series[61] – had an unclothed Warren Mitchell as Alf Garnett in pride of place (albeit covering up his genitalia with hands and tobacco-pipe) and a caption thanking John Lennon for "pioneering this form of publicity".

It resonated too at the reception following Cilla Black's wedding in 1969 to her longtime fiancé, Robert Willis. Reading a congratulatory telegram from John and Yoko, the bride got a cheap laugh by adding the addendum "Stay nude!" (the same scansion as 'Hey Jude' – get it?).

On 1 March that year too, whilst fronting The Doors at Miami's Dinner Key Auditorium, 'Lizard King' Jim Morrison's ritualised cavortings ended with his arrest for "lewd and lascivious behaviour". According to the group's keyboard player, Ray Manzarek, the former Albuquerque public schoolboy was sending up his sex-symbol status with a routine involving a towel, and may have accidentally exposed himself. Backstage opinion intimated that the consequent charge was trumped-up by local authorities, anxious to strike a blow for common decency against another anti-establishment icon that, since 1966, had been corrupting their children – who had often been as disgusted as their parents by his behaviour.

John Lennon's intimates had not associated penis display with one who, only three years earlier, had seethed, "You don't do that in front of the birds!" when he, Cynthia and the Harrisons had been confronted by a drunken Allen Ginsberg wearing only underpants – on his head – at a London *soirée* held on the beatnik bard's birthday.[62]

That was before LSD entered Lennon's life. *Two Virgins* might have been rooted in too much acid triggering onsets of self-imposed humiliations. He and Yoko were also to start on heroin, now a more popular chemical handmaiden to creativity for certain songwriters than hallucinogens. 1969's chart debut by David Bowie, 'Space Oddity', was regarded in some quarters as a paean to heroin, and a sense of longing rather than self-loathing emanated from the addict in 'Sister Morphine' by Marianne Faithfull, whose wretched bouts of heroin addiction would blight periodic comebacks now that 1965's 'Summer Nights' had waved her out of sight of the UK Top Ten forever. A newer female star, Linda Ronstadt, would brag that "I can sing better after shooting smack [heroin] in both my arms."[63] Yet there was strong hostility to drug culture from many musicians, both in interview and record grooves – such as those of Frank Zappa's later 'Cocaine Decisions', a swipe at a stimulant in more general use within the music industry in the 1970s.

It was feasible that, as well as consumption of hard drugs, John Lennon's conduct also had a connection with St Francis of Assisi, who was given to sometimes preaching the gospel in the nude as an act of self-abasing godliness. Though it was the sort of statement he might have made, it was not St Francis but Lennon who assured *Melody Maker* editor Ray Coleman, "I try to live as Christ lived. It's tough, I can tell you."[27] Furthermore, a few months prior to the cloak-and-dagger release of *Two Virgins* – and the day before he consummated his desire for Yoko in Weybridge – it was said that Lennon had summoned McCartney, Harrison and Starr behind closed doors in an Apple board room in order to proclaim himself the Messiah. He wasn't being funny ha-ha either.

Paul had been persuaded to write a commendation (if it was one) that called Lennon and Yoko "saints" for the *Two Virgins* cover, but he and his new girlfriend, Linda Eastman – a showbiz photographer from a family of US attorneys – were, reportedly, most offended by the entire affair.

Of all the other Beatle couples, Ringo and Maureen swooped most unquestioningly to Lennon's defence. The *Two Virgins* sleeve was, concluded Ringo, "just John being John. It's very clean."[64] Yoko became "incredible". No one doubted it either. "We'd be pleased when people realise that she's not trying to be the fifth Beatle," Starr continued[64] – though, when waiting to console Yoko before Lennon's cremation 12 years later, he was supposedly overheard to mutter, "It was her who started all this."[65] This indicated an adjustment of his previously stated opinion, as late as 1971, that her and John's *amour* had not taken priority over group commitments. "Ringo was a little confused," deduced Klaus Voorman, "because John's closeness to Yoko was sad to him. John and Yoko were one person, which was difficult for him to accept."[66]

George Harrison, however, wasn't confused at all. One day at Savile Row, he could no longer contain his resentment, particularly as Yoko was now taking an active hand in the running of Apple. She'd been the one, for example, who'd interviewed Freddie Garrity (!). George burst into the couple's office and came straight to the point. Naming Bob Dylan among those with a low opinion of Yoko, Harrison went on to complain about the present "bad vibes" within The Beatles' empire, which were correlated with her coming. "We both sat through it," said John, "and I didn't hit him. I don't know why."[2]

Soon, John's extreme broadness of gesture – which extended to changing his middle name by deed poll from "Winston" to "Ono" – was an embarrassment to the world outside The Beatles clique too. Perhaps the more resolute gentlefolk of the press got wind of the "Messiah" nonsense, because early in December 1969 it was reported in the *Daily Express* and then in several other domestic newspapers that John was "considering" an offer to play the title role in a forthcoming musical, *Jesus Christ Superstar*, but only on condition that Yoko star too as "Mary Magdalene". All this was a surprise to composer Andrew Lloyd Webber and his lyricist, a former EMI production assistant named Tim Rice, who issued a terrified denial straightaway.

The *Express* feature was, allegedly, the first John heard of the matter too, but he didn't mind. It gilded the image of him as the coolest cat ever to walk the planet, the most messianic symbol of hipness since Bob Dylan, the most way-out star in the firmament – though not a star in the sense of sending teenage girls into paroxysms of screaming ecstasy any more. *Two Virgins* had put paid to that – as articulated in the hookline of the topical disc "John You Went Too Far This Time" by Rainbo, alias Hollywood starlet Sissy Spacek: "Since I saw that picture, my love will never be the same."

A special "Groupies" edition of *Rolling Stone* in 1969 concerned female music-lovers renowned for evading the most stringent security barriers to impose themselves on rock stars. The more free-spirited of these "groupies" (not "scrubbers" anymore) remained interested in John Lennon sexually – "It'd be a privilege for him to even notice me," said one[67] – but others were wary of one who had mutated from object of desire to not so much a spoken-for all-father as a universal batty uncle: not a clown prince of pop like Freddie Garrity had been – far from it – but a Holy Fool, a sort of clown godhead of pop.

In reciprocation, a fur-coated woman had shouted, "You are a very holy man," when he and Yoko had emerged on 28 November 1968 from Marylebone Magistrates Court, where John had been fined after pleading guilty to possession of substances contrary to the provisions of the 1966 Dangerous Drugs Act, section 42.

He and a pregnant Yoko had been recipients of a Narcotics Squad pounce the previous month after they'd found a temporary refuge from self-aggravated media attention in a rented maisonette a few blocks from Regent's Park. Unacceptable to the officer in charge was John's excuse that the cannabis he and his men – and a sniffer dog – had discovered was the lost property of some earlier tenant, maybe Jimi Hendrix or novelist William Burroughs.

The first Beatle of three to be "busted", Lennon was no longer above the law, MBE or not. The rip-tide of the drama – "an offence of moral turpitude" – was to wash over his attempts in the next decade to settle permanently in the United States, but in 1968 he accepted it as part of life's small change and he didn't find the furore completely unwelcome.

He seemed so bound up in himself and Yoko that every occurrence and emotion was worth broadcasting to as wide a forum as possible, just as it happened – just as, in microcosm, Rory Storm was prone to do in the old days, ensuring that his birthday celebrations were public events, and being nabbed by a porter spray-painting "I Love Rory" on a wall at Bootle railway station.

With the means to go infinitely further, John Lennon ordered the issue on Zapple, Apple's short-lived "experimental" subsidiary label, of his second LP with Yoko, *Unfinished Music No 2: Life With The Lions*. The back cover was a *Daily Mirror* photograph of him with his arm around a distressed Yoko in the midst of policemen and morbid inquisitiveness outside the Marylebone court room. The disc's content, however, was concerned principally with Yoko's subsequent miscarriage – and included the dying foetus's heartbeat, which was offered to and rejected by *Student* magazine as a giveaway flexidisc.

Most self-obsessed of all was autumn 1969's *Wedding Album*. One side of this feast of entertainment was the two's repeated utterances of each other's name suspended over their own pounding heartbeats – though there was a blurry link, I suppose, with Marcel Duchamp's "ready-made" art and the provocation of Dada just after the Great War.

If that was the case, then *Self-Portrait* paralleled Duchamp's *Fountain*, a urinal with "R Mutt 1917" painted on it ("which is just out of this world", gasped John[2]). *Self-Portrait*, a 42-minute movie starring Lennon's famous cock – and some fluid that dribbled from it – was screened at London's Institute of Contemporary Arts in September 1969 as one of several British premieres of Warhol-esque films of similar non-events made by John and the more seasoned movie director, Yoko. Like other Ono–Lennon artistic collaborations during this period, most of them were laboured, inconsequential and generally misconstrued comedy. The chief exception was *Rape*, a disturbing hour or so of an obtrusive cameraman following an increasingly alarmed foreign student around London. *Rape* aside, however, some viewers tried to fool themselves that Yoko and John's celluloid ventures were quite absorbing in parts, even as others fidgeted in their seats.

Rape was broadcast on Austrian television on 31 March 1969, as just-married Yoko and John were completing their first "Bed-In for Peace". Now with centre-parted hair splayed halfway down his back, bearded to the cheekbones and defiantly round-spectacled, John had smoked a cigarette during a quiet, white-costumed wedding in Gibraltar on 20 March. It was followed at the Amsterdam Hilton's luxurious honeymoon suite by the Bed-In. They hoped that lying about for a week whilst entertaining the press would stop the atrocities in Vietnam and Biafra more effectively than any post-flower-power protest march or student sit-in.

Both the ceremony and the Bed-In were mentioned in 'The Ballad Of John And Yoko', The Beatles' final British Number One. That each chorus began with the interjection "Christ!" – him again – restricted airplay, and the entire narrative confirmed the Lennons' status as a Scandalous Couple on a par with Serge Gainsbourg and Jane Birkin, makers of that summer's 'Je T'Aime...Moi Non Plus', on which an easy-listening arrangement seeped incongruously beneath their grunts, moans, whispers and half-crooned lines like one that translates as "You are the wave: I, the bare island. You go, you go and you come between my loins" as prospects of imminent sexual climax increased towards the fade. In spite of an outright BBC ban, it ended Creedence Clearwater Revival's reign at Number One in Britain, and reaped even fatter harvests *sur le continent* (though it wilted at *Position Soixante-Neuf* – if you'll pardon my French – in the US Hot 100). 'Je T'Aime...' sold an eventual million copies and continued to fill dance floors with groping smoochers as surely as 10cc's 'I'm Not In Love' after it.

Ono and Lennon's canoodling went beyond the bounds of generally acceptable ickiness too. Moreover, to say things most people didn't want to hear or understand, they'd made their headline-hogging lives an even more open and ludicrous book with further eye-stretching pranks such as press conferences from inside kingsize white sacks; the slapdash letter to the Queen that would accompany John's renouncement of his MBE; sending acorns to world leaders; his scrawly lithographs of themselves having sex; and ordering the plastering of billboards proclaiming "War Is Over!" all over 11 city centres. The Ancient Greeks had a word for such conduct: *hubris*, which defies succinct translation, but alludes to a heroically foolish defiance rooted in a feeling that one is beyond the reaches of authority and convention.

In response, a lot of the "War Is Over!" signs were defaced within a day of their appearing. However, something those who did so could comprehend more readily, if not sympathise with, had emerged from another crowded "Bed-In" – this time in Toronto – where Lennon's 'Give Peace A Chance' was taped. Though "Lennon–McCartney" was given as the composing credit on the record label, this was his first smash – Number Two in Britain, 14 in the USA – without Paul, George and Ringo, attributed as it was to the ad hoc "Plastic Ono Band". The subsequent full-page advertisement in the music papers informed readers "*You* are The Plastic Ono Band!" Yet, over 30 years later, I still haven't received any royalties for 'Give Peace A Chance'. Have you?

Never mind, it was a catchy effort, even if the verses were just syllables strung together to fill enough 2/4 bars to separate each instantly familiar *omnes fortissimo* chorus – which if nothing else carried the message of the title across.

The contradiction between Lennon's twee projection of himself and Yoko as "Mr and Mrs Peace" and his beery unpleasantness towards members of The Terry Young Six, another act on the Helen Shapiro tour, raised a derisive laugh from the Six's keyboard player, Barry Booth, who recalled him as "a nasty bastard then". Moreover, prior to the Bed-Ins, John had been active only after a detached, pop-starrish fashion in verbal support of pacifism, sharing the general disenchantment with the hippie counter-culture following the Sharon Tate bloodbath and the general dissipation of flower-power idealism. He said as much in an interview with *Student*'s editor, Richard Branson, a former pupil at Stowe Public School, where The Beatles had played that curious recital in 1963.

Lennon had earned the approbation of *Student*'s leftish readership partly through the B-side to 1968's 'Hey Jude', 'Revolution'. However irresolute it would seem in retrospect, it was John's most far-reaching assessment in song of any of the cultural, political and other undercurrents pertinent to the culmination of the Swinging '60s – though there was also an abstraction of this in 'Revolution 9', the longest track on The Beatles' eponymous first Apple album – a double – which may be heard as a rendering in sound of one of Stuart Sutcliffe's latter-day paintings in that it was trying to express a unconscious emotion.

Selected at the insistence of Lennon, who created almost all of it with Yoko, only the recurring "number nine" announcement lends 'Revolution 9' even vague orthodox form – though Lennon was to aver that "It has the basic rhythm of the original 'Revolution' [a different take of the B-side that begins side four of *The Beatles*], going on with some 20 tape loops we put on, things from the archives of EMI. There were about ten machines with people holding pencils on the loops. I did a few mixes until I got one I liked. I spent more time on 'Revolution 9' than I did on half the other songs I ever wrote."[21]

This patchwork of noises that the man in the street wouldn't think of as musical is comparable to Varèse's *La Pòeme Électronique*, a montage commissioned to accompany an exhibit at the 1958 World's Fair in Brussels. This too was assembled literally second by second from seemingly random sources. 'Revolution 9' was lauded too by Barry Miles in the *International Times* as a send-up of John Cage's 'Fontana Mix', an 11-minute "chance operation" tape collage recorded in 1958 and a classic of its kind, like his more famous "silent piece", '4'33''', which requires a pianist to sit before a keyboard without touching it for that length of time. Coughs, the rustling of programmes and the huff of footsteps walking out of the auditorium are part of the performance.

'Revolution 9' ("an aural litmus of unfocused paranoia", concluded *Rolling Stone*[68]) reached a far, far larger audience than all its avant-garde antecedents combined – antecedents of which most of its buyers were unaware. Hence its dismissal as "rubbish" by those who were bored, irritated and, now and then, inadvertently amused by what they heard only as scribble between 'Cry Baby Cry' and 'Goodnight'. Others, including me, weren't so sure, and listened again – and again and again – until 'Revolution 9' reached out and held them forever.

The outlines between The Beatles and Lennon's undertakings with "Mrs Peace" were fast dissolving and yet widening the chasm between him and his old comrades. "I don't think you could have broken up four very strong people like that," countered Yoko. "There must have been something that happened within them – not an outside force at all."[21] The disbandment of The Beatles would connect with their own inner natures and desires – and when it dawned on them that not everything they did was great – but the new brides of John Lennon and Paul McCartney were among catalysts that enabled it.

With all pretensions of The Beatles' four-man brotherhood now gone, Yoko's constant and baleful adherence to John at Abbey Road entitled Paul McCartney to bring along Linda Eastman, soon to be Linda McCartney. While she and the older Yoko had both attended school in the same well-to-do New York suburb, they didn't have much else in common, although they were both to marry their respective English *beaux* during the same month. There were moments of congeniality, but generally the lukewarm rapport between the chief Beatles' immovable women was just one of Ringo's "little niggly things"[69], which cropped up as the group worked through *The Beatles* and then *Let It Be*: "the most miserable session on Earth", scowled John.[2]

Yoko and Linda, however, were but two guest participants as the group vacillated between the colour-supplement artwork of *Sgt Pepper* and a vain endeavour to get back to their Merseybeat womb. They were trying too not to alienate those for whom pop meant little until a belated admiration for a disintegrating Beatles' "joyful music-making that only the ignorant will not hear". Thus read a King's New Clothes-ish critique of the 'White Album' in *The Observer*.[70]

Perhaps the least "joyful" music they'd ever made, *Let It Be* was intended as purposeful veering away from the string quartets, backwards-running tapes, horn sections, sitars and Mike Sammes Singers of yore. The idea had been to tape nothing that couldn't be reproduced onstage. "It would be honest," so George Martin had understood, "no overdubbing, no editing, truly live, almost amateurish."[7]

It was, therefore, to be The Beatles pared down to just vocals, guitars, bass and drums, plus keyboards where necessary. These were fingered by Paul – and Billy Preston, whose joviality and energetic instrumental dexterity had first impressed The Beatles in 1961, when he was Little Richard's organist at the Star-Club.

No matter how deferential they were towards Billy during the making of *Let It Be*, The Beatles subjected George Martin – no longer the imposing figure he'd been in 1962 – to the same oafish discourtesies they were rendering each other. This was among reasons why he became as fed up with the project as they were.

Therefore, rather than a disinclined Martin, Phil Spector was drafted in to edit, spruce up and mix what was to be described as a "new-phase Beatles album".[71]

Of all of them, John Lennon and George Harrison had been the keenest on the record productions of this undersized if self-important New Yorker. He'd been hot property in the early 1960s for his spatial "wall of sound" technique, whereby he'd multi track an apocalyptic *mélange* – replete with everything, bar the proverbial kitchen sink – behind beehive-and-net-petticoat vocal groups The Crystals and The Ronettes and other artists who'd submitted to his masterplan.

In the wake of the British Invasion, he let it be known that he wanted to work with The Beatles – and several years later, they let him.

As heard on numerous bootlegs, Spector's raw material for *Let It Be* had resulted from weeks of loose jamming, musical ambles down memory lane and hitting trouble whenever John, Paul and George came up against each other's new compositions.

In keeping with a flagrant spirit of self-interest, discord and intrigue, anything that needed too much thought got a thumbs-down. The strained atmosphere had alleviated slightly with the wheeling-in of Preston, who also joined in the celebrated, and unannounced, afternoon performance – The Beatles' last ever – on the flat roof of 3 Savile Row on 30 January 1969.

Afterwards, the participants, their musical appetites ruined by the project as a whole, were tempted to jettison the frayed miles of *Let It Be* tapes, but the fastidious Phil's doctoring satisfied even – at least, in the first instance – Paul McCartney, albeit not the keenest Spector fan. Yet Paul was to demand – to little effect – that the *Let It Be* album be divested of the superimposed orchestral and choral grandiloquence he regarded as gratuitous frills that both attempted to smother ugly moments (such as Lennon's poor bass playing on 'The Long And Winding Road') and contradicted George Martin's original uncluttered production criterion. In the pungent words of Abbey Road engineer Glyn Johns, Spector "overdubbed a lot of bullshit all over it, strings and choirs and yuck".[72]

Johns – and McCartney – may have considered this the case with 'Let It Be' itself and 'The Long And Winding Road', but in a statistically commercial sense, these songs were triumphs in that, like the comparatively unvarnished 'Get Back', they both topped the US Hot 100 as spin-off singles.

Nevertheless, Spector was out of the picture when the team – Lennon, McCartney, Harrison, Starr and Martin – rallied for the *Abbey Road* finale, which the discerning Frank Zappa regarded as "probably the best mastered, best engineered rock 'n' roll record I've heard," albeit adding, "which has nothing to do with the material on it".[73]

When *Abbey Road* was hot off the press, John was approached to compère an open-air pop festival in Canada with a majority of olde-tyme rock 'n' rollers – Fats Domino, Little Richard, Chuck Berry, Gene Vincent and Bo Diddley – on the bill. Instead, he, Yoko and some hurriedly rehearsed Plastic Ono Bandsmen – guitarist Eric Clapton, drummer Alan White (from The Alan Price Set) and, on bass, Klaus Voorman – performed at midnight on Saturday 13 September 1969. Issued as *Live Peace In Toronto 1969*, their ragged set consisted mainly of 1950s classic rock, a nascent arrangement of 'Cold Turkey' – a forthcoming new Plastic Ono Band single – 'Give Peace A Chance' and Yoko's screech-singing.

Manning the barricades in front of the stage, the Hell's Angels stewardry called Ono and Lennon dirty names. In the wings, however, Gene Vincent was weeping with emotion as, overweight and in a grey-faced, boozy haze, he tried to forget both a worrying demand for maintenance from a former wife and certain knowledge that his now steadfastly painful crippled leg would have to be amputated.

The ill-starred Gene's appearance at Toronto astonished those who thought that he was already dead – and he would be within a month – but the bigger event for most was the Plastic Ono bash. Regardless of its content, it was enough for most of the 20,000-odd onlookers that it happened at all. If not on the scale of Moses re-appearing before the Israelites from the clouded summit of Mount Sinai, it was the proverbial "something to tell your grandchildren about": John Lennon's first major concert – the first by any Beatle – since the showdown at Candlestick Park.

For all that, the album sold but moderately, ie less than a million, while 'Cold Turkey' touched a high of between 10 and 30 in most charts by Christmas. Its B-side was Yoko's 'Don't Worry Kyoko (Mummy's Only Looking For Her Hand In The Snow)' – which could have been about anything – or nothing. However, a Beatle-ologist might conjecture that it was an exaggerated commemoration of John missing a bend and rolling over a hired Austin Maxi somewhere in the Scottish highlands during a brief holiday the previous July. Only one passenger – six-year-old Julian – escaped uninjured; Yoko, John and Kyoko, Yoko's daughter by a previous marriage, needed stitches.

Lennon found 'Don't Worry Kyoko' as potent as his adolescent self had Little Richard's 'Tutti Frutti'. Indefatigable work-outs of 'Don't Worry Kyoko' and 'Cold Turkey' filled his last stage appearance in Britain – with a Plastic Ono *Supergroup* containing the bemused likes of George

Harrison and The Who's madcap drummer, Keith Moon – at London's Lyceum ballroom in December 1969.

They'd done it for charity, even though no one was sure or not if Lennon was joking in a recent interview that he was "down to my last 50,000".[74] If ever he'd believed that his means were infinite, a letter from The Beatles' accountants had disabused him of this. His overdraft on the corporate account was £64,988 – and those of the other three were of comparable amounts. Worse, they'd lost control of Apple, where embezzlement and more open theft – such as that of the television and fitted carpet in the room the Lennons had commandeered at Savile Row – was rife.

Matters improved with the arrival and consequent purge by go-getting Allen Klein – "like the archetypal villain in a film", according to Ray Davies.[43] Klein's reputation as the "Robin Hood of pop" stood on his recouping of disregarded millions for his clients from seemingly irrefutable recording company percentages. Grateful clients included Bobby Vinton, Bobby Darin – and Phil Spector.

When the '60s started swinging, he'd made himself as useful to The Dave Clark Five, The Kinks and the uncut rubies – including The Animals and Herman's Hermits – that had been processed for the charts by freelance producer Mickie Most. The Rolling Stones had also bitten, grinned Most, after "they'd seen me driving around in a Rolls and owning a yacht, and started wondering where their money was going".[75]

Then Klein sought to win the biggest prize of all. He began hovering over John, Paul, George and Ringo like a vulture over a horseless cowboy with an empty canteen staggering across the burning desert. The subject of a small wager between Mickie's wife and Allen was that he'd be superintending The Beatles by Christmas 1967. Indeed, he'd gathered that Paul McCartney had been particularly impressed by his wheedling of an unprecedently high advance from Decca for the Stones two years earlier.

"Allen tried to come in when Brian was there, just as a business manager, and not run our lives," Ringo Starr would recall, "and Brian would have nothing to do with him."[52] Klein wasn't popular amongst other moguls as he wasted no time with small-talk while driving hard and unrelenting bargains on the telephone and in the boardroom. Nonetheless, though no love was lost between them, EMI chairman Sir Joseph Lockwood said, "In fairness to Klein, I ended up doing deals that I have never regretted."[76]

To Lockwood and the rest of EMI's executive body, Klein was everything that Brian Epstein wasn't. An observer of a routine ruled by the clock, he was an impassive, reflective type at home, who liked to distance himself from the office – and his clients because "otherwise you can really get on each other's nerves".[77] Yet, though to him pop was simply a commodity to be bought, sold and replaced when worn out, he wasn't self-deprecating about his knowledge and love of it, and when his wooing of The Beatles moved into top gear, Klein – like a certain Eastern mystic they'd encountered – underwent a crash-course in their music to better butter them up and, by 1969, his prophecy that he'd one day represent the group seemed to be fulfilling itself.

One of many bluff homilies attributed to Klein was "What's the point of Utopia if it don't make a profit?"[77] – and Apple was living proof. In its white-walled, green-carpeted headquarters, it had been a boom time for the more self-serving members of staff after they'd assimilated the heedlessness of their paymasters' expenditure and guessed – erroneously – that their means were limitless. A dam burst for a river of wastefulness to carry off gluttonous restaurant lunches; bottle after bottle of expensive liquor; illicit trunk calls to other continents; and wanton purchases of trendy caprices to lie swiftly forgotten in desk drawers. Not far from the truth would be a scene from 1978's spoof Beatles bio-pic *All You Need Is Cash*, in which a thinly disguised Apple Corps is pillaged by its employees while in the foreground its press agent chats to a television news commentator (played, incidentally, by George Harrison).

Out of his depth, John Lennon, with Yoko, had stuck to conventional office hours and played company director until the novelty wore off. Initially, he'd looked away from the revolting realities of the half-eaten steak sandwich in a litter bin; the receptionist rolling a spliff of best Afghan hash; the typist who span out a single letter (in the house style of no exclamation marks!) all morning before "popping out" at noon and not returning until the next day.

A great light dawned, but as neither John nor any other individual Beatle felt responsible for straightening out a venture that had taken mere weeks to snowball into chaos, the task had fallen to Allen Klein. Yet, though Lennon, Harrison and Starr yielded to Allen's contractual seduction, McCartney, once his champion, preferred to believe his lawyer brother-in-law's tales of Klein's sharp practices, high-handedness and low cunning.

McCartney, however, had to applaud the purge that discontinued sinecures and unviable ventures. Among the first within the organisation to go had been The Fool and Magic Alex – and there'd be no more "Unfinished Music" on Zapple, which "seized up before it really got going", grimaced George Harrison, "as with so many things at Apple". With commendable honesty, Harrison confessed that "both of the Zapple albums that did come out were a load of rubbish"[78] – namely *Life With The Lions* and George's own self-indulgence, *Electronic Sounds*.

Even Apple Records, starkly the enterprise's only money-spinner, was to be subject to inevitable cuts as unviable releases were cancelled, contracts unrenewed, and retainers stopped. After Mary Hopkin, Billy Preston and Badfinger's chart strikes for Apple were over, all that remained were The Beatles, together and apart.

In the offices too, personnel were subject to Klein's pruning stick; a clocking-on system was installed and the fiddling curbed. Overnight, glib unconcern had deferred to pointed questions. Why does that typist ring New Zealand every afternoon at 5:15pm on the dot? Why has so-and-so given himself a rise of £60 a week? Why is he seen only on pay day? Suddenly, lunch meant bringing in sandwiches instead of ordering a taxi to a fancy *brasserie* up West.

The Beatles had to bite back on sentiment when the ruthlessness also meant the casting adrift of old retainers by Klein, who, becoming something of a pop personality in his own right – as Epstein had been – confirmed in a *Melody Maker* interview his scheme "to make Apple financially successful and tailored to The Beatles' own specifications, but when you get a lot of energy wasted, it doesn't make for an efficient organisation".[79]

However, Allen Klein's streamlining of Apple was nothing compared to his renegotiation of a royalty rate with Capitol that amassed millions for The Beatles – albeit a Beatles that would disband within months.

11 *"An Escape Valve From The Beatles"*

In 1969, John Lennon won an *NME* poll in which other famous vocalists had each been asked to nominate their own three favourites. He was, debatably, as adept as he'd ever be by the late 1960s – as illustrated by the coda of the White Album's 'Happiness Is A Warm Gun' when he swerved cleanly into falsetto, having already built from muttered trepidation to strident intensity earlier in the song, tackling its surreal lyrics without affectation.

Yet self-doubt about his singing skills was to persist as an ex-Beatle who allowed Phil Spector and a later producer, Jack Douglas, to smother his vocals in what became a trademark echo, not only in the mix but even as he sang onto tape, refusing to open his mouth unless this was so. "After he left me, he did all his own distortion to his heart's content," lamented George Martin, "and I didn't like that. After all, the raw material was so good."[27]

With vocal vehemence taking precedent throughout over nicety of intonation, the studio version of 'Cold Turkey' was issued, so Lennon put it, "as an escape valve from The Beatles",[2] from whom he'd cast his net furthest. He was also absenting himself from press calls, business meetings and record dates just as the similarly lovestruck Stuart Sutcliffe had stints on the Top Ten stage in Hamburg.

As if in prophecy, John wasn't around for what seemed to be The Beatles' final recording date on 3 January 1970. In skittish mood during this tying-up of a *Let It Be* loose end, George Harrison – whose progress as a composer was among other factors that had led to the present state of affairs – indulged in a little taped tomfoolery at John's expense: "You all will have read that Dave Dee is no longer with us, but Micky, Tich and I would like to carry on the good work that's always gone down at (Studio) Number Two."[80]

On hearing of this, John grinned askance and told the wife – and Allen Klein, now his official manager. As fatigued as everyone else was of the fraternal animosity, Lennon had been relieved that the atmosphere during the making of *Abbey Road* was more co-operative than it had been for *Let It Be*. The subtext, of course, was a tacit agreement that *Abbey Road* was to be the last LP, and they might as well go out under a flag of truce.

Of each Beatle's preparations for the end, John's had been the most lucrative – on vinyl anyway. Even *Two Virgins* had inched into the lower reaches of the US album list. Yet, while *Let It Be* – issued out of chronological sequence after *Abbey Road* – lorded it over the likes of *Led Zeppelin II*, Andy Williams' *Greatest Hits* and the latest from The Who, Crosby, Stills, Nash And Young and Simon And Garfunkel in May 1970's charts, Paul McCartney's eponymous solo debut and Ringo's *Sentimental Journey* were in there too – though neither spawned a spin-off 45.

Like children of parents who stay together just because neither has yet quite enough motivation to leave, Ringo and George – who'd both quit briefly already – were waiting for one of the other two to marshall his words and dare the speech everyone knew he'd been agonising over for months. While *McCartney* was still at the pressing plant, Paul had been preparing a press release that almost, but not quite, proclaimed the end of The Beatles. Behind closed doors, he'd also been setting wheels in motion for the formal dissolution of Messrs Harrison, Lennon, McCartney and Starkey as a business enterprise. Yet months before the writs were served, John had slipped a teasing "...when I was a Beatle" into an interview with *Disc*,[81] and, feeling as little regret, had announced privately his own exit well before Paul – though this had been hushed up, mainly for fear of it cramping Allen Klein's bullying of Capitol.

Having said it at last, much of the tension of the preceding months had flowed from John Lennon. An unsettled chapter in his life had just ended. If a lot of his problems had been self-aggravated, it had been a stressful and demanding time that he wouldn't wish on anyone else. Now he could get on with the rest of his life. How could he have known then that he had only ten years left?

Moreover, having soundtracked the 1960s, he and the others wouldn't be able as solo stars and ex-Beatles to so minister to the next decade when all but the most snowblinded would understand how ordinary, even disagreeable, the mere mortals behind the myth could be. "George was the most normal and friendly of men," said Richard Reed, the architect who restored Harrison's newly purchased mansion in Henley-on-Thames. "He introduced me to John Lennon. He was shorter than I expected and not as pleasant as George. He just shook my hand and turned away."[82]

In the wake of February 1970's echo-drenched 'Instant Karma' – recorded and mastered within a day of its composition – I discovered quite early on how yawnsome Lennon was becoming via an associated interview headlined "Shut Up And Listen!: The Thoughts Of Chairman John" in *Record Mirror*.[83] What I could not articulate to myself then was that I was being tested by a horrified realisation of being unendurably bored by his pontifications about The Plastic Ono Band, his and Yoko's new short haircuts, his peace mission and an oscillating commitment to other worthy (or not) causes – the *Oz* trial, say, or the clearing of convicted murderer James Hanratty – he was espousing with varying degrees of pragmatism at the rate of roughly one a week.

Readers paid attention, however, because, even as 'Power To The People', his first 45 as a *bona fide* ex-Beatle, penetrated the UK Top 40 on 20 March 1971, somewhere in such discussions Lennon might fan the dull embers of The Beatles' future, which were becoming duller by the day. While clouds of litigation gathered, he and the others had been "tight, nervous, everyone watching everyone else", noticed the forgiving Cynthia, who, before her ostracism from that most innermost of 1960s in-crowds, was "at home" one afternoon for guests that included her increasingly distant Beatle pals and ex-husband.

Yet the illusion of reconciliation that was *Abbey Road* had tricked the general public into believing that The Beatles weren't over. Indeed, until well into the 1970s, not a week would pass without some twit or other asking John, George, Paul or Ringo when the four of them were going to get together again in the studio. It was seen as almost inevitable by even the most marginally hopeful outsider for whom the concept of collecting every record The Beatles ever made was not yet economically unsound. Thus an ex-Beatle was assured of at least a minor hit, even with substandard merchandise.

In 1976, when all four happened to be on the same land mass at the same time, they would be tempted to call the bluff of Lorne Michaels, producer of *Saturday Night Live* (a TV satire transmitted from New York), who said that, if they agreed to play together before his cameras for the prescribed Musicians' Union fee, he'd squeeze them onto the show. Depending on whose account you read, unfortunately – or, perhaps, not so unfortunately – Lennon and McCartney ordered a taxi, but decided they were too tired. Alternatively, Paul, Ringo and George arrived for the show, but John's chauffeur drove to the wrong studio, thereby capsizing what might have been the ultimate practical joke.

As things turned out, a Ringo Starr album of 1972 would be the nearest the living members would ever come to a reunion on disc, embracing as it did compositions and active participation by all four, albeit not at the same time. Lennon's main contribution, 'I'm The Greatest', came close as it featured himself, Starr and Harrison at Los Angeles' Sunset Sound Studio. McCartney had been amenable to pitching in too, but was refused a US visa owing to a recent conviction for possessing narcotics, which had been seized during a European tour with Wings, his new outfit, in which Linda fingered the keyboards.

Entitled *Ringo*, the LP was coloured, therefore, as a bastardised Beatles collection, supplemented as it was by Klaus Voorman's *Sgt Pepper*-esque lithograph and Starr's teasing insertion of the odd Lennon–McCartney song title into its lyrics. That the Fab Four were theoretically together on the same piece of plastic was sufficient to feed fans' expectations that soon everything would be OK again, and The Beatles would regroup formally to tour and release the chart-toppers that John and Paul – all friends again – would be churning out once more.

Pressed on the subject, glam-rock overlord Gary Glitter hit the nail on the head: "They'll have to come back as a bigger creative force than before, which will be very difficult indeed."[84] As difficult had been

Muhammad Ali regaining his world heavyweight title in 1975. Possibly, The Beatles might have regained theirs, even though the world had become wiser to their individual weaknesses – and the fact that, after picking and choosing from both illustrious chums and the trendiest and most nonchalantly squeaky-clean studio musicians, none of them would ever accomplish what The Beatles, for all their casually strewn errors, had committed to tape instinctively and without complacency.

With their wealth now secure, John, Paul, George and Ringo were all above the tour-album-tour sandwiches incumbent upon poorer stars, and each could wait until he felt like going on the road again or making a new record. However, an unkempt-looking Lennon still took the trouble to plug 'Instant Karma' – a "live" vocal over a backing tape – twice on *Top Of The Pops*, with that creepy Yoko next to him on a stool, either blindfolded and holding up her scrawled signs with PEACE, SMILE, BREATHE and other cryptadia on them, knitting a jumper, or mouthing silently into a microphone. Weird, eh?

Yet George Harrison, the former Beatle least addicted to the limelight, had been first off the starting line after sifting through a backlog of around 40 compositions for a new LP, a double, even a triple if he felt like it – which he did. This he titled *All Things Must Pass*, which was completed with more than a little help from an insufferably smug cabal of "heavy friends" and Phil Spector applying his spent "genius" to the console.

The first *All Things Must Pass* single, 'My Sweet Lord', sold millions, certainly more than 'Instant Karma', but both were reflective of a turn-of-the-decade fad for spirituality. Born-again fervour saw evangelical marches up high streets, the Bible on hip bookshelves, the Scriptures quoted at parties, and record deals for outfits like The Water-Into-Wine Band, from England's West Country, whose come-to-Jesus output was epitomised by 'Song Of The Cross', a 1971 album track that was quite moving in a *Ben Hur*-ish sort of way. On the other side of the same coin, Graham Bond led an early 1970s unit, Magick, which focused on his fascination with the occult and was as different from The Graham Bond Organisation, once the toast of London's mid-1960s in-clubs, as the Moon from the Earth.

The same comparison might be made between Lennon's first post-Beatles album and *Abbey Road*. Like its vinyl companion, *Yoko Ono/Plastic*

Ono Band, John Lennon/Plastic Ono Band was the cathartic outcome of a course of Primal Scream therapy under Los Angeles psychologist Dr Arthur Janov. Its basic premise, that all neuroses stemmed from deprivation of parental love, enabled John to look up from the bottom of his 30-year-old pit and imagine that he saw a strip of blue sky with God peering over the edge. It wasn't Him but the good doctor who made a half-hearted attempt to film a sitting with the famous pop star for use, he said, in a documentary – presumably to rope in further well-heeled patients.

John would be smiled in and smiled out of such consultations, which overflowed with extravagant lamentations and, ideally, rejoicings too. All the pain John had been carrying since the departure of his father and the death of Julia was supposed to disappear like the sack of woe falling from Christian in *The Pilgrim's Progress*.

With the starkest instrumentation, and the exhilaration of the impromptu prized more than technical accuracy, the Primal Scream experience came to a head in the songs he'd written for *John Lennon/Plastic Ono Band*. There was also a point of contact with Sleepy John Estes, Lightnin' Hopkins and other black bluesmen who trafficked in individual visions of an immediate world, about which they strove to say enough without too much lingering intimacy or any of that "oh gawd!" tweeness that characterised Melanie, Nick Drake and any other precious post-Woodstock balladeer, seated singing to a guitar and beaming a small, sad smile every now and then.

John's personal exorcisms, like 'Mother' and 'Isolation', mingled with stark rejections of former heroes and ideals – notably in "God" – and 'Working Class Hero', an acoustic ballad that railed against the mysterious "they", and got itself banned from most daytime radio stations for its use of the f-word, even if Lennon was no more the salt of the earth than Mick Jagger, also a scion of privet-hedged suburbia. He came on even more falsely as a workin' class 'ero, albeit in an affected raw Cockney instead of thickened Scouse.

Ripe language and soul baring were apparent in Lennon's newspaper interviews too – as was the almost audible snigger whenever he sniped at McCartney. His old comrade was pilloried further in 'How Do You Sleep' from 1971's *Imagine*, though the two had still been on speaking terms, with John ringing Paul when the track was on point of release. By contrast, *Imagine* also contained paeans of uxorious bent (such as 'Oh Yoko', 'Oh My Love' and the apologetic 'Jealous Guy') as well as a utopian title track, fairy-dusted with strings, that, for better or worse, was to endure as Lennon's most memorable post-Beatles opus.

'How Do You Sleep' had had George Harrison in support on lead guitar – and the month before the release of *Imagine* in September 1971, George was to invite John to participate in his Concerts *For Bangla Desh* in New York, but only on the understanding there'd be no place in the set for a number or two from Yoko as well. As the evil hour when her husband was actually going to perform without her crept closer, the humidity in New York thickened to what The Lovin' Spoonful had sung about in 'Summer In The City'. No breeze blew, and Yoko's forehead and upper lip was bestowed with pinpricks of sweat. It was weather that breeds maggots in dustbins and Ono's tantrum was so violent that, crushing his spectacles in his fist, John had slammed out of their hotel for the next flight back to Europe.

Harrison's giant step for Bangla Desh took place regardless and, in one throw, he outshone all the Lennons' more mystifying tactics to right the wrongs of mankind. Perhaps in a spirit of resentful competitiveness, John spoke briefly of a Wembley show for a worthy cause with him, Yoko and their sort of people instead of George and his crowd.

No time was better for Lennon to be charitable on such a scale. With *Imagine* soon to be at Number One in the States, no time was better either for him to make hay with a world tour too, but both ideas – if they were ever even considered seriously – had been jettisoned by the time he left his country of birth forever for the United States on 3 September 1971.

The first album – a double – from his "American period" was 1972's *Sometime In New York City*. He and Yoko were backed by Elephant's Memory, a local band fresh from a maiden Hot 100 strike. This joint venture also embraced excerpts from both the Lyceum extravaganza and a guest spot at the Fillmore East with Frank Zappa's Mothers Of Invention. Nevertheless, apart from the odd inspired moment, notably a driving revival of The Olympics' 'Well (Baby Please Don't Go)' with

Zappa, the kindest critics agreed that *Sometime In New York City* was documentary rather than recreational.

The essence of it was slogan-ridden musical journalism that had less in common with 'John You Went Too Far This Time' than the likes of 'He's Gonna Step On You Again' and 'Tokoloshe Man', UK hit singles the previous year by John Kongos, a South African – and a *Wedding Album*-period John Lennon lookalike – who freighted his songs with uncompromising lyrics born of the socio-political situation back home.

The music was strong enough for Kongos to ride roughshod over the principal worry about topical ditties: what becomes of them when they are no longer topical or the topic becomes tedious? That's how it was with John and Yoko's statements about the National Guard shooting rioting convicts in an upstate "correctional facility" ('Attica State'); a bloke receiving a ten-year gaol sentence for possession of an inappreciable amount of dope ('John Sinclair'); the troubles in Northern Ireland ('Sunday Bloody Sunday', 'The Luck Of The Irish'); and further current – and, generally, very North American – events and scandals.

Lennon was the central figure of one such *cause célèbre* himself. Though respected – or at least patronised – by powerful allies, his attempts to settle on US soil were hindered by, purportedly, ceaseless official harassment provoked by anti-government sentiments on *Sometime In New York City*, and his and Yoko's active part – an acoustic set – in a concert-*cum*-political rally in Ann Arbor, Michigan, on 10 December 1971 on behalf of marijuana miscreant John Sinclair, who was freed three days later.

The following August, the Lennons hosted a bigger spectacular, *One To One*, at Madison Square Garden for a children's charity, but that didn't serve as *quid pro quo* for the quashing of John's "moral turpitude" offence back in 1968. How can we ever know whether his splendid *One To One* effort – and a personal donation of $60,000 on top of the nigh-on $2 million dollars raised – was prompted by a simple desire to help or an ulterior motive? It was the same equation as those pop stars who pranced before the world at Live Aid in 1984.

Whatever the reason, it wouldn't wash with the US Immigration Department. This meant that John still had to keep reapplying for an extension of his visa to stay in the USA.

For all *Sometime In New York City*'s display of marital and artistic unity, the deportation notice that hung like a sword of Damocles over Lennon was among factors that were causing trouble in his marriage – so much trouble that he left Yoko in New York in 1973 for a 15-month "lost weekend" in California, where he lived with May Pang, her Chinese secretary, in a well-appointed ocean-side chalet, once owned by the Kennedys, in Santa Monica beneath the woodland sweep of the Hollywood hills. The place was open house for his circle of friends and friends of friends as well as callers like Alice Cooper, once and future Monkee Mickey Dolenz – and Paul McCartney.

Far more permanent a guest was Harry Nilsson, whose pop-star mystique had accumulated since *Aerial Ballet*, owing to out-of-focus publicity photographs and a reluctance to be interviewed. After Grammy -winning 'Everybody's Talkin'', more (mostly US) hits followed. The first of these was 'I Guess The Lord Must Be In New York City' from *Harry*, a third album that had been lauded in *Stereo Review* as "America's equivalent of *Sgt Pepper*".[85]

Surprisingly, Nilsson chose an interpretation of ten Randy Newman songs for his next album. After the market failure of *Nilsson Sings Newman* and an overlooked score for the film *Jenny*, he signed briefly – and never again – with a management company who procured him a role as a wandering folk singer in an episode of the television series *The Ghost Of Mrs Muir,* but "it was awful". He was of the same opinion of Otto Preminger's *Skidoo*, "possibly the worst film ever", but sodden with big names such as Groucho Marx, Mickey Rooney and George Raft – and a Nilsson soundtrack. Next came his "treatment" for *The Point*, the first ever feature-length cartoon film for television. It won many awards, and yielded another US chart entry in 'Me And My Arrow'.

Then Nilsson enjoyed a major international breakthrough (if mixed reviews) with 1971's *Nilsson Schmilsson*, recorded in London in June 1971 with help from famous mates. This contained three hit 45s, 'Without You' (a British and US Number One, written by two members of Badfinger), 'Coconut' and 'Jump Into The Fire'. He liked England enough to live there for a while, dwelling in the exclusive metropolitan flat where John and Yoko had holed up during the divorce from Cynthia – and where Keith Moon was to die. Some 50 old folk from a nearby Darby and Joan club would be featured as the choir on 'I'd Rather Be Dead' on *Son Of Schmilsson*, which, Nilsson's commercial tide-mark, brought another US Top 30 single, 'Spaceman'. The album was promoted in Britain via *Nilsson In Concert*, which, on the proviso that there would be no studio audience, was taped and shown on BBC2 – along with *The Point* – on New Year's Day 1972.

He failed to consolidate his success owing to an unsound decision to record *A Little Touch Of Schmilsson In The Night*, an album – possibly satirical – of orchestrated standards like 'Over The Rainbow', 'Makin' Whoopee' and 'As Time Goes By'. Produced by Derek Taylor, rejected tracks included 'Auld Lang Syne', 'I'm Always Chasing Rainbows' and 'Hey Jude'. Nilsson also overhauled selections from his first two LPs – as *Aerial Pandemonium Ballet*. I dare say it's heresy to say so to those in a 1960s repetend, but in nearly every case, it was a change for the better.

Yet, however much his critical standing had, on balance, improved, Nilsson's marriage, like John Lennon's, was failing. In much the same boat, Ringo Starr also strung along with John and Harry for three-in-the-morning bar-hopping followed by late-afternoon mutual grogginess by the Santa Monica swimming pool. Joining in the fun too was Keith Moon, The Who's chief show-off, whose buffoonery would often deteriorate into a nonsensical frenzy and, eventually, it would make headlines: explosives in hotel suites, slashing his wrists at the drop of a hat, and applying a lighter to his £150 pay packet for a day's film work (in days when £150 was worth something).

After accidentally running over and killing his chauffeur in 1970, Keith began punishing up to four decanters of spirits a day. More likely to fling a bottle at a television screen as rise from the armchair to switch it off, his fee for his last UK tour with The Who would be a paltry £40 on subtracting compensation for damage he'd inflicted along the way.

The instant fortune that had come his way since insinuating his way into the group in 1963 permitted Moon to think nothing of such costly indulgence. Mal Evans, however, was obliged to be more circumspect when, missing the activity and reflected glory of being a Beatles runaround, he left the family home in Surrey for sunny California, where, imagining his former masters needed him still, he rented an apartment near Santa Monica.

With Mal on board, the gang and its hangers-on were regular frequenters of topless bars, and were prone to gatecrashing parties and kerb-crawling. It wasn't uncommon for any one of them to wake with a hangover in a strange bed, unable to recollect the circumstances that had brought him there. Just as stories about Lennon in Hamburg had improved with age, so too did those of the Santa Monica coterie's escapades. Among these was one evolving from Moon coming across his boyhood hero, surf guitarist Dick Dale, at the Whiskey-A-Go-Go. "I was in the middle of a song," related Dick, "when he walked up on stage with Mal Evans. He was stoned, and he grabbed the mike right out of my face and said, 'Dick Dale, I'm Keith Moon of The Who.' Who? I'd never heard of The Who, but he told me – and everyone else – that he'd got John Lennon and Ringo on his solo album, *Both Sides Of The Moon*, and if Dick Dale didn't play on it, he'd junk the whole project."

As dilettantish were projects like Nilsson's slovenly *Pussycats*, which got underway simply because he, his Irish girlfriend, Lennon and May Pang "were sitting around with nothing to do, so we said, 'Let's do an album.'" With Starr, Moon and all the usual shower, he and producer John wrapped up *Pussycats* in New York after the sessions in Los Angeles had collapsed in a fog of drug abuse, which was discernible on a record that veered fitfully from long, leaden melodies to strident but oddly flat cracks at such as Dylan's 'Subterranean Homesick Blues', a mickey-taking 'Loop-De-Loop' – a fly-by-night rival to the Twist by one Johnny Thunder[86] – and a 'Rock Around The Clock', which was "speedy" in every sense of the word.

On the swift follow-up, *God's Greatest Hits* (retitled *Duit On Mon Dei* to placate the record company), Nilsson and his accomplices were also audibly half-seas over in an assortment of sub-'Without You' *Lieder* and unfunny gabblings on such as 'Good For God' and other perpetuations of an arrogance that encapsulated at its most loathsome the self-destructive disdain of the "superstar" for the record-buying public.

Further endeavours to stay the phantoms of middle age included Ringo securing an actress much given to exposing her bust, to recite Shakespeare during John's 34th birthday celebrations, and John's excessively worshipful and inebriated audience with Jerry Lee Lewis – whose own over-indulgence, brushes with the law and extreme domestic ructions had only enhanced the legend.

More widely reported was Lennon's ejection on 12 March 1974 – two years to the day after his US visa was revoked – from west Los Angeles' Troubadour, where, whilst drinking heavily, he had been constantly interrupting a show by The Smothers Brothers with interjections that included swearing and a recurrent "I'm John Lennon!" There were also allegations that he had assaulted both the comedy duo's manager and – with a sanitary towel attached to his forehead – one of the night club's waitresses, who was to file a complaint against him to the city's district attorney. Once outside the building, Lennon instigated another scuffle with a waiting photographer.

John managed to keep a civil tongue in his head the following night, when he and May Pang attended an American Film Institute dinner in honour of James Cagney, and a few weeks later, when he got together with Paul McCartney for a chat in the light of appeals from the United Nations for them, Ringo and George to do their bit for the Vietnamese boat people. There'd also been someone with more money than sense who was ready to shell out $50 million for just one more Beatles performance, even if there was a danger that what he'd hear might not be magic, just music.

Lennon was then in the throes of producing *Pussycats* at Los Angeles' suburban Burbank Studios, whilst taping demos back at Santa Monica. "We picked songs off the top of our heads and just did them,"[21] he shrugged. This strategy was very much in force when McCartney, staying at the Beverly Hilton Hotel, looked in – with Linda – at what were becoming fiascos at Burbank on Thursday 28 March 1974. Paul helped in trying to salvage an arrangement of 'Midnight Special', which was once in The Quarry Men's skiffle repertoire, and was invited to a musical evening the following Sunday at Lennon's house.

Present too would be Nilsson, guitarist Jesse Ed Davis – Eric Clapton's understudy at the Concerts *For Bangla Desh* – "supersideman" saxophonist Bobby Keyes and blind singing multi-instrumentalist Stevie Wonder, Tamla Motown's cosseted former child star, who'd notched up his first US hit, 'Fingertips', in 1963. He'd been on the bill with Lennon for both the John Sinclair benefit and the One To One concert.

As there were so many distinguished participants at Santa Monica, it was decided to keep a tape rolling for posterity – and the inevitable bootlegs – on equipment borrowed from Burbank. With McCartney choosing to beat the drums, they cranked out an interminable quasi-reggae version of Ben E King's much-covered 'Stand By Me', a slow and raucous 'Lucille' and, with Wonder to the fore, a medley of Sam Cooke's 'Cupid' and 'Chain Gang'.

These were punctuated by various meanderings during which were heard the intermittent strains of Bobby Byrd's 'Little Bitty Pretty One' – revived two years earlier by The Jackson Five – and, beneath, improvised lyrics by Paul, Santo and Johnny's 'Sleepwalk' instrumental from 1959, as well as blues-derived chord cycles over which Lennon, who bellyached throughout about the low volume of his voice in the headphones, kicked off an extrapolation that touched on his immigration woes.

None of the sung or spoken dialogue was anywhere as entertaining as that on the fêted "Troggs Tape" (an illicit recording in London of a cross purposes studio discussion riddled with rude words) and, musically, the clouds parting on the gods at play over in California revealed nothing more remarkable than what you might hear whenever any idle session crew warms up with loose jamming not intended for public ears.

Regardless of quality, however, it – and 'Midnight Special' at Burbank – amounted to a Lennon and McCartney reunion of sorts, though it wasn't the harbinger of any permanent amalgamation. Yet, if time hadn't healed, there lingered still memories of the struggle back in Liverpool and its unbelievable consequence. McCartney let slip that he wouldn't mind working with Lennon again on a less casual basis, while John was now saying how wrong it had been for the group to have split so decisively.

What's more, though the lines drawn over Allen Klein were among reasons for it, all the ex-Beatles were now of the same mind about one who'd overseen the solo careers of Lennon, Harrison and Starr until 1973. That's when their mustering of legal forces supported a new willingness to credit provocative tales – not all of them true – by their friends and various of Klein's incensed former clients of shifty manoeuvres and artful transfer of cash into his own account, passed off later by Keith Richards as "the price of an education".[87]

Klein was, nevertheless, not as greedy as he might have been – on paper anyway. Compared to some of his peers, who'd made themselves entitled to over half of everything their artists earned, the Robin Hood of Pop took but a fifth of what he'd actually secured. Yet, as John, George and Ringo unravelled enough supposed evidence of "excessive commissions" from Klein's mazy balance sheets to justify a court case, so the counter-suing Allen, once a hero, had been dyed a villain of the darkest hue by the time the blizzard of writs settled the various incoming monies into complex but defined financial streams running towards the respective deltas of Klein and each involved ex-Beatle's present and separate business executor – that is, George's Denis O'Brien, Ringo's Hilary Gerrard and John's Yoko.

Yet, while administrative matters were being resolved, Lennon, McCartney, Harrison and Starr's very vacillation over a reunion in the studio and, less likely, on the boards, indicated neither destitution nor any real enthusiasm. John and Ringo went back to the woozy vortex of Santa Monica, Paul to Wings and the simple life on his Sussex farm, and George to an ill-judged North American tour.

John was the only former Beatle to send George a bouquet of first-night flowers, and the two had nattered affably enough at one post-concert party. At another, however, everything turned red as hell for Harrison, and he saw himself rounding on Lennon and the flat of his hand shooting out in an arc to make glancing contact with John's spectacles. These clacked onto the ground and, while John was grubbing for them, George was loud enough to be heard in Liverpool. The subsequent tongue-lashing streamlined what had become, in Lennon's estimation, "a love-hate relationship of a younger follower and older guy. I think George still bears resentment towards me for being a daddy who left home."[21] This time, the "hate" sprang specifically from John's procrastination over signing some papers relating to The Beatles – and that John hadn't taken up an open invitation to join George onstage one night during the troubled tour to do a turn as a surprise treat for the fans.

No more the tough guy that he'd never been, Lennon "saw George going through pain – and I know what pain is – so I let him do it".[27]

The hatchet was never quite buried, and, as the months turned into years, only infrequent postcards filtered between Harrison and Lennon. Other than that, they knew each other only via hearsay and stray paragraphs in the press – and John was to be wounded by the "glaring omissions"[21] of him from George's pricey autobiography, *I Me Mine*.[88]

This volume was published early in 1980 when a musical, *Beatlemania*, shattered box-office records in London's West End and a sign appeared outside Mendips – from which Aunt Mimi had long gone – reading OFFICIAL NOTICE. PRIVATE. NO ADMISSION. MERSEYSIDE COUNTY COUNCIL for the benefit of foreign visitors, mostly from the USA and Japan, pouring huge amounts into the English Tourist Board's coffers for conducted treks round Liverpool to such shrines.

By 1980 too, Beatles conventions had become annual fixtures in cities across the globe, complete with guest speakers, archive film and forums for fans to reveal "My Beatles Experiences" as well as trivia quizzes, "celebrity" discussion panels, showings of ancient film footage, sound-alike contests and continual community singing to acoustic guitars. Life-size displays of LP covers might enable you to "be photographed with the Boys", and a mock-up of Abbey Road studio plus 40 pre-recorded Xeroxes of Beatle backing tracks may cater for less tangible fantasies. Along a single corridor at one such extravaganza, I passed a Cynthia Lennon lookalike, a high-buttoned moptop and a Sgt Pepper bandsman.

All the major conventions hire groups that are, if anything, even more contrived than Los Shakers, The Beatlettes, The Monkees *et al*, with their big-nosed drummers, moon-faced bass players; handles like "Walrus", "Cavern", "The Blue Meanies", "Abbey Road" and "The Beetle Brothers"; and *raisons d'être* centred on impersonating the founders of the feast, note for note, word for word, mannerism for mannerism. On a global scale, the most famous are The Bootleg Beatles, formed from the cast of *Beatlemania*. Maybe the most accurate copycats anywhere, they cover every phase, from the coming of Ringo to the end of the Swinging '60s, via cleverly co-ordinated costume changes.

While the ex-Beatles themselves have proffered saleable artefacts for charity auctions at these events, none – bar Pete Best – has ever attended one. Instead, "special guests" have been drawn from old colleagues, former employees – and, scraping the barrel, authors of Beatle biographies. A typical example is Sam Leach, an unsung hero of Merseybeat when compared to the Brian Epsteins and Bill Harrys of this world. However, as perhaps the era's most adventurous promoter – the one responsible for John, Paul, George and Pete's terrible journey to Aldershot – Sam cut a popular figure at a 1992 convention in Chicago. The Yanks couldn't get enough of him retelling anecdotes from the old days in his lush wacker dialect, and presenting well-argued theories about the Liverpool beat explosion and its aftermath, whether on the podium in the ballroom or whilst signing books and posters at his stall in a memorabilia fleamarket, which dwarfed any in Britain, even Liverpool's *Merseybeatle* weekend.

Customers covered a waterfront and ranged from babes-in-arms to pensioners, but mostly young marrieds disenfranchised by post-*Abbey Road* pop and older individuals who once might have been part of a screaming mass as amorphous as frogspawn at this or that stop on a Beatles US tour. Since then, they'd settled into jobs and parenthood – but while 'She Loves You' or 'I Feel Fine' yet spins its little life away, balding Weybridge stockbrokers and face-lifted Minneapolis hairdressers will become irresponsible Swinging '60s teenagers again.

Nothing by The Beatles had ever been deleted, and because EMI/Capitol still owned the master tapes, it had been able to run riot with posthumous million-selling double albums like the all up-tempo *Rock 'n' Roll Music*, which, in the States, spawned a smash 45 in 'Got To Get You Into My Life', culled from *Revolver*. Meanwhile, Britain experienced the chart-swamping aftermath of 20 Beatles singles being repromoted on the same spring day in 1976, almost a quarter of a century after 'Love Me Do'. Perusing the UK Top 40, a correspondent from *Time* magazine enquired rhetorically, "Has a successor to The Beatles finally been found? Not at all – it is The Beatles themselves."[89]

12 *"Who'd Want To Be An 80-Year-Old Beatle?"*

Guest speakers at Beatles conventions are two-a-penny compared to the diehard fan who can tell you at a second's notice, say, the B-side of the Australian pressing of 'Cry For A Shadow'. Many doctors regard such a skill as a mental disorder, even giving it a name, Asperger's Syndrome. Being mad about The Beatles, however, is a more socially acceptable pastime – even obsession – than, say, accumulating information about donkeys' false teeth, collating the reference matrixes of electricity pylons or, as is the case of a lady from Sunderland, believing that, by entering the loins of her (now estranged) husband, the ghost of a certain country and western entertainer whose records she collected had impregnated her with the son she would have baptised "Jim Reeves".

How did yours start? Was it because your first remotely romantic encounter – a chaperoned kiss under the mistletoe – was soundtracked by The Dave Clark Five's 'Do You Love Me'? Maybe a patrol leader you had a crush on at Girl Guides mentioned that she was keen on Bolton Wanderers or Sean Connery. You plan your life and bank balance around a soccer team's away matches. You watch the same movie so often that you can recite the script by heart. You holiday in a different overseas resort every summer just to seek out and buy your favourite group's discs issued by an alien company. Attic floors groan beneath the weight of memorabilia.

The worst aspects of Beatles idolatry are likely to be represented forever by the homicidal Mark David Chapman – but, as Bob Dylan reminds us in 'The Times They Are A-Changin'', we shouldn't criticise what we can't understand. When John, Paul, George and Ringo landed in New York in 1964, Chapman was eight and living with his parents and younger sister in Atlanta, Georgia. He compiled the first of many scrapbooks that kept track of The Beatles' ever-unfolding career. By the time Mark's voice broke, every nook and cranny of his bedroom was crammed with Beatles' merchandise: pictures of them all over the walls, and piles of records with label variations, foreign picture sleeves and the canons of associated artists: the Word made vinyl in the comfort of his own home. His function then was to remain uninvolved directly, just to absorb the signals as they came.

For hundreds, thousands of hours, he'd file, catalogue and gloat over his acquisitions, finding much to notice, study and compare. Discs by The Beatles, corporate and solo, from different countries made the same sounds, but there were visual differences. When 'I Feel Fine' was released in the Netherlands, Dutch Parlophone was in the final months of using the old logo – with the firm's name in large capital letters across the top of the label, and an additional "45" prefix at the start of the catalogue number. The second pressing stuck to the same fundamental design, except that it was printed in a more compact typeface. This is most noticeable on the song title. Another intriguing feature is that "McCartney" is misspelt in the composing credits. The Dutch 'I Feel Fine' also had a push-out rather than solid centre.

Should you express polite interest, Mark would probably explain apologetically that nobody got to *look* at it, much less *hear* it. The Beatles wasn't about enjoyment any more, but being addicted as surely as someone else can be to heroin. Wanting to learn everything possible about them, no piece of information was too insignificant to be less than totally absorbing. Mark could dwell very eloquently and with great authority on his interest, but couldn't grasp why fellow pupils at Columbia High School were not as captivated. The ones kind enough not to look fed up regarded the rather pudgy youth in round John Lennon glasses as otherwise "just a real quiet, normal guy".[5] Descriptions of him by others ranged from "slightly eccentric" to "a creeping Jesus", but Mark had taken his Beatles' fixation too far now to care any more than a chimp in the zoo does about what the people looking through the bars think.

When he graduated in 1973, the Fat Owl of Columbia High had experienced both LSD and, fleetingly, the glory and the stupidity of being in a pop group. In keeping with a mood of the early 1970s, he was now professing to be a born-again Christian. Two years later, Mark was working amongst Vietnamese refugees on a reservation in Arkansas, pleasing his superiors with his diligence and aptitude for the most onerous of tasks. Through the love of a good woman, he was contemplating enrolling at a theological college. No longer outwardly living his life through The Beatles, it was a period that he'd recognise as the nearest he'd ever come to contentment.

Chapman's future victim, however, was in a bad state. Flitting between California and New York, John Lennon had grown fatter, if less publicly ridiculous. Glassy-eyed musings and vocational turbulence also slopped over onto albums like *Pussycats* and Ringo's *Goodnight Vienna* – with a title track by Lennon. Because both he and Ringo were enthusiastic listeners to Johnny Winter, a boss-eyed and albino Texan bluesman who'd had been catapulted from regional celebrity to the front page of *Rolling Stone*, Lennon contributed 'Rock 'n' Roll People' for 1974's *John Dawson Winter* album, a delayed reaction to a captivation with 1969's Grammy winning 'The Thrill Is Gone,' the only mainstream pop hit by BB King, one of the few surviving links between post-war blues and mid-1970s rock.

John's own *Mind Games* in 1973, however, was as so-so as *Goodnight Vienna*; yet *Walls And Bridges*, if rehashing some old ideas, still effused potent singles in ethereal 'Number Nine Dream' – which, as usual, climbed far higher in North American charts than anywhere else – and, also in 1974, the US Number One 'Whatever Gets You Through The Night'. This was recorded with help from Elton John, a now famous singing pianist, who had first become known to Lennon when Xeroxing the hits of others for EMI's *Music For Pleasure* budget label (to which *Mind Games* was to be consigned one day) before metamorphosing into a cross between Liberace and a male Edna Everage.

Another British star omnipresent in the States then was David Bowie, no longer a glam rocker, but touring as a blue-eyed soul man, a fair indication of the direction he was to pursue on his forthcoming *Young*

Americans album. It was through this that John Lennon made his most iconoclastic contribution to 1970s popular culture. As his "lost weekend" approached its Sunday evensong, he'd been invited to a Bowie session for a resuscitation of 'Across The Universe' – from *Let It Be* – in New York. There, he ended up co-writing 'Fame', *Young Americans*' infectious US chart topper, with David and an awe-struck Carlos Alomar, a highly waged guitarist of urgent precision and inventiveness. This and his apprenticeship in James Brown's employ qualified him for the house band at the trend-setting Sigma Sound complex, from which had emanated Philadelphia's feathery soul style earlier in the decade.

All three writers of 'Fame' were present at a Grammy awards ceremony at the Uris Hotel in New York on 1 March 1975. John was sporting a lapel badge that read "ELVIS" – who, back on the concert platform, displayed ardour for little but the most conservative post-Beatles pop. Moreover, in an amazing and ramblingly respectful letter to President Nixon, he had requested enrolment as a federal agent in order to fight "the Hippie Element".

Unconscious of his boyhood hero's reactionary tendencies, John Lennon – who evidently typified all that he detested – was seen at one of a dismayingly portly Memphis Flash's grandiloquent pageants at 20,000-capacity Madison Square Garden, where the King included songs that had fuelled the ex-Beatle's adolescent imaginings. His stock-in-trade, however, was mainly country pop ('Kentucky Rain', 'Sweet Caroline' *et al*) plus bursts of patriotism like 'American Trilogy' and just plain 'America' – and the last that John, like most people, would ever see of him would be in the white garb of a rhinestone cowboy *sans* stetson.

As regressive in its way as seeing Presley was Lennon's growing collection of Beatles bootlegs – dating as far back as rehearsals in early 1960 with Paul, George and Stuart – and recording 1975's non-original *Rock 'n' Roll*, its content telegraphed on the sleeve by a photograph of 1961 Hamburg vintage and the artist's own sentiment: "You should have been there".

Its spin-off single – which rose to Number 20 in the States, 30 in Britain – was another stab at 'Stand By Me'. As well as the Ben E King prototype from 1961, Lennon was also up against moderately successful covers later in the 1960s by Kenny Lynch and Cassius Clay (Muhammad Ali). Viewers of BBC 2's *Old Grey Whistle Test* on 18 April 1975 were treated to an *in situ* film of Lennon at the microphone in New York's Record Plant, delivering both an exaggerated broad wink at the camera and 'Stand By Me' with its curiously stentorian vocal. Neither were very appealing.

Having gone full-cycle professionally with this plus other favourites that The Beatles may or may not have performed in the Hamburg era, and a greatest hits collection entitled *Shaved Fish*, Lennon chose to take a year off to master his inner chaos and take professional and personal stock. At a press conference back in 1964, he'd answered a question about retirement with a rhetorical "Who'd want to be an 80-year-old Beatle?"[90] Well, he was nearly halfway there now.

Reunited with Yoko – who'd been with him at the Grammy Awards at the Uris Hotel – John was finally granted US residential status. His and his wife's happiness was completed by the arrival of their only surviving baby, Sean, by caesarian section on John's 35th birthday. The very proud father judged this to be an appropriate moment to extend the "year off" indefinitely to become Yoko's quasi-incommunicado "house husband" in the apartments they'd purchased in New York's snooty Dakota block. This retreat was, he felt, the "karmic reaction" to the holocaust of pop, summed up by his much-quoted, "Don't bother trying to make it, because when you do there's nothing to make".[91]

Besides, the gang had broken up long ago. Having gained no contentment from following John and Ringo to California, Mal Evans's slaughter on 5 January 1976 by gun-toting police – after a woman alleged he'd threatened her with what turned out to be an air-pistol – was said by some to have been a form of suicide.

While Mal's extinction was unexpected, few were caught unawares entirely on 7 September 1978 by Keith Moon's body's final rebellion after a lifetime of violation. As he drifted away on the tide of twice the recognised lethal intake of a potion to combat his alcoholism, his last utterance was to tell his girlfriend to get lost.

However, with remarriage and the birth of his eldest son, Harry Nilsson – as heavy a drinker as Moon – was perhaps the first of the Santa Monica clique to pull back from the abyss. Artistically, he proved capable still of the odd startling moment, such as the composition of 'Easy For

Me', the strongest track on Ringo Starr's *Goodnight Vienna,* but his living rested mostly on earlier achievements, exemplified by a 1978 stage adaptation of *The Point* in London's West End starring former Monkees Mickey Dolenz and Davy Jones.

Nilsson continued to grind out one album per year until the RCA contract expired. On 1980's *Flash Harry,* he was to mobilise illustrious contemporaries again, among them John Lennon – though their friendship had cooled because he was regarded by then as the proverbial "bad influence" by Yoko. Indeed, he passed much of the next decade jet-setting whilst nursing debilities not unrelated to the stimulants that had been common currency amongst the "superstar" elite in the 1970s.

A proposed 1993 album contained a revival of The Platters' 'Only You' – a rediscovered duet with Lennon, *circa* 1974 – and a huge helping of comic songs like 'UCLA', 'All In The Mind', 'Try' and 'Animal Farm'. Now dried out, Nilsson was making the most of whatever new opportunities came his way whilst looking forward to the past as a regular speaker at Beatle conventions where, before his death in 1994, he engaged in question-and-answer sessions and, surprisingly for one once well known for *never* singing in public, even performed a couple of numbers onstage.

Meanwhile, Lennon had elected not so much to settle cosily into middle age on the consolidated fruits of his success, but to find out what else awaited him on the other side of the Santa Monica interlude, when he'd been unable to make long-term plans. Whatever was wrong appeared to be righting itself. The intolerable adulation, the smash hits, the money down the drain could be transformed to matters of minor importance compared to the peaceful life he felt he deserved, the potential for domestic stability, and providing young Sean with the best of everything, especially more paternal attention than most – certainly far more than John ever had.

It was enough as well to be on the way to tolerable health after all the physical and mental vicissitudes his 35 unquiet years had sustained. In the title track to a 1979 album, *Rust Never Sleeps,* Neil Young, an *après*-Woodstock bedsit bard, was to whinge lines like "It's better to burn out than to fade away", which seemed to laud the banal live-fast-die-young philosophy involuntarily played out by Jimi Hendrix, Jim Morrison, Janis Joplin, Keith Moon, Sid Vicious and like unfortunates chewed upon and spat out by the pop industry. "For what?" inquired John during one of his last interviews. "So that we might rock? If Neil Young admires that sentiment so much, why doesn't he do it?"[21]

Every day he still lived was a bonus now that John Lennon had let go, stopped trying to prove himself – though if he had abandoned the world, the world hadn't abandoned him, not while his work was kept before the public via, say, The Damned's high-velocity overhaul of 'Help!' in 1976, or a revival of 'Working Class Hero' by Marianne Faithfull in a voice grippingly bereft of any former soprano purity on 1979's *Broken English*, an album that was as much a fixture in student halls of residence in the late '70s as a poster of Che Guevara's mug had been years earlier.

A centre-page *NME* article pleaded for if not a full-time return, then Lennon's blessing on the burgeoning punk movement, but it elicited no immediate response from one no longer preoccupied with cooking up marketable food of love and sprinkling it with cheap insight. Nothing from John Lennon, not even another repackaging, would show its face in the charts from a belated appearance of 'Imagine' in the UK Top Ten in November 1975 until '(Just Like) Starting Over' in November 1980. Neither would a solitary new melody or lyric be heard commercially from him after 'Cookin' (In The Kitchen Of Love)', a self-satisfied donation to *Ringo's Rotogravure* in 1976. What right had anyone to expect more? He said as much in a brief and reluctantly granted press conference in Japan a year later.

Lennon's was almost as sweeping an exit from public life as that of the great Belgian *chansonnier* Jacques Brel, who chose to "stop once and for all this idiotic game"[92] – in 1975 too – by fleeing to the last bolt-hole his fans and the media would expect to find him, namely the remote Pacific island where the painter Paul Gauguin had lived out his last years.

Brel and Lennon weren't the only ones to fling it all back in their faces. An unnerving spell of ballroom one-nighters – which included a date at the Star-Club – had caused Twinkle, a swinging London dolly-bird who scored a UK hit with 1965's 'Terry', a 'Leader Of The Pack'-like "death disc", to retire as a full-time pop star at the age of 17.

Once as famous for composing John Leyton's chartbusting 'Johnny Remember Me' in 1960 as Twinkle was for 'Terry', Geoff Goddard was depressed over a messy legal dispute over infringement of copyright in 1964. This brought about his sudden if calculated withdrawal into anonymity in the catering department at the University of Reading, where workmates would deduce from the odd secret smile and what was left unsaid that Geoff had, indeed, Hit The Big Time long ago and far away. A rapid weariness of the shabbier aspects of the record business also led to guitarist Brian Pendleton leaving The Pretty Things in 1965 when he got off a train *en route* to some dates up north. "We went round to his flat afterwards," said Phil May, "and it was like the *Marie-Celeste*."

The *ultima Thule* of pop hermits, however, is Syd Barrett, whose departure from The Pink Floyd in 1968 was on a par with John Lennon, unable to cope with being a Beatle after 'From Me To You', scurrying back to Woolton to dwell in seclusion with Aunt Mimi, or – as actually happened – Chris Curtis washing his hands of The Searchers in 1966 for the security of the civil service.

Hearsay painted the likes of Scott Walker, The Move's charismatic bass player Chris "Ace" Kefford and no less than three Fleetwood Mac guitarists – Peter Green, Jeremy Spencer and Danny Kirwan – in similar hues. They seemed to live outwardly unproductive lives in which nothing much was calculated to happen, year in, year out.

All these examples are the tip of an iceberg of pop artists who, on growing to adulthood in the hothouse of pop's turbulent and endless adolescence, made deliberate attempts to jump the gun and become nobodies again before their time in the limelight was up.

Yet they never quite became nobodies. Self-deception, genuine belief and the balm of ignorance become jumbled as such a recluse's enigma deepens. A legend takes shape, bringing out the strangest yarns. As with the Loch Ness Monster, there'd be purported sightings – of Spencer as a street-corner evangelist, Kirwan as a down-and-out, a brain-scrambled Green as a grave digger. Now something in the City, Brian Pendleton stonewalled a Pretty Things train spotter who accosted him in a Virgin megastore. Someone insists that, wild and pathetic, Walker was prowling an otherwise uninhabited peninsula in the Hebrides like a mad Robinson Crusoe, and that Kefford had revealed his identity during a death-bed confession after spending his final world-weary years in spiritual contemplation. Someone else swears that Jacques Brel had been observed plucking guitar in a cocktail jazz combo as customers chattered in a Hawaiian bar.

Thus it was that, in the teeth of a possibly dull truth, John Lennon continued to fascinate the English-speaking pop world as much as Brel did the Gallic one. Mention of Lennon during his so-called "house husband" years still brings out strange tales of what alleged "insiders" claim they heard and saw.

The mildest of these were that he had albums of The Goons on instant replay, and that he was also "into" new age, the only wave of essentially instrumental music to have reached a mass public since jazz rock in the mid-1970s. You hear it today in hip dental surgeries. Is it merely aural wallpaper or low-stress "music for the whole body" to ease the ravages of modern life? Do you buy it with the same discrimination as you would three pounds of spuds?

A wholesome diet figured prominently in Lennon's new life too. When filling in the *NME*'s "Lifelines" questionnaire early in 1963, George, Paul and Ringo had all chosen chicken, lamb and steak cuisine as their favourite foods while John went for non-committal "curry and jelly".[93] He had acquired such a comparatively exotic taste via Pete Best's Indian mother and, later, in a Britain where most restaurants that served a late-night square meal were Indian or Chinese. Otherwise, during that year's travelling life of snatched and irregular meals, The Beatles' palates had been coarsened by chips with everything in wayside snack bars. It had been the same back in meat-happy Hamburg, where menus in establishments like Der Fludde, Harold's Schnellimbiss and Zum Pferdestalle (which translates as "the Horses' Stable") favoured horsemeat casserole, *Labskaus* (a *mélange* of corned beef, herrings, mashed potato and chopped gherkins, topped with a fried egg) and *Deutsch bifsteak*. A search for a nut roast would be fruitless as all over Europe in the early 1960s vegetarianism was an eccentricity and an inconvenience for dinner-party hosts.

None of The Beatles had, therefore, ever seriously considered adopting vegetarianism, even when they had the means to order more than beans on toast. On the run around the world, gourmet dishes with specious names – *trepang* soup, veal Hawaii, *furst puckler* – pampered stomachs yearning for the greasy comfort of cod and chips eaten with the fingers.

Nevertheless, after the decision to quit touring, Lennon was the first, apparently, to at least try a meat-free diet – though Cynthia and Julian didn't then. Later, he backslid, justifying himself in 1980 with "We're mostly macrobiotic – fish and rice and whole grains – but sometimes I bring the family out for a pizza. Intuition tells you what to eat."[21] Nowadays, he was studying cookery books and baking bread, monitoring Sean's meals with a detail that dictated how many times each bite was to be masticated, and undergoing long fasts when only mineral water and fruit and vegetable juices entered his mouth.

A story leaked out later that he was also swallowing temazepam-like relaxants. Among the side-effects were stream-of-consciousness monologues, directed as much to himself as anyone listening, and mood swings from I'm-a-dirty-dog self-reproach to rhapsodies of peculiar exaltation. Straight up. A mate of mine told me.

By thus internalising, was John Lennon running away from himself in a place where, in his heart of hearts, he didn't want to be? What seems to be true is that, encouraged by his wife, he began spending lonely holidays progressively further afield – Bermuda, Cape Town, Hong Kong, anywhere that was the opposite of the Dakota, where life with Yoko wasn't exactly Phyllis and Corydon in Arcady.

Yoko had become quite the astute business person, ably representing John at Beatles business meetings and investing particularly wisely in properties and agriculture. What he called "work" was attempting to write a third book – "about 200 pages of *In His Own Write*-ish mad stuff"[21] – and now and then tuning his acoustic guitar after breakfast. After strumming and picking for a while, all the fragments of music he was struggling to turn into a composition would sound flat. Then his fingers would start barre-ing the old, old chord changes from when the world was young. Languor would set in and he'd let out an involuntary sigh. Maybe he'd knuckle down to it properly tomorrow. What was the use, in any case, of continuing to mine the same worn-out creative seams over and over again from new angles in wrong-headed expectation of finding gold?

When his former songwriting partner, six-string in hand, attempted to visit the Dakota one day, Paul McCartney was sent away by a harassed John via an intercom message: "Please call before you come over. It's not 1956, and turning up at the door isn't the same any more. You know, just give me a ring."[21] Neither could Lennon bring himself so much as to put his head round the door when McCartney, with Harrison and Starr, met Yoko in the same building to discuss further the division of the empire.

Yet belying a growing legend of Lennon as "The Howard Hughes of Pop", both Mike McCartney – Paul's brother – and Gerry Marsden were able to reach him. "I didn't see John for many years when he was in the States," reminisced Gerry, "or hear much about him other than what I read in the papers. Then once when I was appearing in New York, I called him after a gap of nearly a decade of not communicating, and it was just as if the days of the Seamen's Mission in Hamburg hadn't gone." Moreover, a chance encounter with Lennon in some Bermudan watering-hole caused one journalist to report that not only did the myth-shrouded John stand his round but that his songwriting well wasn't as dry as many imagined. This was confirmed in August 1980, when he and Ono recorded sufficient new material to fill two albums.

The first of these, *Double Fantasy* – which could almost be filed under "Easy Listening" – was issued that autumn, when, from Rip Van Winkle-esque vocational slumber, a fit-looking 40-year-old was suddenly available for interviews again with the unblinking self-assurance of old. He was even talking about a return to the stage, now that such innovations as programmable consoles and graphic equalisers were doing battle against adverse auditorium acoustics. He'd understood too that in sports stadia and exposition centres – especially in the States and Germany – a performance by a pop Methuselah could enthrall Cecil B de Mille-sized crowds. Framed by sky-clawing scaffolding, giant video screens and lighting gantries like oil derricks, you'd be louder and clearer than ever before.

Some of the faithful might have preferred John's to remain an ever-silent "no return" saga rather than him perhaps trying and failing to debunk the myth of an artistic death. However much they might have gainsaid it, they didn't want a comeback from someone who would thrive on goodwill with a side-serving of morbid inquisitiveness, a Judy Garland among Swinging '60s pop heroes. Let's keep the memory of a jewellery- rattling 'Twist And Shout' at the Royal Command Performance and a bow-legged profile defined by an *Ed Sullivan Show* arc light. Otherwise, the sweet mystery will rest in pieces.

It appeared, however, that John Lennon meant business, and maybe, like his pal Elton John, was set to enter middle life as a fully integrated mainstay and wanted party guest of contemporary rock's ruling class. Though May Pang was to maintain that most of the "new" material had been written long before, he seemed rejuvenated as a composer too, as there were plenty of numbers left from both the two albums and stark demos of songs – like 'Free As A Bird' and 'Real Love' – which he'd taped as far back as 1975. There were, indeed, enough for for him to present Life Begins At 40 and three more to Ringo when, in November 1980, the two ex-Beatles spoke for the last time, and parted as good friends.

John Lennon and Mark Chapman were more than good friends – at least, in Mark's mind. Something enormous if perverse had taken place, possibly as a sublimation of the depression brought on by parting with his girlfriend, an unhappy espousal on the rebound, his parents' divorce and a general psychological malaise. With everything else in his life now stripped away, the old Beatles craving had reared up with a vengeance. This time around, however, Mark was perceiving directives from them – to the degree that he was certain that he'd been sent a telepathic message from John. "I know you and you know me," it read. "We understand each other in a secret way." They had become as one.

Chapman was, therefore, no longer someone not far removed from a rabid supporter of a football team. He had evolved too strong a need to affiliate himself to a world of fantasy from which he would never emerge unless he received regular psychiatric monitoring, even residential care – which, in a manner of speaking, he would do, albeit too late.

During the autumn preceding that eerie Christmas in 1980, Mark David decided that the chief Beatle's control of his life could not remain remote, hence, he finished his last shift as a security guard in Hawaii – signing off as "John Lennon" – and appeared in New York as if from nowhere early in December. The needle was in a big haystack, but it was the right haystack.

He was in high spirits, despite the body pressure and the chatter when being jolted from the airport by internal railway to the city centre. It was a moment of quiet joy when he stood at last outside the Dakota, looking upwards, paying muttered homage and wondering what was busying those rooms at that very minute. For hours daily, he stood on that pavement with all his soul in his eyes, totally desensitised to the stares of passers-by as he continued to gaze at what he could make out of outlines that seemed to dart across the Dakota's windows. He felt endlessly patient and vaguely enchanted that his vigil might last forever.

Then something incredible happened! Twilight was falling on Monday 8 December when John – with Yoko – strolled out of the building. Of the few pop stars Mark had ever seen close up, nearly every one had disappointed him. Bob Dylan, for example, had looked like someone who looked a bit like Bob Dylan. However, for all the sunken cheeks and expected ravages of middle age, the person who was crossing the sidewalk, with a slightly pigeon-toed gait and hair frisking in the cold breeze, was 100 per cent John Lennon. The Quarry Bank school tie he'd taken to wearing in recent photographs wasn't in evidence, but he wasn't that much different from the way he'd appeared in "The Beatnik Horror!".

What do you say when you meet God?

Mark did not assume an instant intimacy with one who'd opened a door to his psyche, even though no one knew Lennon like he did. For a split-second, John stared at Mark, almost with dislike, as if he resented his adoration. Obviously, he was suffering from shock and could not grasp the magnitude of the encounter.

Then, in one soundless moment, that adoration was extinguished like a moth in a furnace. After assuming that all he had to do was autograph another copy of *Double Fantasy* – "Is that OK? Is that what you want?"⁵ – John Lennon sort of smirked like Billy Fury had when signing his name for a Silver Beatle in 1960.

That was all. It came and went in the blink of an eye. Yet in that instant, Mark saw a stranger. Had they always been strangers? Had there never been anything special between them in the first place? Lord, I believe: help thou my unbelief. But that was when the being Chapman had worshipped for three decades mutated before him into just The Man Who Used To Be John Lennon.

He sauntered off, and Hell's magnet began to drag Mark David Chapman down. Before the day was done, Mark would be standing on the same spot with a smoking revolver in his hand. Yards away, The Man Who Used To Be John Lennon would be grovelling and open-mouthed with his life's blood puddling out of him.

13 "The Look Of Fated Youth"

In common with everyone else who cared, Gerry Marsden remembers the very moment he received the news. In his house on the Wirral, he was wrenched from sleep at 5am that mind-boggling Tuesday by a call from Liverpool's Radio City. With phlegmatic detachment, Gerry "went back to sleep. It wasn't the kind of information I expected to turn out to be true."

When the world woke up, John Lennon had not recovered from being dead. Marsden decided that "the only thing to do was to carry on with some kind of routine to get rid of the shock". He chose not to cancel a business meeting in Bradford in the face of constant attempts to reach him by the media. Yorkshire Television landed the biggest scoop by persuading Gerry to sing 'Imagine' on *Calendar*, an early-evening magazine programme.

As it was with the early death of Hollywood heart-throb Rudolph Valentino in 1926, the slaying of Lennon had sparked off suicides by mid-morning – though there were to be no reported deed-poll Lennons, bedroom shrines, séances and letters written to him years after 8 December 1980. Furthermore, his death was too public for anyone to manufacture a survival story. John was never to be spotted behind the counter in a Dagenham fish-and-chip shop, moustached and crewcut in a Canberra suburb or opening a bank account in Copenhagen.

Conspiracy theories, nevertheless, had been flying up and down when flags were still at half mast and the wireless was broadcasting the dead man's music continuously in place of listed programmes. Was it an Art Statement more surreal than anything John and Yoko did post-*Two*

Virgins? Had Yoko reneged on an elaborate suicide pact? Was John cursed with "the look of fated youth",[94] as suggested in a *Daily Express* editorial (which thanked fate the next day that it hadn't been the "much more talented"[95] Paul McCartney instead)?

How about a rite by which the kingdom of the "Beatle generation", now with paunches and punk children, was rejuvenated by the sacrifice of its leader – well, one of them – in his prime? The same had happened to certain Greek, Roman and Norse fertility gods as well as King Arthur, Harold Godwinsson, William Rufus, Charles I – beheaded in his climacteric seven-times-seventh year – and John F Kennedy. The Victim's awareness of his role is irrelevant. The point is that the common people – some of them, anyway – believed that he had been slaughtered for them and their land. It said as much in *The Golden Bough*, and it was visible on general release in *The Wicker Man*, a 1973 B-feature that Lennon – and Mark David Chapman – may well have seen, in which a far-flung Scottish island reverts to pagan ways in hope of rich harvests.

For all the mystical, arty and political analogies that went the rounds, most people reckoned that John Lennon had been killed simply because Chapman, who'd also been sighted sniffing around Bob Dylan, was as nutty as a fruitcake – though he was to be confined not to a mental institution but gaol after he pleaded guilty, saying in effect, "I insist on being incarcerated for at least the next 20 years."

In New York's Attica Correctional Facility – the setting of Lennon's 'Attica State' from *Sometime In New York City* – Mark served his sentence, spending most of it separated from other prisoners for the sake of his own safety, particularly when he seemed to be becoming something of a celebrity as the focal point of a video documentary and numerous magazine features.

However, eligible for parole again, an apparently remorseful and rehabilitated Chapman is, if freed, likely to become, advisedly, as reclusive as his victim was during the "house husband years". In prison, he'd refused written requests for autographs, remarking, "This tells you something is truly sick in our society. I didn't kill John to become famous, and I'm horrified by these people."[5]

When Mark Chapman first began amassing this supposedly unlooked-for immortality, John's side of the tragedy had bequeathed unto *Double Fantasy* and its follow-up, *Milk And Honey*, an undeserved "beautiful sadness" – with particular reference to tender 'Beautiful Boy', which told five-year-old Sean Lennon of "what happens to you when you're busy making other plans", and 'Hard Times Are Over' with its line about "you and I walking together round a street corner".

Elsewhere, 'Watching The Wheels', 'Nobody Told Me' – which borrowed the tune of 'Mama Said', a Shirelles B-side – and the remaindered 'Help Me To Help Myself' were riven with an amused, grace-saving cynicism, while the first *Double Fantasy* single, '(Just Like) Starting Over', hinted at Lennon's Merseybeat genesis.

Overall, however, both *Double Fantasy* and *Milk And Honey* were bland, middle-of-the-road efforts musically – with the former's 'Woman' reminding me vaguely of Bread's slushy 1970 hit, 'Make It With You'. As for the lyrics, smug, slight statements were made by a rich, refined couple long detached from the everyday. Once, their antics had been wilder than those of any punk rocker, but with 1981 approaching, John and Yoko had been derided by punks and hippies alike as indolent, Americanised breadheads.

Be that as it may, Lennon's passing was a boom time for those with vested interest – who regarded his absence as no more of a hindrance than Elvis Presley's stint of square bashing in Germany had been for Colonel Tom Parker. Indeed, when the King died suddenly in 1977, record-store windows had bloomed with his splendour. He was scarcely off Top 40 radio and was swamping many national charts six or seven repromoted singles and albums at a time.

Likewise, universal grief and an element of ghoulish Beatlemania was to reverse the fall of *Double Fantasy* and '(Just Like) Starting Over' from their respective listings as Christmas petered out, and John Lennon would score a hat-trick of British Number Ones within weeks, an achievement that matched that of his Beatles in the dear, dead Swinging '60s. Out of sympathy too, Yoko engineered her only solo Top 40 entry – with 'Walking On Thin Ice' – in February 1981, thus lending further credence to the cruel old joke: death is a good career move.

The next time her poor husband made the charts, however, was in 1982 when 'Beatles Movie Medley' reached the Top 20 in both Britain and the States. Always it boiled down to The Beatles. Yet, in interview, George Harrison in particular underlined his boredom with the ceaseless fascination with the group – a fascination that was to escalate with the runaway success in 1994 of *Live At The BBC*, a compilation of early broadcasts.

This prefaced an official proclamation of a coming anthology of further items from the vaults. These were to be hand picked by George, Paul and Ringo themselves for issue over the period of a year on nine albums (in packs of three) as appendant commodities to a six-hour documentary film to be spread over three weeks on ITV, and presented likewise on foreign television.

Then came talk of the Fab Three recording new material for the project. The general feeling, however, was that it wouldn't be the same without Lennon. Yet, after a fashion, a regrouping of Harrison, Starr and McCartney in the later 1990s wasn't without him. Their labours in George's and Paul's respective private studios yielded the grafting of new music onto John's voice-piano tapes of 'Free As A Bird' and 'Real Love', provided by Yoko after much negotiation.

With Harrison's producer, Jeff Lynne, rather than elderly George Martin, at the console, 'Free As A Bird' took shape as near as dammit to to a new Beatles record, complete with a guitar break from George, Ringo's trademark pudding drums and Paul emoting a freshly composed bridge as a sparkling contrast to John's downbeat verses. The result was certainly better than 'Can't Buy Me Love' and 'The Ballad Of John And Yoko', A-sides released by The Beatles when Lennon was still alive.

For me, however, 'Free As A Bird' wasn't as piquant as either a briefly reformed Sex Pistols on *Top Of The Pops* in 1996, or the launch of *Zombie Heaven*, a four-CD retrospective, at London's Jazz Café that November. Trooping onstage at 10:45pm in this nicotine-clouded club were, yes, organist Rod Argent, bass player Chris White, singer Colin Blunstone, drummer Hugh Grundy and, still jet-lagged after flying in from the USA, guitarist Paul Atkinson. Rough and ready they may have been for their first performance in 28 years, but like Lennon in Toronto in 1969, it was sufficient that the original Zombies were merely there.

All the same, I was among the multitudes willing 'Free As A Bird' to leap straight in at Number One as Beatles singles were supposed to – and as a verification of the lost value of the performance of a song as opposed to the producing of a production. Yet for all the amassing of anticipation via no sneak previews, and a half-hour TV special building up to its first spin over a remarkable video, it stalled in second place in Britain's Christmas chart. The 'Real Love' follow-up reached the UK Top Ten more grudgingly.

Who could not understand Paul, George and Ringo's mingled regret and elation when the *Anthology* albums shifted millions, affirming that almost but not quite reaching the top in the UK singles chart was but a surface manifestation of enduring interest in The Beatles that made even this abundance of out-takes, demos and other leftovers as much of a joy forever as *Zombie Heaven* and similar produce issued around the same time by The Beach Boys and The Doors?

In deference to the years before the coming of Ringo, the first *Anthology* package contained tracks with Beatles who'd left the fold one way or another. Such inclusions were of no use to Stuart Sutcliffe, mouldering in a Liverpool parish cemetery for 35 years – or John Lennon. The group's sacked drummer, however, could foresee that the attention would enable his Pete Best Band to broaden its work spectrum. Thus a busy 1996 schedule covered 18 countries as well as bigger UK venues than before – Barnsley Civic, Margate Winter Gardens, London's Bottom Line, Southport Floral Hall, you name 'em.

Assisted by Bill Harry, Pete recovered further scrapings of his stolen heritage through *The Best Years Of The Beatles*,[96] a timely second memoir just over a decade after his long-awaited *Beatle!*.[97] The other living ex-Beatles covered their respective tenures with the group with the publication of the pricey *Anthology* autobiography in 2000. Several years in gestation, it was a "Beatles story told for the first time in their own words and pictures".[98] Whereas Ringo, George and Paul's were from turn-of-the-century taped reminiscences, with no anchoring narrative, John's were from media archives and, therefore, not influenced by the fact of being observed: *litera scripta manet*.[99] He came over, therefore, as less of a straightforward, unspoilt Merseyside lad than any of the other three.

If an engaging and sometimes courageous account – and a thought-provoking companion to this one – it was aimed at fans who prefer not to learn too much about what kind of people their idols are in private. Too many illusions will be shattered, and the music may never sound the same. The more salacious amongst us were, therefore, to be discomfited: Though you'd think that, like a fisherman boasting about a catch, the stories (particularly about Hamburg) would get more eye-stretching with each passing year, the sex and drugs were actually played down.

On other matters, however, there were not so much new twists in the plot as further snippets of detail. Finally, while the Swinging '60s are hardly the Schleswig-Holstein question (the most complex matter ever to perplex European politics), *Anthology*, despite an unavoidable subjectiveness, was certainly a more palatable way to at least scratch the surface of what the fuss was about than 1,000 Open University treatises.

With its weight on a par with that of a paving slab, *Anthology* amassed enough advance orders to slam it straight in at Number One in *The Sunday Times* book chart, a feat duplicated across the world. It was still doing well while EMI co-ordinated its biggest-ever marketing campaign. Eight million copies of *1*, a compilation of The Beatles' 27 British and US chart-toppers, were shipped around the world. The fastest-selling CD ever, *1* reached that number in the charts in Britain, Japan, Germany and Canada within a week of its issue.

What victory was John Lennon's? "The leader of the band's arrived!" *NME* reader's letter had bawled back in the aftershock of 8 December 1980, presuming that John was being conducted to the table head in some pop Valhalla. A spiritualist *au fait* with Lennon's afterlife adventures knew of his affair with a long-departed Hollywood screen idol – intelligence that might have inflamed his volcanic widow whose *Season Of Glass* album sleeve in 1981 had depicted a pair of bloodstained spectacles – while the following year's *It's Alright (I See Rainbows)* employed trick photography whereby a spectral John stood next to her and Sean in what looks like a recreation ground.

Even before the necessarily hasty cremation, although a Coalition To Stop Gun Violence – of which Harry Nilsson was an active supporter – was inaugurated, less altruistic was the bursting of a commercial dam of such force that John Lennon's name would continue to sell almost anything. Publishers liaised with biographers that included a team who had a life of Lennon – entitled *Strawberry Fields Forever* – in the shops inside a fortnight and Albert Goldman, the US journalist whose brief was to portray Lennon as being as certifiable a lunatic as Chapman.

Needless to say, there were also individuals thick skinned enough to start work on a tribute disc within minutes of catching the first bulletin on 9 December. With a bit of luck, it'd be in the shops and on radio playlists in time for mourners to spend their Christmas record tokens on it.

Totally eclipsing efforts like 'Elegy For The Walrus' and 'It Was Nice To Know You, John', George Harrison's 'All Those Years Ago' was the promotional 45 from his *Somewhere In England* album, and the reason why George by association was to end 1981 seven places behind Lennon as tenth Top Male Vocalist in *Billboard*'s annual poll. Regardless of this singalong canter's mediocrity, another incentive for buyers was the superimposed presence of Ringo and Paul, who, with Wings, had taken a break from another project in George Martin's Monserrat complex to add their contributions when the unmixed 'All Those Years Ago' arrived from Harrison.

It's futile to hypothesise about John's beyond-the-grave verdict on George's first big hit since 'Give Me Love (Give Me Peace On Earth)' in 1973, but I like to think that he would have preferred Roxy Music's go at 'Jealous Guy'. Lennon was, after all, an artist with whom the group's Bryan Ferry, via a *Melody Maker* article, expressed a wish to collaborate. Bryan may have told the man himself when, in 1974, he dined with John, George and Ringo in New York. Touring Germany with Roxy Music the week after the slaying, Ferry suggested closing the show with 'Jealous Guy'. A German record company executive ventured that it would be a sound choice for the next Roxy Music single, but Bryan felt it might appear tasteless. Nevertheless, after further deliberation, the outfit tried an arrangement during an exploratory studio session. With the oblique message "A Tribute" on the picture sleeve, the sole reference to its main purpose, 'Jealous Guy' scudded all the way up the UK charts, the only Roxy Music 45 to so do, by March 1981.

Sean Lennon's godfather, Elton John got no further than Number 51 with his 'Empty Garden' tribute in 1982. Though he procrastinated for even longer, Mike 'Tubular Bells' Oldfield – with sister Sally on lead vocals – slummed it on *Top Of The Pops* with 1983's 'Moonlight Shadow', which addressed itself to the horror outside the Dakota on the night it happened. Waiting a decent interval, more deserving of a chart placing was the title song of The Downliners Sect's *A Light Went Out In New York*, a 1993 album that mingled remakes of some of the reformed British R&B combo's old tracks and Beatle obscurities. Dare I suggest that the Sect actually improve upon 'I'll Keep You Satisfied', 'That Means A Lot' *et al*? Also, that 'A Light Went Out In New York' – composed by the Sect's own Paul Tiller – may be the most moving Lennon oblation ever released, knocking the likes of 'All Those Years Ago', 'Empty Garden' and po-faced 'Moonlight Shadow' into a cocked hat?

The principal subject of Mike Oldfield's ditty was not John but Yoko Ono, who was to sanction and partly compère 1990's televised and international concert tribute to John at Liverpool's Pier Head. Since 1980, Yoko has not retreated from public life. As recently as summer 2002, she endeavoured to re-invent herself as a disco diva with a remix of 'Open Your Box', her self-composed flip-side to 'Power To The People'. While this was still being advertised via posters in London underground stations, Ono was presented to the Queen during Her Majesty's golden jubilee visit to Liverpool's John Lennon – formerly Speke – Airport. It's likely that I've got Yoko all wrong but, to me, she gives an impression of hurrying her duties by John out of the way in as bombastic a manner as possible while simultaneously using him as leverage to further her own artistic ends: kind of "Yes, he was quite a guy, but listen…"

The ease with which Yoko's step-son secured a British Top Ten hit in 1984 might be the most renowned instance of affinity to The Beatles kick-starting a musical career. In April of the following year, Julian Lennon also played three nights in a theatre in New York. During this brief residency, he and his mother Cynthia were spotted at a dining table, sharing the proverbial joke with his half-brother and Yoko Ono. "It was after Julian's first appearance in New York," Cynthia elucidated, "and he and I, Yoko and Sean were there – so for the photographers, it was a classic coup, but though we both wed the same man and both had a child by him, we were and still are worlds apart."

A more convivial repast was eaten by Cynthia with Maureen, Ringo's late ex-wife, at Lennon's, Cynthia's short-lived Covent Garden restaurant, which bored journalists made out to be in fierce competition with ex-Rolling Stone Bill Wyman's Kensington eaterie, Sticky Fingers. The two well-dressed, "liberated" divorcees might have hardly recognised their younger Merseyside selves. "We'd remained best friends through thick, thin, births, deaths and marriages," smiled Cynthia. "I happened to be staying with Maureen when Ringo rang at dawn with the news of John's death. She was also my last link with The Beatles. I'm out of their social orbit completely now."

Though Cynthia had gained a lucrative design contract in 1984 on the strength of her Art College qualifications, her memoir, *A Twist Of Lennon*, had done brisk business when published in 1978. Another account may follow "because so much has happened since then. It would be very easy to get in a ghost writer, but, because the first one was all my own work, it'd have to be in the same vein, in the way that I saw it – not the way other people want to see it. In the film *Backbeat*, I was a simple girl who wore tweed coats and head scarves, and that all I ever wanted in life was marriage, babies and a house – which was totally untrue. I was training to be an art teacher for four years, and it was only when I became pregnant that marriage followed, and The Beatles followed after that.

"People think of The Beatles in terms of millions of dollars. I don't see those dollars. What dollars I see are from my own damned hard work since I was out on my own after the divorce. From being so protected by millions that I never saw, and having a secure family, it was desperate really."

Yoko held the purse strings of John's fortune, but, after much to-ing and fro-ing of solicitors' letters, Julian Lennon received assorted – and, according to him, long overdue – monies. There was, therefore, no love lost between him and his father's relict. While noting that she and Sean attended 88-year-old Aunt Mimi's funeral in December 1991, another of John's blood relations felt the same as Julian about Yoko Ono. "Dad bought his half-sister Julia and her family a house to live in," snarled Julian by way of example. "As soon as Dad passed away, Yoko went and took their home that had been given to them by him, and then gave it to charity with no compensation for them."[5]

The second Mrs Lennon didn't appear to be very popular with John's former workmates either. On 27 April 1981, Yoko had been conspicuously absent from Ringo Starr's wedding to film actress Barbara Bach. Furthermore, George Harrison was to have nothing to do with Ono's Pier Head shenanigans and, while Paul and Ringo each sent a filmed piece, they declined to show up in person.

No Merseybeat groups "who'd got drunk with him"[100] had been invited even to warm up for Kylie Minogue, Christopher "Superman" Reeve, Roberta Flack, Hall And Oates, Cyndi Lauper and the rest of Yoko's star turns. Some, however, paid their respects that same year in a John Lennon Memorial Concert at the Philharmonic Hall. Blowing the dust off their instruments, many of those on the boards on that night of nights were belying daytime occupations as pen pushers, charge hands and captains of industry.

Old friendships and rivalries had been renewed likewise in May 1989 at the Grafton Rooms, scene of many a rough night in the early days, during the inaugural evening of Merseycats, a committee formed by Don Andrew, once of The Remo Four, to facilitate reunions of Merseybeat groups in support of KIND (Kids In Need and Distress), an organisation that provides activity holidays for seriously ill and handicapped local children.

Brian Epstein, "John Lennon of The Beatles" and "Stuart Sutcliffe of The Beatles" were pictured amongst "absent friends" in the souvenir programme. The latter two were also central to *Backbeat*, the 1994 bio-pic from the makers of *Letter To Brezhnev* – set in Liverpool – and *The Crying Game*. The action took place against the background of the *vie bohème* of Liverpool and Hamburg and concentrated on the often volatile relationships between John, Stuart and Astrid (and, to a lesser degree, Cynthia).

Backbeat's commercial success helped Sutcliffe close the gap on John as the most popular dead Beatle – at least, until George Harrison was taken by cancer in 2001. During the early 1990s, small fortunes changed hands for both a letter to Stuart from George and a Sutcliffe oil painting, not in the murmur of a museum or art gallery committee rooms but the bustle of a pop-memorabilia auction – for, regardless of how regrettable a loss he was to the world of Fine Art, as a figure in time's fabric Sutcliffe's period as a Beatle remains central to most considerations of him.

Conversely, their own merits, more than their association with The Beatles, have enabled Gerry Marsden and Billy J Kramer to be among the few of the old Merseybeat school who have managed to cling on to recording careers. In 1998, they delivered respectively Take That's 'A Million Love Songs' and REM's 'Losing My Religion' with more guts than the originals on *Sixties Sing Nineties*, an album on which hits by callow apprentices were given the masters' touch.

Tidy-minded (or lazy) journalists were mostly responsible for the habit of finding 1960s opposite numbers to Britpop acts that bestrode the UK Top 40 in the mid- to late 1990s. It was, however, too black and white to categorise, say, Oasis – whose 'Don't Look Back In Anger' was covered by Dave Dee on *Sixties Sing Nineties* – as the day's Beatles. Nevertheless, a few similarities are noticeable. For instance, their Liam Gallagher seems to have inherited a singing style that crosses that of John Lennon – after whom his eldest child is named – and Allan Clarke, once of The Hollies.

Yet Britpop belonged to a radically different economic, sociological and technological climate than the decade in which a provincial youth's decision to grow his hair even *With The Beatles* length, prefaced years of incomprehension, lamentation, deprivation, uproar, assault and oppressive domestic "atmospheres". At Aldershot Magistrates Court in 1965, a soldier accused of beating up a total stranger offered the plea, "Well, he had long hair, hadn't he?" Men don't have periods and can't get pregnant, but pillars of women's liberation might note how difficult the issue of hair could be for boys in the 1960s. You had to fight every literal inch of the way.

As a result, those who suffered this and other repressions were much more liberal when, as former Mods, Rockers and hippies, they became parents themselves and bought MIDI equipment for 16th birthday presents. More insidiously, the notion of the two-guitars-bass-drums line-up of a self-contained group was instilled from the cradle for many of their offspring. This was partly why 1960s outfits still operational in what was no longer such a nostalgia netherworld began drawing a remarkably young crowd that, not wanting its 1960s medicine neat, mouth the words of what little new songs are performed as accurately as the ancient smashes.

The latter, however, had dominated proceedings at the John Lennon Memorial Concert. Gerry Marsden was present but not participating beyond a brief cameo at the end. Nonetheless, the Philharmonic Hall's resident orchestra helped him do his bit in 2001 with Much Missed Man, a remarkable CD that, clocking in at just over 20 minutes, hung on a title requiem for Lennon with lyrics by Joe Flannery, once Brian Epstein's friend and business associate.

Within weeks of 8 December 1980, Flannery had written 'Much Missed Man' with Marsden in mind. "I felt it was too soon for a tribute from me then," thought Gerry. "However, when the anniversary of John's 60th birthday was coming up in 2000, Joe rang and asked me to give it another listen as he felt that the time might be right for me to record it – and he was right. The words said what I thought about John. People who like John will like the record."

Most of the playing time, however, would consist of a chronologically illogical collage of John holding forth amid a recitation of one of his poems and interruptions by Yoko and persons unknown (among them a "street-corner evangelist" that I suspect might be McCartney). There's fun to be had dating these excerpts, which seem to stretch from final interviews back to the "Jesus" press conference in Chicago in 1966.

As for 'Much Missed Man' itself, a fragment of dialogue by Lennon and an 'Imagine'-esque piano figure sequed into a lush and adventurous arrangement behind a serenade that is on a heartfelt par with 'A Light Went Out In New York'.

To a greater degree than The Downliners Sect, Gerry Marsden still earns good money as an entertainer. He certainly has as warm a rapport with the audience as he did way back when, even if the rehearsed jokes told by both him and the latest edition of the Pacemakers about his age, weight and love life are received nearly as well as 'How Do You Do It', 'Ferry 'Cross The Mersey' and all the rest of them.

Getting laughs was more important than the music for Ricky Richards, albeit as "Rick Hardy" nowadays, though his act as a singing comedian betrays hardly any link whatsoever with the rock 'n' roll he, Tony Sheridan and the other Jets punched out in Hamburg. A decade on, a similar chicken-in-a-basket circuit was interrupted for The Searchers by two well-received albums of new material for the new-wave label Sire. Since then, The Searchers have split into two separate factions, each claiming to be the most *bona fide* line-up.

The still-functioning Merseysippi Jazz Band bloomed again too and, as demonstrated by the very existence of locally published *Sweeping The Blues Away*, a "celebration" of their first half-century by BBC Radio Merseyside's Spencer Leigh, the unit have become as much of a Liverpool institution in their way as the long-lost Beatles – and, once upon a time, Lord Woodbine.

He, however, was all but lost to the archives of oblivion, although daughter Barbara was to surface as a playwright whose work includes episodes for Channel Four's Merseyside soap opera, *Brookside*. If well-placed to grow fat on Beatlemania, her father chose instead to continue living on his wits around Toxteth. Yet, before he perished with his wife Helen in a house fire on 5 July 2000, Lord Woodbine sold a rather bitter story to *The Observer*, but – perhaps surprisingly – he never guested at any Beatles conventions and, unlike others less entitled, resisted further incentives to cash in on The Beatles ticket.

Who could begrudge Lennon's ex-wife from doing so with unprecedented abundance? A 1999 exhibition of her paintings at the KDK Gallery down London's Portobello Road was only part of it. Was I attending a preview or a cocktail party? White wine, please. Red gives me heartburn. Do those canapés contain meat? Don't look now, but wasn't that fellow with the camera once in The Troggs? Is that Mick Hucknell or one of Kula Shaker? That bloke I can't quite place: I'm sure he played Lennon in some play or other?

Actually, he *was* Lennon. Julian was there supporting his mother and Phyllis McKenzie, friends since student days in Liverpool when they breathed the air around others occupying that wide territory between realism and abstract expressionism: Phyllis leaning closer to the latter form than Cynthia – who freighted *A Twist Of Lennon* with her own illustrations.

The originals were on display in KDK for most of the summer, along with further visual mementos of her life at the storm centre of 1960s pop as well as later pictures bereft of such reference.

Cynthia Lennon was not nominated for that year's Turner prize. Nevertheless, her work had a charm that begs the question: does only the surname prevent her from being an artist in her own right? Maybe, but in such matters, your opinion is as worthy as mine, and beyond both of us, the only approbation KDK, McKenzie and Lennon need really are those whose time is utilised interestingly in an experience that, through my eyes, was as much aesthetic as historical.

Three years earlier, while it may not have reactivated the Cynthia Lennon Fan Club, the release of a debut single, a revival of Mary Hopkin's chart-topping 'Those Were The Days', had precipitated a more far-reaching reassessment. Produced by Isle of Man neighbour Chris Norman, formerly of Smokie, for his own Dice Music label, Cynthia's was not one of those discs that you buy for the wrong reasons – not like her former father-in-law's unmelodious 'That's My Life' in 1965.

Fifty-five-year-old Cynthia turned in a surprisingly appealing vocal – though perhaps not so surprising considering that "from the age of 10 until I was 14, I was in the Hoylake Parish Girls' Choir, and I ended up as soloist. "As an adult, I had no aspirations to be a singer. I didn't even sing around the house or in the bath, but a fax came through from a German record company who wanted to get in touch with Julian. So Jim, my partner, phoned back and said sarcastically, 'Julian's not here, but you can have his mother' – a throwaway comment that they answered in all seriousness, 'We can't do anything unless we know whether she can sing.' My voice had dropped about two octaves – probably because of all the cigarettes I smoke – but I'm game for anything nowadays, so

I taped a selection of songs *a cappella*. Chris asked to hear it out of curiosity and said, 'Let's give it a whirl.'

"Chris thought 'Those Were The Days' would be a good song for a person of my age, and very pertinent, looking back – though I resisted a temptation to sing, 'Once upon a time, there was a *Cavern*' on disc. For weeks after the session, I was on cloud nine. I was so pleased with it – and it was so creative for me. Six months earlier, if somebody had told me a record of mine was going to be on the radio, I'd have fallen about on the floor in hysterics, but – what's John's expression on *Double Fantasy*? – 'Life is what happens when you're busy making other plans.' At nearly every interview I've done, I've got one of the same two questions. 'Don't you think you're jumping on the bandwagon?' 'Won't people think you're cashing in?' I've tried for intelligent answers that don't sound aggressive, but no one other than me will ever understand. 'Cashing in' is earning a living as far as I'm concerned. Why should you feel guilty for working?"

With this in mind, Cynthia took the show on the road as novelty headliner of With A Little Help From Their Friends, a revue that you shouldn't have missed but probably did, judging by the half-capacity audience at any given theatre *en route* around Britain. Other "insiders" on the bill were more hardened to both poor turn-out and general stage exposure than Cynthia – notably The Merseybeats, who appeared with her ex-husband's group more times than anyone else.

Subtitled "a celebration of The Beatles by those who were part of the story", this package was not a convention-like evening of selective reminiscences, but a musical spectacular coalesced by scripted patter and short cameos like Cynthia's then-boyfriend Jim Christie scuttling on as "Brian Epstein" during a spot by the soundalike Silver Beatles', who focus on their namesake's apogee as a local attraction. The fab-gear winsomeness was flawless, but ropey mouth-organ blowing from "John", "Ringo's" too plummy vocal on 'Boys', and, the most common problem of the clone groups, a right-handed "Paul", might have been distracting for some. For me, however, these were of no more account than, say, the real Lennon's loosened tie, Paul's frequent five-o'-clock shadow – and, of course, the wavering tempos and fluffed riffs that the Fab Four themselves delivered onstage.

The Silver Beatles captured the required ramshackle grandeur. Other With A Little Help From Their Friends antics, however, appear lame or peculiar in cold print today – such as a sketch in which matronly Cynthia was embraced by The Silver Beatles' Andy Powell as youthful "John" in his high-buttoned suit – but they made sound sense in the context of proceedings that closed on an emotional high with the assembled cast joining The Merseybeats and a jubilant audience, blasting up chorus after rowdy dah dah chorus of 'Hey Jude'.

It seemed that, the older you were, the louder you clapped and shouted, the more you waved your arms about. Everyone whose life has been soundtracked by The Beatles should have attended, but the Congress Theatre, Eastbourne, on 14 March 1996 was the last opportunity to do so as cancellation of the remaining dates was the only way to staunch the financial losses that the trek had suffered since opening in February.

At the last hurrah in Eastbourne, a palpable wave of goodwill had washed over Mrs Lennon the instant she walked centre-stage before a backdrop mock-up of the graffiti-covered Cavern wall. From being a softly spoken outcast after the world and his wife were confronted with a John they'd never known before in 1968, Cynthia, if no Ken Dodd, proved a self-assured, likeable MC. Moreover, the former chorister also dropped sufficient reserve to open the second half with 'Those Were The Days'. Shorn of the Welsh soprano's incongruous maidenly innocence, Cynthia's pining for past times was as poignant as 'Free As A Bird'.

The customers, typically English, loved Cynthia for being a survivor – and for reaching her half-century in such great shape, too. The same applied to another lady on the bill, Twinkle, who couldn't let the evening go without giving 'em a stirring 'Terry', which had left the charts 31 years ago almost to the day.

On a *Ready Steady Go* nostalgia tour two summers earlier, Twinkle has been accompanied by her 1965 Top 20 contemporaries, The Four Pennies – who weren't quite the full shilling, containing only one original member, bass player Mike Wilsh. Perhaps mitigating this shortfall for 1960s purists was the onstage presence of a certain John Charles Duff Lowe, the selfsame pianist with The Quarry Men. He was combining Four Pennies duties with an attempted relaunch of if not *The* Quarry

Men, then *a* Quarry Men. A 1994 debut album, *Open For Engagements*, mixed items from the 1958 edition's repertoire with some startling originals, more *Sgt Pepper* than 'In Spite Of All The Danger'.

"In 1975, I'd moved to Bristol," John explained. "We always had a piano, and I used to play a lot, so I never lost interest in music. In 1991, I received a call from Mike Wilsh, who until then hadn't realised that I lived only two miles away from him. I was rehearsing with The Four Pennies within three or four days. I spoke at a *Merseybeatle* convention in Liverpool in 1992, and the following year we played at a party at the Cavern as 'The Quarry Men'. Later that year, were asked to do a recording by a producer named Tony Davidson, who had done one with The Four Pennies.

"That all came to nothing, but early in 1994, John Ozoroff, The Four Pennies' guitarist, wanted to do a solo album in a Bristol studio. Three tracks were done with me on keyboards, and we decided to turn it into a Quarry Men album, to be put out on my own Kewbank Records. It was mastered at Abbey Road by Nick Webb, who, incidentally, was assistant engineer on *Yellow Submarine*, the 'White Album' and *Abbey Road*. Of the new songs on *Open For Engagements*, there's a tribute to John Lennon, 'John Winston'.

"Rod Davis came over from his home in Uxbridge to play rhythm guitar on the sessions, but I took over the mantle of The Quarry Men. A number of other people could have done it. They didn't; I did – therefore, I run the present-day Quarry Men. I've got plans for another six Quarry Men albums."

It was to be The Quarry Men's task to kick-start With A Little Help From Their Friends with a brief skiffle prelude before Lowe swapped washboard for his more customary state-of-the-art keyboards for the remainder of the longest half hour of the show. Olde-tyme rock 'n' roll was adulterated by Lowe's synthesiser and Ozoroff's guitar solos, which reacted to underlying chord patterns rather than the melodic and lyrical intent of any number.

Yet there was a clever Cajun arrangement of Chuck Berry's 'Sweet Little Sixteen' with programmed accordion and Rod on inaudible fiddle; a daring 'History' from *Open For Engagements*; a competent rendition of 'Woman', with quotes from The Searchers' 'Don't Throw Your Love Away'; and an *a cappella* finale with 'In My Life', taken from *Rubber Soul*.

Theirs was an almost scholarly recital, which provoked clapping rather than screams. More agreeable a venture was when Rod Davis and others still alive from the Woolton fete line-up were heard 43 years after the event on *Get Back Together*, 15 tracks of rocked-up skiffle from the opening 'Mean Woman Blues' through to the apposite 'Lost John' valediction. As lead singer, Len Garry coped better with, say, Bing Crosby's 'Have I Told You Lately That I Love You' than Eddie Cochran's 'Twenty Flight Rock', but, on his solitary vocal, 'When The Sun Goes Down', Rod – hedging his bets – was as uncannily close to the Donegan template as John Lennon was with 'Putting On The Style' on the rediscovered tape from the day when the Lennon–McCartney partnership began.

On the whole, there wasn't as much grit as I'd have liked – but perhaps that's not the point for incorrigible old rockers with no other cards left to play. If nothing else, *Get Back Together* – with a teenage Lennon in pride of place on the front cover – sounds like it was fun to record, even if that particular brand of fun isn't a thing that money can't buy anymore.

Epilogue

"And Now, Thank Christ, It's Over"

How different could John Lennon's life have been? This is probably a senseless hypothetical exercise, but let's transfer to a parallel dimension for a few minutes.

Sean Connery has failed his screen test for *Dr No*; Cassius Clay didn't beat the count when knocked down by Henry Cooper, and, in summer 1966, Dave Dee, Dozy, Beaky, Mick And Tich top the US Hot 100, the first British act to do so since The Tornados.

Around the same time, John Lennon quits The Beatles, an also-ran beat group, for a hand-to-mouth existence as a jobbing commercial artist back in Liverpool. For a while, he's on the periphery of the Liverpool scene, a mixed-media aggregation, before a supplicatory chat with Arthur Ballard lands him a post as technician in Ballard's department at the college.

As his marriage to Cynthia deteriorates, John becomes a fixture in Ye Cracke, still a student pub, where he often rambles on with rueful and misplaced pride about The Beatles' meagre achievements. On one maudlin evening, he brings in his photo album – "us with Tony Sheridan", "me and George with Ringo Starr in the Top Ten. Ringo was in Georgie Fame's Blue Flames later on, you know…" Most regulars find both John's reminiscences and the pictures mind-stultifyingly boring.

For beer money and a laugh, Lennon reforms The Beatles for bookings in local watering-holes. They became as peculiar to Liverpool alone as Mickey Finn, a comedian unknown nationally but guaranteed work for as long as he can stand on Merseyside. A typical engagement is providing music after Finn's entertainment at a dinner and dance at Gateacre Labour Club on 8 December 1980. The group's personnel on that night of nights consists of Pete Best, deputy manager at Garston Job Centre on drums; George Harrison, a Southport curate, on guitar; Paul McCartney, a Radio Merseyside presenter and amateur songwriter, on bass; and Lennon, his singing voice darker and attractively shorn of 1960s ingenuity, now a slightly batty art lecturer who'd wed a Japanese performance artist he'd seen at a 1967 "happening" at the college.

The four leave a dancing audience wanting more after a finale of a 1965 Oriole B-side, 'I'm A Loser', during which Lennon accommodated suitable – and often amusing – gestures and facial expressions as well as wailing an endlessly inventive harmonica. He also displayed a commendable sense of historical perspective during humorous continuity. Meanwhile, George delivered workman-like solos, and Paul sent frissons through middle-aged female nervous systems with his pretty 'Till There Was You', but a more unsung hero of the night was Pete, ministering unobtrusively to overall effect and, in his way, a virtuoso.

Brought back for an encore, The Beatles affirm their staying power once more. None of their few records ever sold much beyond Merseyside but, as an eminently danceable live act, they've outlasted most of their local rivals – and there's every reason to suppose that they'll still be around in the next millennium.

Unreal life isn't like that – at least, it wasn't for John, whose unmeasurable fame had accorded unto him a magnificently god-like certainty about everything he said and did for invisible armies of fans, old and new, whose adoration will never dwindle. As pressured denizens of the media cobbled together hasty obituaries on the morning of 9 December 1980, one of the more memorable comments any of them reported was by the recently retired Arthur Ballard: "I think his death is more significant than that of a leading politician. Like Michelangelo has never been forgotten, neither will John Lennon be."[101]

Shall we try again with an interview with John Winston Lennon,

MBE, retired musician and composer at Fort Belvedere, Sunningdale, Berkshire, on 9 December 2002...

To the click-clack of his own approaching footsteps, the former Beatle sings what sounds like "Softly, softly spreads the grunion/thinner thorn our saviour's feet..." to the tune of 'Johnny Todd', title theme to the old BBC television series Z-Cars.

"Welcome to the inner sanctuary," he begins. "Better not shake hands. I've just given the old feller a swift dekko at the scenery. My MBE's on the wall in the bog, y'know. Best place for it. I only asked the Queen for it back to cheer up my auntie during her last illness.

"Do I seem larger than life? Don't worry. That'll change as this chat progresses. I'm ordinary, modest, boring and all too human since that arsehole winged me outside the Dakota in 1980. Quite spoiled Christmas, it did – though it was that other gun-slinging get who did for Reagan in '82 that finally put the tin lid on my 'American period'.

"I miss New York sometimes, and I got pissed off recently with Berkshire County Council or whoever they are, when they turned their noses up at the plans to modernise this place. Used to belong to Edward and Mrs Simpson, don't-ye-know? All the same, I'm unlikely to live out of England ever again – especially since getting back together with Cyn and his Holiness down in Sussex, even if the old chart-busting magic isn't there any more.

"Never mind, we made our contribution to society a 100 times over in the '60s, and I reckon now that the four of us should have been put out to grass as soon as we split up the first time. But the game dragged on, didn't it? And now, thank Christ, it's over. Live Aid was a laugh, but all it proved was that looking forward to the past isn't healthy for any bunch of musicians, let alone John, Paul, George and Pete. Anyway, I wouldn't want to be an 80-year-old Beatle..."

Author's Note

While John Lennon's deeds and personality have become more ambiguous and nebulous in retrospect, care has been taken to define as widely as possible the myriad social, cultural, economic, environmental and other factors that polarise and prejudice what is generally known about him already, and the new and rediscovered evidence and information that recent research has brought to light. Often pop biography – and that is all this account is – has tended to shy away from these areas, even though they form a more tangible basis for investigation than, as I said in the prologue, treating the subject's most flippant public remarks as gospel.

Those whose lives are devoted to collating facts about The Beatles may pounce on mistakes and omissions while scrutinising this work. All I can say to them is that it's as accurate as it can be after the synthesis of personal memories and interviews with some of the key *dramatis personae* – not to mention a filing cabinet of Lennonia, and exercise books full of doctor's prescription-like scribble drawn from press archives – some of them quite obscure.

Please put your hands together for Penny Braybrooke, Iain MacGregor, Michelle Knight, Laura Brudenell, Chris Harvey, Alan Heal, Chris Bradford and Michael Wilson and the rest of the team at Sanctuary, who went far beyond the call of duty from this biography's sluggish genesis to its final publication.

I am also grateful to Rod Davis, Rick Hardy (Ricky Richards), Bill Harry, Cynthia Lennon, John Duff Lowe, Gerry Marsden, the late Harry Nilsson and Tony Sheridan for conversations and interviews that took place before this project was commissioned.

Whether they too were aware of providing assistance or not, let's have a round of applause too for these musicians: Frank Allen, Ian "Tich" Amey, Don Andrew, Roger Barnes, Alan Barwise, Cliff Bennett, Dave Berry, Colin Blunstone, Barry Booth, Clem Cattini, Don Craine, Tony Crane, Dick Dale, Trevor "Dozy" Davies, Rod Davis, Dave Dee, the late Lonnie Donegan, Vince Eager (Roy Taylor), Freddie Garrity, "Wreckless" Eric Goulden, Keith Grant, Mike Hart, Brian Hinton, Donald Hirst, Tony Jackson, Garry Jones, Billy Kinsley, Phil May, Jim McCarty, Mike Pender, Brian Poole, Mike Smith, Norman Smith, Mike and Anja Stax, the late Lord David Sutch, the late Vivian Stanshall, Dick Taylor, John Townsend, Paul Tucker, Fran Wood and Twinkle.

Equally invaluable was the clear insight and intelligent argument of my principal researcher, Ian Drummond.

It may be obvious to the reader that I have received much information from sources that prefer not to be mentioned. Nevertheless, I wish to thank them – as well as B & T Typewriters, Bemish Business Machines, Stuart and Kathryn Booth, Maryann Borgon, Eva Marie Brunner, the late Ray Coleman, Kevin Delaney, Peter Doggett, Katy Foster-Moore, Ann Freer, Gary Gold, Louise Harrison, Dave Humphries, Rob Johnstone, Allan Jones, Graham Larkbey, Spencer Leigh, Russell Newmark, Mike Ober, Mike Robinson, Mark Stokes and Ted Woodings – plus Inese, Jack and Harry Clayson for letting me get on with it.

Selective Bibliography

Such is the volume of literary spin-offs after his death that someone ought to write a book about books about John Lennon. These have ranged from scurrilous trash to well-researched, scholarly works that any historical figure of his stature would warrant. There have also surfaced countless volumes containing raw information that only the most crazed devotee would not find too insignificant to be interesting.

Therefore, rather than attempt a long – and probably incomplete – list of dry titles for further reading, it makes more sense to compile a selection with brief commentary of items that either I found helpful or are prototypical of specific aspects of John Lennon and The Beatles.

BADMAN, KEITH: *The Beatles After The Break-Up* (Omnibus, 1999). This reference work provides comprehensive facts about Lennon's life as an ex-Beatle.

CLAYSON, ALAN and SUTCLIFFE, PAULINE: *Backbeat – Stuart Sutcliffe: The Lost Beatle* (Pan-Macmillan, 1994). Ostensibly a film tie-in, this serves as an insight into the social and academic atmosphere from which The Beatles emerged.

COLEMAN, RAY: *John Winston Lennon, Volume 1 1940–1966* (Sidgwick & Jackson, 1984); *John Ono Lennon, Volume 2 1967–1980* (Sidgwick & Jackson, 1984). The antithesis of the Goldman job, these are very much the sort of books of which John himself might have approved. Take that how you like.

GOLDMAN, ALBERT: *The Lives Of John Lennon* (William Morris, 1988). Intricately researched muck-raking, this must be read on the understanding that the good doctor disliked Lennon, The Beatles and pop, and that he did it for the money.

HARRY, BILL: *John Lennon Encyclopedia* (Virgin, 2000). A vast and detailed tome by an art-school crony of John Lennon, editor of *Mersey Beat* and pal of The Beatles up to and beyond their disbandment.

NORMAN, PHILIP: *Shout! The True Story Of The Beatles* (Elm Tree, 1981). Despite factual errors, this is still accepted by most as the standard work on the group.

SEAMAN, FREDERIC: *Borrowed Time* (Xanadu, 1991). One of the more compassionate "insider" efforts.

SHEFF, DAVID (with John Lennon and Yoko Ono, edited by G Barry Olson): *The Playboy Interviews* (New English Library, 1982). One of the final interviews, and perhaps the lengthiest ever, it delves into many important areas, including memories of nearly every song he ever composed.

SHEPHERD, BILLY: *The True Story Of The Beatles* (Beat Publications, 1964). Neither a triumph of linguistic ability nor a penetrating insight into the human condition, this assignment was, nevertheless, the first of more Beatles biographies than anyone in 1964 could ever have comprehended.

Notes

In addition to my own correspondence and interviews, I have used the following sources, which I would like to credit:-

1. *Today*, BBC Radio Four, 9 December 1980
2. *Lennon Remembers: The Rolling Stone Interviews* by J Wenner (Penguin, 1980)
3. *Six O'Clock News*, BBC 1, 9 December 1980
4. Richmal Crompton was to be short-listed for inclusion on the *Sgt Pepper's Lonely Hearts Club Band* montage.
5. *The John Lennon Encyclopaedia* by B Harry (Virgin, 2000)
6. *Record Mirror*, 21 January 1956
7. *Backbeat: Die Stuart Sutcliffe Story* by A Clayson and S Sutcliffe (Bastei Lubbe, 1994), a translation of the original manuscript of *Backbeat – Stuart Sutcliffe: The Lost Beatle* by the same authors (Pan-Macmillan, 1994)
8. *Arthur Ballard* by P Davies (Old Bakehouse, 1998)
9. By coincidence, a photograph of another 1960s pop-star-in-waiting, Dave Berry, was published that same week in the *Daily Mirror* above a non-story about his big feet.
10. 1975 letter to Stuart Sutcliffe's mother
11. *Liverpool Daily Post*, 19 March 1964
12. *Disc And Music Echo*, 6 November 1970
13. *Trinity Parish Magazine*, August 1960
14. Renamed "The John Lennon" in 1964, during the Rickenbacker firm's period of greatest prosperity – because Lennon was still picking at his Model 1996 at the height of world-wide Beatlemania. If employed but rarely for soloing, it was unique for its jangling effect as rhythm *arpeggio*.
15. *Hamburg: The Cradle Of British Rock* by A Clayson (Sanctuary, 1997)
16. *The Beat Goes On*, February 1992
17. *Let's All Go Down The Cavern* by S Leigh and P Frame (Vermilion, 1984)

18. And later butt of Lennon's paraphrasing of a 1967 B-side hook-line – "baby, you're a rich man too" – as "baby, you're a rich fag Jew", a dig at the public school undercurrents of anti-Semitism and homo-eroticism that helped make Brian Epstein what he was.

19. *Brian Epstein: The Man Who Made The Beatles* by R Coleman (Viking, 1989)

20. *Serge Gainsbourg: View From The Exterior* by A Clayson (Sanctuary, 1998)

21. *The Playboy Interviews* ed G Barry Golson (New English Library, 1982)

22. *The Beatles: The Authorized Biography* by H Davies (Heinemann, 1970)

23. Once, Brian Poole And The Tremeloes were said to have been the ones Decca chose instead of The Beatles when, allegedly, both groups auditioned on New Year's Day 1962. According to Brian Poole himself, however, "Our studio test took place sometime in 1961 – not the day The Beatles did theirs. How did that story get around? Maybe one of our publicists made it up.

    "You check the release dates. Our first LP was *Big Big Hits Of 1962* – the first ever party-dance compilation mix, by the way – so we had to have been recording quite a bit before that to be allowed to do an album in those days. Also, George Martin told me later that The Beatles were still in Germany when we were recording as a backing vocal group for Decca – at EMI Studios."

24. *Peterborough Standard*, 7 December 1962

25. Lennon's sleeve notes to *Off The Beatle Track* by The George Martin Orchestra (Parlophone PC5 3057, 1964)

26. *Melody Maker*, 31 March 1973

27. *Lennon* by R Coleman (McGraw Hill, 1984)

28. *New Musical Express*, 1 February 1963

29. *Radio Luxembourg Book Of The Stars No 2* ed J Fishman (Souvenir Press, 1963)

30. *Tribute To The Big O*, BBC Radio Two, 5 January 1989

31. *Melody Maker*, 7 May 1963

32. *Melody Maker*, 9 March 1963

33. With a title borrowed from Walt Disney's *Snow White And The Seven Dwarfs*, 1937

34. *Mersey Beat*, 29 November 1963

35. *Melody Maker*, 3 August 1963

36. *Andover Advertiser*, 3 January 1965

37. Not the Johnny Sandon And The Remo Four number.

38. Third track, side two of *Memphis Beat* by Jerry Lee Lewis (Philips, 1966)

39. *Mojo: The Psychedelic Beatles: Special Edition*, 2001

40. Quoted in *Heroes And Villains: The True Story Of The Beach Boys* by S Gaines (Grafton, 1986)

41. *Playboy*, 19 October 1964

42. Even in the light of John Lennon's laddish comment to Brian de Courcy, Melbourne concert promoter: "Christ, Brian! You've got a grip like a fucking bear. I bet you're

not a poofter." (Quoted in *The Spinning Wheels: The Story Of A Melbourne Rhythm And Blues Band* by D Hirst, published by Park Fraser, 2002.)

43. *X-Ray* by R Davies (Viking, 1994)

44. Quoted in Alex Palao's booklet to *Zombie Heaven* CD box set (Big Beat ZOMBOX 7, 1997)

45. To Ray Coleman

46. *Paul McCartney: Many Years From Now* by B Miles (Vintage, 1998)

47. *New Musical Express*, 25 June 1966

48. *Don't Let Me Be Misunderstood* by E Burdon and J Marshall Craig (Thunder Mouth, 2001)

49. *Frank Zappa In His Own Words* ed B Miles (Omnibus, 1994)

50. *National Rock Star*, 18 December 1976

51. *Revolution In The Head: The Beatles' Records And The Sixties* by I MacDonald (Fourth Estate, 1994)

52. *Melody Maker*, 7 August 1971

53. *Rolling Stone*, 14 December 1967

54. *Time Out*, 4 September 1988

55. *Sunday Times*, 27 February 1983

56. Published by Pierian Press, 1983

57. *Disc And Music Echo*, 16 December 1967

58. Excerpt from Yoko Ono's opening address at her exhibition at the Everson Museum of Art, 9 October 1971

59. *Disc and Music Echo*, 12 August 1968

60. *Beatles Monthly*, July 1968

61. Adapted in the USA as *All In The Family*

62. *Ginsberg: A Biography* by B Miles (Viking, 1996)

63. Quoted in *Loose Talk* ed L Botts (Rolling Stone Press, 1980)

64. *Daily Express*, precise date obscured, 1969

65. *Chicago Tribune*, March 1981

66. *Rolling Stone*, 27 August 1987

67. *Rolling Stone*, 15 February 1969

68. *Rolling Stone*, 22 January 1981

69. *Rolling Stone*, 30 April 1981

70. *The Observer*, 27 November 1968

71. Sleeve note to *Let It Be* (Apple PXS/PCS 7096, 1970)

72. *Beatles Unlimited*, February 1977

73. To Giovanni Dadamo

74. *Daily Express*, 3 May 1969

75. *Disc And Music Echo*, 22 March 1969

76. To Michael Wale

77. *Daily Express*, 5 May 1987

78. *Musician*, November 1987

79. *Melody Maker*, 19 July 1969

80. *Zabadak* No 7, July 1994

81. *Disc And Music Echo*, 9 November 1969

82. *Henley Standard*, 30 August 2002

83. *Record Mirror*, 14 February 1970

84. *Melody Maker*, 27 April 1974

85. *Stereo Review*, November 1969

86. Covered in Britain by Frankie Vaughan

87. *Arena*, BBC2, 27 November 1989

88. To be issued in mass-market paperback by Simon & Schuster, 1988

89. *Time*, 21 May 1976

90. *New York Times*, 20 December 1964

91. Quoted by Chris "Ace" Kefford in *Record Collector*, No 179, July 1994

92. Translated from *Jacques Brel: Un Vie* by O Todd (Robert Laffont, 1984)

93. *New Musical Express*, 15 February 1963

94. *Daily Express*, 10 December 1980

95. *Daily Express*, 11 December 1980

96. Published by Headline, 1996

97. Published by Plexus, 1985

98. *Anthology* by The Beatles (Cassell, 2000)

99. "The written word remains"

100. *Sunday Times*, 6 May 1990

101. *Reading Evening Post*, 9 December 1980

Index